INDUSTRIAL
PUBLICITY

INDUSTRIAL PUBLICITY

Joseph C. Quinlan

 VAN NOSTRAND REINHOLD COMPANY
NEW YORK   CINCINNATI   TORONTO   LONDON   MELBOURNE

Library of Congress Catalog Card Number: 82-8363
ISBN: 0-442-27781-4

Manufactured in the United States of America

Published by Van Nostrand Reinhold Company Inc.
135 West 50th Street, New York, N.Y. 10020

Van Nostrand Reinhold Publishing
1410 Birchmount Road
Scarborough, Ontario M1P 2E7, Canada

Van Nostrand Reinhold
480 Latrobe Street
Melbourne, Victoria 3000, Australia

Van Nostrand Reinhold Company Limited
Molly Millars Lane
Wokingham, Berkshire, England

15 14 13 12 11 10 9 8 7 6 5 4 3 2 1

Library of Congress Cataloging in Publication Data

Quinlan, Joseph C.
    Industrial publicity.

    Includes index.
    1. Industrial publicity. I. Title.
HD59.Q56   1983   659.2   82-8363
ISBN 0-442-27781-4   AACR2

To Marjorie

*With gratitude for her support and encouragement,
and for enduring without complaint
the life of a "writer's widow."*

Preface

This book is meant to serve as a how-to guide for practitioners, particularly beginners, in the field of industrial publicity. Not a textbook in the usual sense, the book presents tips gleaned from my years of experience with three manufacturers, a public relations agency, and an industrial magazine. The book is subjective, opinionated, and at times blunt—a personal statement on a fascinating, challenging function.

In these pages, I have not attempted to cover the immense, nebulous subject of public relations. With one or two exceptions, the book deals solely with publicity as a communications tool for industrial marketing.

Today many of industrial publicity's practitioners, including some of the most capable, are women. I hope my female readers will not be offended by my exclusive use of masculine pronouns throughout the book. I've done this strictly for brevity and convenience.

The tone of the book is directive, full of statements such as "do this" and "don't do that." I trust you won't be irked by this bossy tone of voice, which was adopted for its simplicity and straightforwardness. Besides, if a novice is looking for solid direction, he doesn't want to be confused and encumbered by a swarm of options, qualifiers, and other forms of obfuscation. Subtle complexities will become evident with experience.

Whatever I know about industrial publicity I learned partly from personal involvement and partly from observing and conversing with editors and publicity practitioners. I owe thanks to professional publicists James Strenski, James McCarthy, Charles Higgins, and Peter Budzilovich, and to the dozens of knowledgeable, helpful editors with whom I have dealt over the years.

In particular, I wish to thank Paul Rolnick, for reviewing the entire manuscript; Bernie Knill, for his valuable comments on Chapter 11; and Mike Vasilakes, for his contributions to Chapter 13 and his encouragement during the early stages of the book, when the road was rocky.

J.Q.
Cleveland

Credits

Some of the material in this book was originally published in slightly different form as magazine articles. The previously published material appears here with the permission of the publishers.

The section of Chapter 2 called "Nine ways to stretch the [press release] budget" appeared in *Public Relations Journal,* November 1977.

Chapter 3, "Illustrating the Product Press Release," ran as an article in *Industrial Photography,* May 1979.

Chapter 4, "Why Releases Fail," appeared in *Public Relations Journal,* January 1980.

Chapter 6, "Seventeen Ways to Stretch the Case History Budget," ran in *Industrial Marketing,* September 1977. Copyright 1977 by Crain Communications, Inc., Chicago, Illinois.

Contents

INDUSTRIAL PUBLICITY

Chapter 1

Introduction to Publicity as a Marketing Communications Tool

Publicity is one of the tools you can use to spread the word about your new products, product improvements, staff personnel changes, applications of products and engineering, technical advances, service and manufacturing facilities and capabilities, new franchises, new catalogs, and a host of other subjects.

Publicity for the print media — magazines, newspapers, house organs, etc. — appears in the form of news stories or articles. Photos, drawings, charts, or tables may be used to illustrate the text. Publicity for the broadcast media — radio or TV — appears in the form of a spoken script. (More about the forms of publicity in the next section.)

Good publicity rests on its own merits as news or feature material. If it doesn't have legitimate, current news value, or if it isn't interesting, useful feature material, then it isn't good publicity. Phony, weak material is called "puff," and editors won't disseminate it. They don't even want to see it.

In a sense, when you produce publicity material, you are acting as an assistant editor for the media. If you attune your thinking to the needs and wants of the editors and broadcast directors, you will get better and more frequent exposure in their media.

HOW PUBLICITY DIFFERS FROM ADVERTISING

Publicity is "free" editorial space or broadcast time; advertising is paid space or time.

The word "free" is put in quotes because you always incur some expenses in producing the material for publication. With publicity, though, you do not pay the periodical or broadcast medium. If the editors think your news or feature material will interest their readers, listeners, or viewers, they will run it free of charge.

When you want advertising, on the other hand, you pay for a certain amount of space or broadcast time, and it is guaranteed that you will get it. You enter into a contract with a company.

Occasionally an editor will ask for a specific news story or article. In this case, if you submit good material, you can be fairly certain it will be published. For the most part, though, publicity material is submitted on speculation. It rests on its own merits and on the needs of the periodical or broadcaster at that particular time. The better the material, the better your chances of having it published.

One big advantage of advertising is that it enables you to use showmanship — attractive pictures, big headlines, smart layouts, hard-sell copy.

Publicity is more staid in its format. It tells the facts in a simple, straightforward manner, without overt sales-talk. It gets your message across subtly, in a low tone of voice, without a lot of fanfare.

When properly edited and presented by the media, publicity is more believable than advertising. The reader, listener, or viewer accepts publicity more readily; he doesn't put up his guard as he does when assaulted by a hard-working ad.

What's more, when publicity material is published or broadcast, it appears to carry the endorsement of the editors. It is presented in an editorial format — the same format used for material prepared by the staff members themselves. This is one of the big advantages, the main strengths, of publicity.

THE FORMS OF PUBLICITY

News Releases

The news release is the most important and useful form of publicity; much of your publicity effort will be directed toward producing releases. Written in a terse, vigorous style, the news release announces something that is important, useful, and — as the name implies — new.

If you want to convey information not related to announcing a new development, you should consider another form, such as a letter, bulletin, brochure, or manual.

News releases can do many things for you. Here are some of them:

1. *Let people know that you exist* — your products, services, distributors, plants, and so on. Creating this awareness is of prime importance, because if your prospects don't know about your products, etc., they can hardly be expected to become interested in them, order them, or prefer them.

2. *Maintain an awareness* of your products, organization, etc. Creating awareness comes first; then you must maintain that awareness. Job analysts tell us that there is a 30% to 33% turnover in management positions each year. This means you are trying to get the attention and awareness of a passing parade rather than a static, captive audience.

Today you make John Doe aware of your existence, but tomorrow Doe is promoted, transferred, or retired, or he changes employers. There's a very strong chance that his successor has never heard of you.

As a result, one news release, one ad, or one mailing — even a whole campaign — may not be enough. You must keep hammering in your name, your products, your features and benefits, your very existence, time and time again. A continuous flow of news releases can help do this for you, at low cost.

3. Tell your customers and prospects about your *new products, improvements in products, and new product literature* — and pull inquiries about them. You can get inquiries in many ways; ads, trade shows, direct mail, and personal calls are some of them. The news release is only one of many methods; you may want to use it in combination with others.

You will find, however, that the news release is one of the most efficient methods. It is without doubt the most economical — one you should consider particularly when your budget is tight.

4. Tell customers, prospects, distributors, employees, and other publics about your *new methods and facilities for distribution, new plants and facilities, changes in your staff* and other news items of interest.

Again, you can use other methods. But to get your message across to a widespread audience, at low cost per person contacted, you won't find another method that can match the news release. Besides, what other form of message is as believable, and has such an aura of importance, as a story printed in a magazine or newspaper?

5. *Strengthen your organization,* and thus help boost your sales. Publishing and/or broadcasting news about your distributors, staff personnel, and plants will help build and maintain morale, good will, and "esprit de compagnie." It has been well established that this kind of publicity is one of the most effective and necessary forms of good public relations.

Articles

News releases form the backbone of any publicity effort, but articles, too, are needed to give it substance and depth. Moreover, articles give you benefits that cannot be gained through other forms of communication. Here are some of the types of articles you will want to consider:

1. *Product application ("case history") articles.* As the name tells you, a case history article informs the reader about an application or installation of your products or services in a customer's facility. A case history may deal with how original equipment manufacturer (OEM) customers make use of your products in their products. In another form, it may describe how an individual user such as a plant engineer or maintenance chief is making use of your products in his machinery, systems, or facility. Either way, your customer plays the starring role, with you supporting as a helpful supplier.

You will find the application article especially useful in telling prospects about your experience in their fields. A continuous flow of application stories will convey the fact that you have had broad experience and that you're an active leader in the industry.

Application stories that tell about a customer's problem, and how you — your engineers, salesmen, distributors, and products — helped to solve it, are particularly effective. So are stories that include quoted testimonials from the customer.

A variation on this form is the "design case history," in which you take the reader through a design problem-and-solution narrative step by step, with lots of technical detail. Product design and application engineers appreciate receiving this kind of information.

2. *"Design idea" articles.* Whenever you bring out a new, unique, and interesting product design, a design idea article is one good way to let machine and system designers know about it.

The design idea article is complete in technical detail, with well-illustrated explanations of configuration, materials, operation, potential uses, operating ranges, etc. (Of course, you don't reveal any more than you want to, or any more than is protected by patents.)

In some cases, a magazine editor will write the article for you. Otherwise, you or your agent can handle the project. Either way, the cost to you is low, and reprints, available at reasonable rates from the magazine, will make excellent mailers for your product promotional campaign.

3. *Feature-length bylined technical articles.* Bylined articles are a bit harder to produce than are some other kinds of publicity, but they pay off by effectively conveying the impression that your company or client is an expert in its field.

This kind of article usually gives a thorough, detailed look at a technical subject of interest to key buyers in your industry. There are many types of potential subject matter; for a partial list, see Chapter 8.

You can write the technical article yourself or merely make rough notes and then let your agent ghostwrite it for you, with an appropriate byline. Your agent can also help you create suitable drawings, graphs, tables, etc., and place the material in a magazine of your choice.

Take a look around; you'll probably find much material for technical articles already on hand. Conference papers, audiovisual presentations, training materials, and lab reports often contain information and illustrations that can be converted into valuable, interesting articles.

When debating whether or not to present a given subject in the form of an article, don't forget the benefits you can receive not only from the initial publication in a magazine, but also later on from distribution of reprints. You can put these to good use as salesmen's talk-pieces, trade-show giveaways, training literature, mailers, and even ad premiums.

One old pro I know maintains that "it feels good when that article first appears, but a company doesn't get one-tenth of the potential benefits from an article unless it's reprinted and distributed." And that old pro doesn't own a printing press.

4. *Short technical articles.* Some call them "technical releases," others call them "fillers"; whatever you call them, though, they're without doubt one of the best bargains in publicity. You get a lot of editorial exposure per dollar invested.

Essentially, a technical release is a condensed version of a full-length technical article. You take a good article that has already been published, boil it down, and reduce the number of illustrations. Then you shotgun the material to several noncompeting, vertical trade periodicals. In the cover letters, you explain to the editors that you're offering the material as exclusive in the field.

The type of full-length article best suited to adaptation as a shorter technical release is one that presents how-to material or tips on a subject such as selection, installation, assembly, servicing, or troubleshooting. Titles of some technical releases issued recently for a Cleveland manufacturer include: *"Tips on Maintenance of Mobile Hydraulic Systems," "Ten Tips on Tube Clamping," "Sizing Quick-Disconnects for Shop Air Systems," "Reduce Your Equipment Downtime With Skiveless Hose and Reusable Fittings,"* and *"Take Good Care of Your (Hose) Carcass."*

Used in conjunction with new-product releases, new-literature releases and product-application stories, the technical release provides an excellent tool for reaching prospects in many vertical segments of your overall markets. The technical release gives you credible editorial exposure, usually in increments averaging a full page, at a very low cost per impression.

You'll want to consider employing the technical release, along with other forms of publicity, if your advertising budget is tight but you still need to reach a wide variety of potential buyers. This way, you can concentrate your ad dollars in the major periodicals serving your field.

Some chapters in this book explain the various types of releases and feature articles in detail and tell you how to write and place them. Other chapters relate editors' opinions on various aspects of industrial publicity and give you tips on managing publicity programs, budgets, and department operations.

Chapter 2
The Press Release

What is a "press release," or, as it is often called, a "news release"?

It is an announcement of an event — the introduction of a product or catalog, the appointment of a manager, the opening of a plant — which is (1) newsworthy and (2) of interest or importance to a large number of people. Essential characteristics of the release include the following:

1. The event is recent. Something that happened six months ago doesn't qualify as news, unless the story was withheld for some important reason. That in itself may be the basis for a story.

2. The event is newsworthy. Changing the design of the company nameplate likely doesn't qualify. Changing the nature of the finish on a product may qualify, however; the reason for the change could be important to customers.

3. The story is written in a terse, vigorous, straightforward news-style. Your prose should tell, not sell.

4. It is brief. Most releases should be as short as possible. Usually, one and one-half to two typewritten pages, double-spaced, are plenty. Give the editor and readers all essential information, however. The editor shouldn't have to call in order to obtain vital data missing from the story.

5. Usually, a press release is mass produced and mailed (or in some cases hand carried) to more than one periodical or broadcast station. At times, though, you may want to offer a news story as an exclusive.

The range of possible topics for press releases is virtually limitless. See Table 2-1 for a partial listing.

THE PRODUCT PRESS RELEASE

For companies that manufacture and sell products — or market products made by other companies — the product press release affords an easy, effective, inexpensive means of generating inquiries.

Many inquiries can be qualified as sales leads. Others will be mere expressions of interest or curiosity, with little or no sales potential.

Dollar for dollar, though, the product press release can generate more sales leads, at lower cost per lead, than can any other form of promotion. The judicious marketing manager will want to include releases, along with ads, direct mail, trade shows, and other formats, in his plans.

What the Release Should Tell

An effective product press release will provide the following information:

Name and model number of product; other identifying information.
Name and location of company introducing product.
Actual and potential uses of product.
Outstanding features and advantages.
The significance of those features and advantages, in terms of benefits to the user.
What is first, different, or otherwise superlative about the product.
Variations available: sizes, weights, colors, etc.
Where product may be purchased: company outlets, distributors, dealers, etc.
Typical list prices, if product is standardized.
Where to write for more information; phone number to call.
Name and number of literature to request.

Design and Sequence

Newspaper reporters have traditionally cast their news stories in the form of an inverted pyramid. That is, the most important facts are

Table 2-1. What You Can Publicize

PRODUCTS, SERVICES, TECHNOLOGY

Products – single products or complete
   new lines
Major improvements in existing products
New-found applications for existing
   products
New materials, processes, or techniques
   used in a product or its manufacture
Services
Trends in the uses of products
Demonstration equipment, facilities

**LITERATURE AND
RELATED MATERIALS**

Catalogs, brochures, bulletins, pamphlets
   – on products, services, company
   facilities and capabilities
Technical reference material
Manuals – operation, maintenance,
   troubleshooting
Calculators, other aids for the user
Motion picture films, slide films, other
   audiovisual materials
Reprints of useful technical articles

TRAINING

Courses offered to qualified customers,
   others
Seminars
Training materials available on loan or for
   sale or rent

**MANUFACTURING,
ENGINEERING, R&D**

New capital equipment, process lines
New or unusual procedures in testing,
   quality control
Superlative operations – largest, smallest,
   newest, etc.
New R&D facilities, procedures, equipment

PERSONNEL CHANGES

Appointments
Promotions
Transfers

PERSONNEL CHANGES (Continued)

Unusual jobs
Awards
Retirements
Service anniversaries

MARKETING

Newly awarded franchises
New territories, regions
New warehouses, service centers
Packaging news
Shipping procedures
Major sales meetings
Trade show participations; unusual displays
Noteworthy exhibits, mobile classrooms
Major sales programs and campaigns,
   including winners

PUBLIC RELATIONS

Speeches and technical papers by company
   officials, experts
Books and articles by company members
Open house, plant tours
Visits by VIP's, school groups
Significant ad campaigns
Donations, trust funds, scholarships, grants
Employee benefit programs
Favorable labor relations

GENERAL CORPORATE NEWS

New plants, additions to plants
Acquisitions
Financial news – e.g., quarterly and
   annual dividends
Energy conservation
Pollution control
Unusual operations
International activities
Metrication

WAREHOUSING AND TRAFFIC

New crating, palletizing
New handling and shipping procedures
Improvements in inventory control,
   order handling

compressed into the first paragraph or two; then facts of slightly less importance are given; and so on in descending order.

Writing the story in this form serves two purposes. First, it gives the reader the meat of the story quickly, at the start; and second, it enables the editor to trim the story from the bottom, in accordance with the story's value and timeliness and the space available.

The publicist announcing a new product can use this inverted pyramid design, but only to a point. Information vital to one reader may be less important to the next.

Generally speaking, you'll want to pack the key facts into the first paragraph and follow this with a paragraph on the actual and potential uses of the product. After that, the sequence doesn't make much difference, except for the last paragraph.

As vital as the first or lead paragraph, the last one or two paragraphs should tell:

• Where to write for more information, including street address and zip code.
• Name of person to contact, if a person has been designated. If a certain department handles inquiries, specify.
• Telephone number to call for information.
• Variations available, if any.
• Whether or not literature on the new product is available. If it is (it should be), give the publication title and number.

Example

Following is an example of a product press release from a fictitious manufacturer of electrical apparatus. I give this release not as an example of an ideal or perfect piece of work, but rather as typifying the structure of a release. Note that the release provides all the information specified under "What the Release Should Tell."

Illustrating the product press release properly and imaginatively is an art in itself. See Chapter 3 for a full discussion.

New Air-Operated Limit Switch Announced by Alva Electric

A new, air-operated, oiltight limit switch for machine–tool control applications — the first switch of its kind on the market — is now available from Alva Electric Company, Edison, NJ.

Unlike standard limit switches, the new device (catalog number 10TP) is operated by air pressure rather than by travel of an actuating device. The 10TP has a threaded, 1/8"-diameter opening in the top of its operating head. Here the user can connect the switch to a machine tool's air line by means of tubing or hose.

If pressure in the air line rises to 25 psi (± 25%), a mechanism in the switch head causes the contact block to operate. The switch will reset itself when pressure in the line drops to 15 psi (± 25%). A patented, snap-action blade in the block, common to all Alva limit switches, provides fast, positive switching for both parts of the switching cycle.

The latest addition to Alva's Series 10 line, the 10TP has two normally open and two normally closed contacts. Pilot duty ratings are: AC — 6 amps, 110 volts to 1.2 amps, 550 volts; DC — 0.4 amp, 115 volts to 0.1 amp, 550 volts.

A small hole in the side of the switch head releases excess pressure. This prevents high-pressure air from pushing out around the gaskets and breaking the oiltight seal.

Standard features of the 10TP include a sturdy aluminum case with steel cover; neoprene gaskets to ensure complete, oiltight sealing; and the rugged, snap-action contact block that provides positive switching and high contact force. The double-break contacts, made of silver alloy, will operate many millions of times without requiring attention.

The list price of the basic 10TP limit switch with threaded 1/8" top opening is $98.00.

For more information, get in touch with Guy Depuy, Alva Electric Company, 21 Orange Avenue, Edison, NJ 12345. Tel. 201/777-5151. Ask for Bulletin 10TP-80.

-30-

Enclosed: One photo
         One diagram

THE PERSONNEL PRESS RELEASE

Most industrial companies, as well as other types of organizations, find it advantageous to publicize personnel changes. Doing so keeps the company name before the various publics and also helps to boost and maintain employee morale.

What the Release Should Tell

A personnel press release gives the following information:

Full name of person, including middle initial. If the subject is known by a nickname, that should appear, too.

Nature of change: appointment, promotion, transfer, retirement, etc.

Nature of the job – plant manager, director of research, superintendent of a department.

Name of person who previously held position, if not a new one, and this person's new position or affiliation.

Name and title of person making the announcement.

Subject's duties in new position.

Nature of subject's previous position.

Subject's previous work experience.

Subject's schooling, degree(s), military service, memberships, other affiliations.

Special achievements such as awards, articles, books, patents; also, elected and appointive offices.

Family data.

Example

Following is an example showing the wording and sequence in a personnel press release. The names of the subject and company are fictitious.

John B. Jones
Named to New Post
at Acme Metals Co.

John B. "Jack" Jones has been promoted to the position of national marketing director at the Acme Metals Company, Buffalo, New York. Jones assumes his new post July 1st.

Previously Acme's regional sales manager for the northeastern U.S., Jones replaces Robert Brown, who left Acme to start his own consulting business.

The announcement comes from William C. Baxter, Acme's vice-president of marketing.

As national marketing director, Jones will manage the activities of Acme's regional field sales force, regional warehouses, and service center outlets. He will also direct the company's advertising and sales promotion activities.

Jones came to Acme in 1974 as a field salesman. He had held a similar position with Mahoning Tube, Youngstown, Ohio.

A 1968 graduate of Purdue University's College of Engineering, Jones is a member of the Society of Manufacturing Engineers.

Jones and his wife Carmella and son Brian reside in Dunkirk, New York.

-30-

Photo enclosed.

FORMAT

Regardless of the subject matter, each release should include the following elements in its format (see Fig. 2-1):

• At the top center of first page, the words "PRESS RELEASE" or "NEWS RELEASE." This tells the editor that he is looking at a release, not a letter, background sheet, or other communication.

• At the top left of first page, if the release comes directly from a company, the company name and address, name of person to contact for more information, and telephone number.

If the release is done for a company by an agency, add a similar block for the agency. Example:

> FOR: Alva Electric Company
> 21 Orange Avenue
> Edison, NJ 12345
> Tel.: 201/777-5151
> Contact: Guy Depuy

> FROM: Cue Publicity
> 1111 Falls Street
> Newark, NJ 12345
> Tel.: 201/111-2020

```
                        NEWS RELEASE

      FOR:  Alva Electric Company    .   FOR IMMEDIATE RELEASE
            21 Orange Avenue
            Edison, NJ  12345            Release No. AE-80-10
              Tel. 201/777-5151
              Contact: Guy Depuy

      FROM:  Cue Publicity
             1111 Falls Street
             Newark, NJ  12345
               Tel. 201/111-2020
               Contact: Mary Doyle




      New air-operated limit switch
      announced by Alva Electric

         A new, air-operated, oiltight limit switch for machine tool

      control applications -- the first switch of its kind on the

      market -- is now available from the Alva Electric Company,

      Edison, NJ.

             Unlike standard limit switches, the new device (catalog
```

Fig. 2-1. Top of sample press release written by an agency for its client. On releases written by a company staff publicist, the lower block would be omitted and the upper block would be labeled "From."

- Release number and/or date.
- The words "For Immediate Release." If you want the release held until a particular date or issue, specify. Examples: "For Release October 1 or Later" or "For October Issue."
- Headline. This should tell the editor what the release is about in a few words. Assume that the editor will rewrite your headline.
- At the bottom of each page except the last, the word "more." This tells the typesetter that there is more copy to follow for this story. In the composing room, the sheets of copy for a story sometimes become separated. The word "more" indicates that the sheet in hand is not the last or only sheet.
- At the top of the second and succeeding pages, an identification or slug such as "Page 2, Air Limit Switch, Alva Electric Co."
- At the bottom of the last page, the number "–30–," the traditional symbol for end of story. A pound sign (#) or the word "End" will serve as well.

If you're sending along an illustration or two, add a notation such as "Photo enclosed" or "Enclosures: One b&w photo print and one color transparency." Sometimes, in the haste of editorial work, a release becomes separated from its illustrations. A footnote on the release will remind the editor to look for the illustrations.

LENGTH

Begin at the beginning, with the meat of the story. Proceed to tell all important details, leaving out sales-puff. When you have finished, stop.

Yes, but how long should it be? You'll find that most personnel-change stories can be told in one double-spaced page or less. Many new-product stories can be told in one page; some will require one and one-half to two pages.

But what if you're announcing a complete, major new product line, or a product that embodies a complex, important new concept?

Write two releases: a two-pager for general release, and a longer, more complete release for the technical magazines in your field that can use all the details.

Why bother with a long release? Because it will provide the editor with all the information that he needs to do a complete report, without having to dig through brochures and manuals to find essential details.

This is the best way to get printed reports of a half-page, a full page, or even more in the technical magazines. I have scored often with full-length, technical press releases; see Fig. 2-2 for an example.

PRINTING

The main requirements here, as in most other printing jobs, are legibility and cleanliness. Short-run offset printing from low-cost plates usually fills the bill.

If your mailing list for a release is relatively short — say, 25 or fewer — consider using dry-copying office equipment such as Xerox or Kodak. Just make sure that the sheets come through relatively clean and free of specks, gray areas, and stray lines. Messy-looking releases often end up in the round file.

THE MAILING LIST

Questions: How do you build a mailing list of editors and news directors, and how long should the list be? Answer: Whom do you

The Leading Edge

Trolley-mounted robot can travel hundreds of feet, do work of several robots

A new robot system for material handling applications which require lateral travel and long horizontal travel was unveiled by PaR Systems, a division of GCA Corp., at the Autofact III expo in Detroit.

Called the XR-6100 robot, the new unit consists of an electro-mechanical robot mounted on a telescoping mast. This is fixed to a trolley which can travel laterally on a rail-mounted bridge. The bridge rides on rails which can be installed on the floor, ceiling or wall.

In effect, the unit is a crane-mounted robot which can travel quickly over hundreds of feet from station to station. With the range afforded by the mast and the traveling bridge, the XR-6100 robot has an extraordinarily large work envelope.

The simple, low-cost friction drive for the bridge and trolley has carefully controlled acceleration and deceleration to prevent skidding. Even with all the moving components involved, the system can position its robot gripper repeatedly within plus or minus 0.020 inch.

The bridge, trolley and mast have a load capacity of 500 pounds and a top speed of 36 inches per second. The robot gripper can lift up to 100 pounds laterally. In special designs, grippers for lifting up to 15 tons have been built.

Wide range of options

PaR Systems offers a wide variety of control and teaching options for the XR-6100. Continuous-path or point-to-point routines may be programmed. Teaching may be performed by any of three standard methods: on-line lead-through with joystick, off-line local and off-line global.

Off-line with 3D animation on a CRT unit can also be provided.

Besides the usual cable controls, PaR offers micro-wave data links between microprocessors in the control console and the traveling robot assembly. PaR has successfully engineered a system with this option for a zinc refinery, where the robot is working over sulphuric acid baths.

Basic design of an XR-6100 robot system with floor-mounted rails.

Debut of an "old pro"

You may not have heard of PaR Systems, but the St. Paul-based company has been engineering manipulator and robot systems, both traveling and stationary, for over 20 years. Many U.S. nuclear power plants use PaR remotely controlled fuel-handling systems.

The XR-6100 represents the company's first venture into the general industrial markets. Purchased in July, 1981, by GCA Corp., Bedford, MA, PaR Systems is expanding its capacity and evaluating potential industrial applications for the XR-6100.

A 24-year-old company, GCA Corp. has about 3000 employees in the U.S. Long a factor in the semiconductor manufacturing, manipulator, instrumentation and vacuum furnace industries, GCA recently formed an industrial systems group. This group will concentrate on the design of advanced material handling and other automation systems for industry.

If you'd like more details on the XR-6100 robot system, PaR manipulator systems or the GCA Corp., circle 158.
— JOE QUINLAN

MATERIAL HANDLING ENGINEERING

Fig. 2-2. Published two-page news story resulting from press kit and trade-show exhibit.

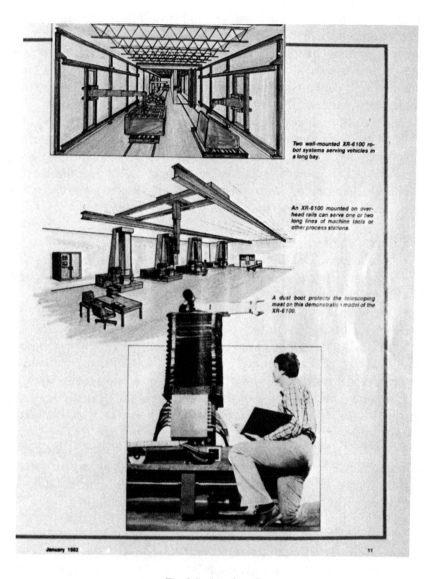

Two wall-mounted XR-6100 robot systems serving vehicles in a long bay.

An XR-6100 mounted on overhead rails can serve one or two long lines of machine tools or other process stations.

A dust boot protects the telescoping mast on this demonstration model of the XR-6100.

Fig. 2-2. (continued)

want to reach with your message, and how much do you want to spend to reach them?

First, decide which publics to target. Consider not only customers and prospects, but also employees, the general public in the cities where you have plants, potential distributors, security analysts, stockholders, and others.

Next, consult directories such as *Bacon's Publicity Checkers,* the *N. W. Ayer Directory of Newspapers and Periodicals,* and the various directories published by Standard Rate & Data Service (SRDS). Don't overlook other sources, such as your local telephone directories, *Gebbie's Directory of House Periodicals,* and *Writer's Market.* Consider periodicals in all pertinent categories, including:

- Trade and technical magazines, tabloids, journals.
- Newspapers — national, city, suburban, small-town.
- Company periodicals — those published by your own company, your suppliers, and your major customers.
- Periodicals published by technical, trade, and professional societies, associations, fraternities.
- In the case of personnel press releases, remember periodicals published by college alumni associations, fraternities, professional societies, religious groups, and other special interest organizations.
- Business periodicals. Consider the benefits of having your story appear in the *Wall Street Journal, Industry Week, Business Week, Forbes,* and so on.
- Wire services. If your story concerns a significant event or development, the release should say so. If it does, maybe you can get a pickup by AP, UPI, Reuters, etc. Consult the phone book for addresses.
- Would the company benefit by having the story broadcast on radio and television? If so, consult telephone directories for addresses of local and nearby stations. Find out the names of the station news directors; if you can't, address the release to "News Director."

Build as complete a list as you can; then pare it down to a manageable, affordable size. Take into account the costs of photoprints and that big one, postage.

THE MAILING

You've printed, collated, and stapled the releases; you've ordered and received the photoprints; the address labels and envelopes are at hand. What's missing?

Cardboard. Don't ship photos through the mail or by U.P.S. without cardboard stiffeners to protect the photos. Editors can't use photoprints on which the emulsion has been cracked.

Three more details:

1. Mail all releases First Class. Any other rate tells the recipient, "I'm not very important."

2. Stamp or preprint the envelopes with the legends "FIRST CLASS" and "PHOTOS – DO NOT BEND."

3. If you're sending 4" x 5" photoprints, don't use No. 10 or No. 11 business envelopes. The Postal Service's automatic machinery chews up business-size envelopes containing stiffeners.

Instead, use 6" x 9" manila envelopes and 5 1/2" x 8 1/2" cardboard stiffeners to protect the photos. Fold the release once, placing the prints in the middle. Label and stamp as you would 9" x 12" envelopes.

NINE WAYS TO STRETCH THE BUDGET

1. Gang illustrations for long releases. Some developments warrant a long release (see Fig. 2-3). Examples include complex products or engineering achievements such as instrumentation and large machines, as well as many types of engineered systems for control, testing, material handling, processing, etc.

For announcements of complex subjects, the editors of the major periodicals serving the fields involved appreciate receiving fairly complete, detailed releases. These may explain the development, construction, and operation of the equipment or system, along with its specifications, applications, and user benefits.

Here a long release saves time for the editor. He doesn't have to dig through lengthy support material or make the time-consuming phone calls to find all the information he wants for a complete story. Sending detailed news releases on complex developments will increase

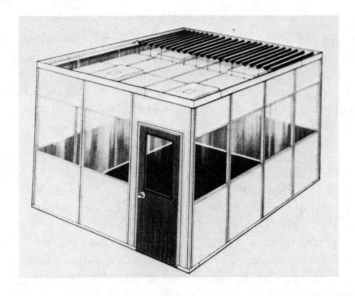

Fig. 2-3. Continuous-tone rendering and photo on one 8″ x 10″ print. Negatives for both illustrations were stripped into one 8″ x 10″ negative.

not only the percentage of pickups, but also the amount of editorial space — the number of column inches — per pickup.

For announcements to be mailed to periodicals not directly involved in the technical aspects of your field, consider sending a condensed, simplified version of the detailed release. *Business Week* and *Industry Week,* for example, may not want all the details going to the technical magazines.

Illustration of long releases calls for more than one photo. For complex subjects, editors like to be able to choose from a number of illustrations and from several kinds of illustrations. These may include not only continuous-tone photos but also plan or elevation drawings, circuit diagrams, cutaways, exploded views, cross-sections, and so on.

Reproducing these illustrations as individual prints could become expensive. To minimize reproduction costs, gang the illustrations whenever it is possible to do so without losing too much detail or clarity.

For example, say you're announcing a new drill press with some interesting design details. You've decided to send a three-quarter-view photo of the machine with a man operating it, a partial cutaway of the drillhead, and a simplified schematic of the control system.

Rather than reproducing these as three separate prints, shoot 4" x 5" negatives of the photo and cutaway, and a 5" x 7" of the schematic. Then have these negatives stripped together (ganged), and print them as a single 8" x 10". The total cost of, say, 100 8" x 10"s will be considerably less than the total for 200 4" x 5'''s and 100 5" x 7'''s.

We're assuming, of course, that the subject matter in the illustrations affords reduction to the sizes mentioned without too much loss of detail or shrinkage of letters, numbers, and symbols. If you save a few dollars by gang printing but miss a large number of pickups because the illustrations are too small or too condensed for good reproduction, then you're not really economizing. Instead, you're throwing away release dollars, and irritating editors to boot.

2. Go for color. When making a mailing of a new-product release, give special consideration to the new-product tabloids. Send each of the relevant tabloids a color transparency in addition to a black-and-white print. The transparency should be 2 1/4" x 2 1/4" or larger.

Why bother with color for the tabloids? Because you'll increase the efficiency of your mailing: the ratio of the total number of inquiries produced to the total cost.

In a letter to the author on this subject, John Van de Water, editor of *Industrial Equipment News,* pointed out that in his tabloid, ". . .color outpulls black & white two to one, on the average." He was referring to color photos printed inside the book.

Color on the front cover does even better. In four issues sampled, front-cover product announcements with color pictures outpulled black-and-white items inside the book by a ratio of four to one, on the average. "These are not isolated figures," stated Van de Water. "We find the pattern constant."

So if you want lots of inquiries − that is, sales leads − go after color pickups in the tabloids. The extra cost of the transparencies will be more than offset by the increased number of inquiries and the resultant drop in cost per inquiry.

3. Keep it "clean." Keep your mailing lists up to date. To be sure, you should add publications that may benefit your marketing efforts, but at the same time, stay on top of editors' transfers, changes in title, changes in publication name or address, cessation of publication, etc.

It's a great temptation to let change notices pile up, with the intent of updating the list on a slow day. That sort of day is slow in coming, though; meanwhile, you're working with an inefficient list. Returned and discarded releases are an outright waste. Make list maintenance a daily or at least a weekly routine.

In addition, go back over your clippings. List the periodicals that are publishing your releases; compare this list with your standard mailing lists.

If you find that a periodical is consistently ignoring your news, and that periodical is of only marginal value, drop it. On the other hand, if the periodical could do you some good, sales-wise, call the editor and level with him. Chances are that if you explain your company's present and potential role in his field, he'll pay more attention to your releases.

4. Standard vs. custom lists. When planning distribution of each release, ask yourself, "Can I use the standard lists, or should I custom-build a list?" Weigh the extra time and other costs of addressing a custom list against the waste that may result from using your standard lists.

Remember, too, that mailing releases to periodicals in nonrelevant fields tends to turn off the editors of those periodicals. "Product doesn't pertain to our field" is one of the reasons editors give most often for rejecting releases. Don't take a chance on having all your releases rejected automatically.

5. Conserve prints. Split your lists into two major parts: periodicals that do use publicity illustrations and those that do not. There's no point in sending pictures to publications that won't print them.

You can quickly and easily determine which periodicals do and don't use pictures by checking a directory of periodicals. *Bacon's Publicity Checker,* for instance, prints a triangle next to the listings of periodicals that do not use publicity photos.

6. Adapt releases from bulletins. Adapt the approved copy and illustrations from your new-product announcement bulletins. Your sales and product managers can use these bulletins to introduce new products to your field salespeople, district managers, distributors, dealers, warehouse people, reps, overseas offices, etc. – even before a detailed bulletin or catalog on the product has been published.

Issuing a new-product bulletin before the press release goes out will let your people know about the product's announcement to the press, well before printed items appear. Nothing is more embarrassing to a distributor or dealer than to have one of his customers query about a new product he hasn't even heard about.

You can keep the costs of the bulletin low by composing the copy on an electric typewriter and printing the photos as halftones. One company I know of sends copies of all their releases, with 8" x 10" glossies attached, to all their sales people.

Considering the costs of glossy prints, printing of multipage releases, 8 1/2" x 11" cardboard stiffeners, 9" x 12" envelopes, and postage, that's an expensive way to go. Setting the copy in cold type and printing the entire release, with photo, on one sheet would cut their announcement costs considerably.

7. Look for other uses. Look for additional ways to utilize your news stories, photos, etc. Likely places include:

• Internal house organ. Your employees want to know, and need to know, what's new in your company.

• External house organ. A vital part of the periodical you mail to customers and prospects is the news department. Besides telling about new products and/or services, this department can include stories and pictures on your company's latest literature, personnel changes, acquisitions, new plants, expansions, etc.

Not only will your customers and prospects appreciate receiving this news, but it will also greatly enhance the promotional value of your periodical. In fact, if you expect your external to pull inquiries, product news is a must.

• Sales house organ. Who needs the news more than the people who are out there on the front lines of your marketing? Even if you issue new-product announcement bulletins, as suggested in Tip No. 6, it won't hurt to repeat the story in your sales house organ.

After all, you have no guarantee that all concerned marketing people will actually receive and read each one of your new-product bulletins. Repeating the material in your sales house organ will increase the percentage of those who do.

8. Clippings help. If you're mailing more than one release a month to more than 50 periodicals, sign up with a clipping service. This is the best way to tell how many pickups you're getting, who's running your stories, how many column inches you're getting, who's using the illustrations, etc.

Only by knowing these facts can you (1) measure the effectiveness of your materials and techniques and (2) obtain guidelines for modifying the materials and techniques to achieve greater effectiveness.

9. Get a critique. At least once a year, put together a sampling of your news releases and have them evaluated for editorial quality by a qualified, disinterested third party, such as a PR agent or an editor. Ask the critic to evaluate your releases for brevity, completeness, punch, and the other elements of good newswriting.

For a small consulting fee, you'll be able to improve your writing and thereby increase the effectiveness of your releases. This in turn means greater economy: a higher percentage of pickups, and a lower cost per pickup and per inquiry.

TWO DOZEN DO'S AND DON'TS

Do

1. Remember that a press-release package is essentially a direct-mail communication to an editor. Follow the rules of strong but tasteful direct mail.

2. Stick to the facts. Don't make claims you can't substantiate.

3. Call the editor; offer additional details, illustrations, other help. Point out possible angles for related feature articles. Extra effort often pays.

4. Provide a good photo, drawing, or illustration for the release. Press releases with pictures stand a better chance of seeing print than do releases without pictures. (More on illustrations in Chapter 3.)

5. Prune your list of editors and news directors. Doing so will save you time and money, give you a higher percentage of pickups, and yield a lower cost per pickup and per inquiry.

6. Indicate actual and potential applications for a product. Don't assume extensive knowledge and imagination in the editors or readers. Spell it out.

7. Before printing your release, have it checked by responsible managers, engineers, etc. The recall of a release is a Royal Pain; so is the last-minute change.

8. Read the important magazines, tabloids, and newspapers serving your company's or client's field. See how they handle releases, what's important to them. Tailor your releases accordingly.

9. Be assured that your release packages will be opened, examined, and read. The staffs of most nonconsumer periodicals are small; the editors want and need your stories and pictures.

10. If you need help, call on a professional publicist, PR counsel, or freelance business journalist. Most ad writers don't know diddly-squat about writing, producing, and mailing effective release packages. Ask for recommendations from the editors; they're in frequent contact with many professionals.

11. For technical developments, write two different releases: one for general and business periodicals, the other for technical periodicals. The extra effort pays off – in ink.

12. Leave room at the top of the first page – room where the editor can write a new head and type specifications.

Don't

1. Call the editor and ask when the release will be published. The editor often doesn't know until the last minute.

2. Waste your time or the editor's on a cover letter that hints or threatens possible advertising. Editors are concerned with providing good editorial coverage; space representatives worry about ad-space

sales or the lack thereof. Let the ad manager do the wheeling and dealing with the space rep.

3. Send the same release to a magazine more than once. Editors will think you're trying to stuff the same story in twice. No fair.

4. Make claims for a product without supporting evidence or references, such as from testing labs.

5. State features of a product without explaining the resultant benefits to users. "Smaller ridges" doesn't mean much by itself; ". . .give better gripping action" answers the question, "So what?"

6. Fail to point out that the product is the first of its kind, largest, smallest, or otherwise significant for any reason. Don't assume the editor or readers will know.

7. Claim that a product is "unique" (one of a kind) or revolutionary unless it truly is. No puff, please.

8. Send a release on a new product until your company is prepared to answer inquiries. Otherwise you'll get burned, and the editors and readers will stoke the fire.

9. Try to represent an old product as new. Play it straight. Editors catch on, eventually, and they have long memories.

10. Ask to "see the item before it runs" or "let us check proofs." No dice.

11. Send onionskin, wet-copy, or heat-copy duplicates of a release. They're too hard to read.

12. Forget to double-check and triple-check spellings, numbers, names, dates. Most magazine issues have a relatively short shelf life, but those pages containing errors seem to hang around forever.

Chapter 3
Illustrating the Product
Press Release

Suppose you mail copies of a product press release to 100 magazines, tabloids, and other periodicals, including an assortment of horizontals, verticals, nationals, regionals, etc. If 25 of those periodicals edit and print the release — and they usually edit severely — you've done quite well. Of course, the quality of the mailing list has a major bearing on your score.

Let's further suppose that an editor at Magazine X has opened the release package you sent to him. What will catch his eye and cause him to not only read the release, but also publish it and the illustration?

Several factors come to his attention, including the general appearance and neatness of the release, the design of the letterhead and format, and recognition of your company's name and logo. These and other factors have an effect.

Without a doubt, though, the most important factor as far as appearance and first impression are concerned is the photo or other illustration.

As the box score (see Table 3-1) tells you, many news releases don't make it. Many well-written releases announcing timely new products end up in the round file.

A good photo helps; a poor photo hinders. Quite often the quality of the photo is the deciding factor.

Henry J. Holtz, editor of *New Equipment Digest,* made a telling statement on this subject. As you probably know, *NED* is one of the nation's major new-product industrial tabloids, with a circulation of

Table 3-1. The Box Score.

PERIODICAL	NUMBER OF RELEASES RECEIVED PER MONTH	NUMBER OF RELEASES PUBLISHED PER MONTH	%
Industrial Equipment News	2000	400	20
Industrial News	500	100	20
Industry Mart	400–500	80	16–20
Industry's Product News	200	75–100	37.5
Materials Engineering	500	100	20
New Equipment Digest	1500–2000	500	25–33.3

Source: Mail survey conducted by author.

about 195,000. When asked, "In deciding whether or not to run a release, how much difference does the photo make (good vs. poor)?", Holtz's reply was, in part: "I'm sure we at least subconsciously reject some product-releases with poor photos. After all, we reject many releases sent without photos, simply because we don't have adequate room for all submissions."

Another editor who voiced that viewpoint was John A. Mock, managing editor of *Materials Engineering*. "A good photo, along with good copy, certainly is a deciding factor in selecting one release over another," Mock said.

So you face a challenging question: What can you put into the picture-idea, exposure, and print that will grab the editor? The question really is: What can you do to help your company's releases get published, pull inquiries, generate sales, and increase profits and prosperity?

Following is a checklist of pointers, drawn from my many years of full-time work and study in industrial editing and publicity, from comments and direction by other pros, and from the spoken and written tips of many other editors.

A word of reassurance: Don't be afraid of becoming bound up by rules. These are guidelines only, not rails you must ride. In PR, as in advertising, there's plenty of room for creative, exciting picture-ideas

PORTABLE EYE WASH UNIT
allows hands-free operation

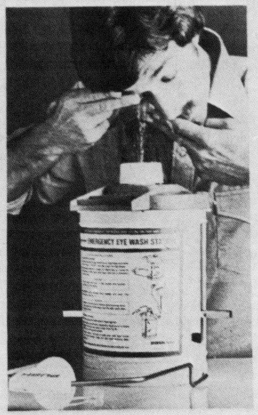

Portable 7½-in.
in. tall emergenc
station made of u
plastic can b
wherever there is
danger. It holds
water, weighs
when filled, and
any position, ir
verted, so that a
down can be hel
Unit operates wi
of the hands
stream has bee
An orifice plug ;
dust cover prev
tion, leaking, and air - borne contamination
75 Panorama Creek Dr., Rochester, N. Y. 1⁴

▲ N

Fig. 3-1. A human using the publicized equipment adds much interest to this photo.

SHOWING THE PRODUCT

1. Illustrate the product clearly. As you can tell by the comments in Table 3-2, lack of clarity is the gripe mentioned most often by the editors polled. What do they mean by "clarity," though? In part, they're referring to the amateurish, poorly lit images they receive from companies that don't know any better or don't want to invest in good photography.

But there's more to clarity than that. Focus should be sharp, not only on the leading edge or surface but all the way back. That calls for adequate depth of field and length of exposure.

Lighting of the product should reveal its textures and as many gradations of tone as possible, as well as all or nearly all important details. Show the reader, in one still view, as much about the product as you can.

Separation from the background is important, too. To show the outlines of the product adequately, avoid white on white, black on black, and middle greys on middle greys. High-key and dusky mood

Table 3-2. Editors' Likes and Dislikes.

Q. What do you look for *most* in product photos?

- "Clarity, detail."
- "Clarity, sharpness of detail."
- "I look for reproduction value in a photo (we use a newsprint stock). Action-scenes demonstrating the product are not essential, but nice. Clarity is important. Lots of photos come in that are fuzzy, muddy and generally useless."
- "Clarity, emphasis on product – preferably in use."
- "Clarity of details, uncluttered background, something that shows size of product (if that's important)."
- "We prefer photos showing some typical uses, or unusual backdrops, or both."

Q. What are your most frequent gripes re product photos?

- " . . . a product photo showing a can of paint, or a tube of adhesive, but nothing more. To us, this type of photo is unimaginative and uninteresting, and is not likely to catch the reader's attention."
- "Fuzzy, cluttered, 'Top' not marked, poor quality (e.g., poor Polaroid print), important details don't show."
- "Black boxes on gray backgrounds; emphasis on girl instead of product; photos without margins for cropping; pictures out of focus, or too grainy, or gray; product container instead of the product itself, or the product in use; prints smaller than 4" x 5"; captions, labels or logos which interfere with cropping and don't show anyway when reduced; and photos pasted on copy-paper."
- "Not close-up enough; can't see enough detail."

shots may work great for fashion and cosmetic ads, where the photos will be printed large, but such shots won't do the job in new-product pages of trade mags.

That brings up a related point: the matter of size. Keep in mind that your beautiful 8″ x 10‴'s will be shrunk mercilessly by the editors, sometimes to a width of less than an inch (see Table 3-3).

In most cases, you'll want the product to occupy half or more of the height or width of the image, whichever is critical. The more detail there is to show, the greater the percentage of image area the product should occupy.

Make a test print and look at it through a reducing glass. Does the product show up large, even in a small image? It should, usually. If the product is simple in appearance, though — simple in contour, lacking fine detail — you can ignore the principle of dominance to some extent.

Are certain physical details all-important? If so, you may want to consider and suggest one of the following:

Photo of detail area alone.
Photo of detail area plus overall view of product; negatives stripped together to make combination print.
Cutaway or cross section of actual product.
Airbrush rendering of cutaway or cross section.
Cutaway or cross section line drawing.
Photo with arrows pointing to, or circles around, key details.

**Table 3-3. Questions to Ask When Planning Illustrations
for Product News Releases**

1. How big is it? Is size important? Should we show a range of sizes or types?
2. What is the end use of the product? How is it applied?
3. Should we show easy installation, application, or operation?
4. Does the product do something special — e.g., make a new kind of part, or achieve a better result? What could we show?
5. Which exterior and interior (hidden) details are most important? Will a close-up or macro photo do the job? Should we consider cutaways, cross sections, drawings, renderings?
6. Do we need extra devices — e.g., callouts, arrows, circles — to tell the story?
7. Who's involved in the use of this product — men, women, or both?
8. Where can we find an actual application of this product in operation or use? Nearby? Photogenic setup? Should we stage a special setup?
9. Would a drawing or rendering do the job better than a photo, or do we want some kind of combination? Will we need photos for reference?
10. If hidden interior details are important, can we get an actual cutaway or cross section of the product made, to photograph? Or is there some suitable art already made?

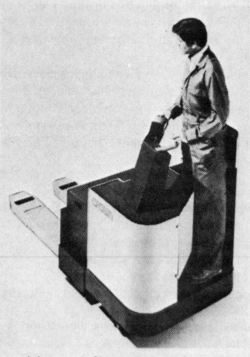

RIDER PALLET TRUCK
6-in. lift, 6,000-lb capacity

Series PR Ri
Truck for hi
material   r
boasts a 6,000
ity and 6-in. li
powered by a
tem and featu
steering and
loaded,   ar
stabilizing c
maneuvering
ple thumb n
activate lift,
horn pushb
trols. Padded
cushioned floor, and foot-operated deadman
standard. **Crown Controls Corp.**, New Bre
45869   ▲ MAF

Fig. 3-2. This illustration gains from the dramatic, high camera angle and the presence of a human operator.

Should you decide on a line drawing, make sure all the lines are thick enough to stand severe reduction. Check them with a reducing glass.

Do you plan to copy a combination involving callouts, arrows, circles, or other added line art? Again, check with a reducing glass. Callouts that reproduce too small only irritate the editor and readers.

Is the installation, application, or operation of the product the key point that should be illustrated? See if you can dream up a way to show it in one shot. True, a sequence of two, three, or more pictures might do the job better, but few editors can give you enough space to show the sequence large enough for effective communication.

Suppose your new product is a material, and you want to show one or more of its desirable properties. Challenge: Come up with a picture-idea that effectively demonstrates the key property.

For instance, is the product a new super-glue? Don't settle for a shot of the tube lying on a tabletop. Show the glue in action, performing a tough holding job.

"I guess our most frequent gripe is the product-photo that shows a can of paint or tube of adhesive, but nothing more," said John Mock of *Materials Engineering,* speaking of the new-product pictures he gets with releases. Show your material in action, or at least in a comparison.

A word of caution on showing your company's logo or nameplate: Keep it where it belongs on the product, and don't make it too pronounced in the photo. Editors don't like to give free plugs to brand names in pictures; they'd rather show the product. Try to jam a logo down an editor's throat, and he may jam the photo — and the release, too — down the chute.

To wrap up this section on showing the product, here are a few short tips regarding composition and lighting:

Keep the highlights away from the edges of the image. Remember, the printing process greys a white to about 10% of black and cuts pure black to about 90%. Highlights on the edges of a printed photo blend into the surrounding paper and are lost.

Many editors prefer that the dominant light fall from the upper left corner of a photo. Their new-product pages often look jumbled; uniform lighting of the product shots helps to minimize the jumbled look.

Light the subject for medium contrast, with a wide range of values, but avoid chalky whites and solid blacks if you can. Also eschew the washed-out, all-grey look.

Align the product with the horizontal, not the vertical.

2. Show the product in use. With some machinery this is easy. Graders can be shown grading and sweepers sweeping. But what about machine tools, plastic molding machines, wood lathes, etc.?

Well, if the machine makes an interesting part, can you include a sample part in the picture, perhaps as an inset? Maybe the end products of the machine are more interesting than the machine itself. If so, let the parts dominate the picture.

Suppose the new product is a component, assembly, part, or material. Here your challenge is greater. If you can show the product installed and functioning, fine; if not, concentrate on creating a grabber of a photo that shows the product alone, and let the text tell about the applications.

3. Show the product's range. If you're announcing a line of products available in a range of sizes or types, show the range. This doesn't mean you must show all the variations. Clutter the picture with too many items, and few details will show.

Suppose your company is introducing a line of air valves in 12 sizes. Show the smallest, the largest, and one specimen from the middle of the range. Three is plenty; more may be too much.

4. Show the relative size of the product(s). You probably know many devices for showing size, including rulers, paper clips, golf balls, hands, fingers, faces, and so on. When choosing an object for size comparison, stick to something common, something not too interesting in itself. Otherwise the reader may ignore your product and concentrate on the object.

One time, in trying to show the size of a new pump, a photographer friend of mine used a live white mouse. The mouse showed the pump's size, all right, but also stole the show. And talk about flak! "Makes our pump look cheesy," grumbled the product manager. "We ain't sellin' no damned rats," groused the sales manager, only half in jest. My friend hasn't used a mouse since.

5. Keep the background simple. Remember, overall simplicity is a prime virtue of good new-product photos. Don't let the background become too busy, too detailed, or even too interesting.

That doesn't mean you must stick to plain backdrop paper. Sometimes the background provides the setting of the application situation that makes the photo meaningful. A skidder dragging a log through

LT RIVET
anchored from top of belt

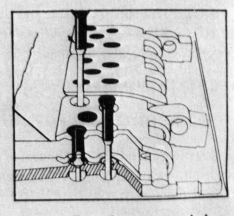

step assembly pro-
 e quickly mates con-
 r belt sections with-
urning the belt over.
 en by Model SR-50
 tool, combination
nail assembly pierces
Portable Model SRT
 ing tool anchors the
 in a long wearing,
 covered hinge pin. Type R5 fastener joins
from ⁷⁄₃₂ to ⁷⁄₁₆ in. thick with working tensions
450 lb per inch of width. Type R6 rivet mates

Fig. 3-3. A simple drawing shows the functions of belt rivets better than a photo could.

the forest, for example, or a cutter head on a milling machine, making
chips — the background is an important part of the message. Just
keep the product up front, dominant.

Want a pretty girl's face beside or behind the product? Try moving
her back a little and using an f-stop or focal length that will throw her
slightly out of focus. She'll still be there, attractive but not intrusive.

6. Include human interest. Try as we may, we have a hard time
making some industrial hardware look interesting. Even the most
interesting hardware is still only that: hardware.

What's more interesting than hardware? People, of course. Engineers, technicians, purchasing agents — they're all people first, then
technical functionaries. Even the most objective, rational, thing-

minded researcher will be attracted more quickly with a photo having human interest.

About that term, "human interest": it's rather vague. What does it include? Well, you can establish "HI" with as little as a fingertip or as much as a crowd of people. Faces have tremendous pulling power; so do close-ups of eyes. And don't forget the magic pull of children, babies, puppies, kittens — and beautiful girls.

The last-named subject, girls, deserves a few extra comments. Here, we're in an area of high subjectivity. Some editors like good girl/product shots; others merely tolerate them; and still others want nothing to do with them.

Small wonder. Editors have been bombarded with so many cheap, sleazy, irrelevant "meat shots" that they want no more dames with the hardware, period.

One such editor is Peter Lichtgern of *Industrial News*. Asked, "What are your most frequent gripes?", he replied: "I loathe cheap-looking women standing in front of or beside some product, pretending they are selling — as in a TV commercial. Models usually cause me to reject a photo.

"This does not mean I reject the photo if there is a purpose for a person being in the shot," Lichtgern added, tempering his previous statement. "It's OK if the product is shown in actual use. I just don't like people pointing to 'interesting' points and features of the product."

You get the point. Let there be a reason for the girl in the picture. Operating a forklift in a warehouse? Sure. Driving a front-end loader? Well, maybe.

What about having a pretty girl holding up a small product? She helps draw attention to the photo, and then to the product — right?

As mentioned, we're in a subjective area. My advice: Let the product, not the girl, dominate the photo.

Now, suppose you're showing a new piece of machinery, and you have a male operator (playing it safe, eh?) running the machine. Two tips: (1) let the operator be dressed in authentic work clothes; (2) before you shoot, make sure he isn't wearing a loud shirt. Wild plaids and checks have a way of dominating a scene.

Clean up before shooting the picture. This is so obvious you'd think it needn't be mentioned. But much film and time have been wasted because someone forgot to remove a pop-can or shop-rag from a scene.

Check for safety — another obvious point worth repeating. Are guards in place on moving parts, goggles on, oil wiped up, cans covered, etc.? This check is worth extra time. Nine people may miss a safety violation in a photo; the tenth, who spots it, may be an OSHA watchdog. Trouble.

MAKING THE PRINTS

Editors prefer 5" x 7", 8" x 10", or 8 1/2" x 11" prints. They're easier to handle, crop, and mark than are the smaller sizes. Moreover, large prints have a stronger impact on the editor, and he's the one you must sell before you reach his readers.

Usually, a news release goes to more than one periodical; hence the name "release." If the total number of periodicals exceeds, say, 100, you may want to consider the more economical, mass-produced, 4" x 5" print size.

Perhaps you have the time and facilities to make large runs. If not, you'll likely want to order from one of the shops that specialize in quantity runs.

Suggestion: Shoot on 4" x 5" film to begin with, or make your own copy negative 4" x 5". That way, you can control the density and you chances of getting high-grade quantity prints will be better.

At various times during my career, I've dealt with six different quantity-print shops. Without exception, their services were fine: fast delivery, good prints, careful packaging, safe return of the negatives — and low price.

A few times, though, I've received prints that were muddy. It could have been human error or mechanical; in either case, the shop should have known better than to ship them.

If you get bad prints, don't sue the lab; don't scrap the prints either. Return them, ask for a rerun, and tell why. You'll lose time, nothing else. Mailing out substandard prints would not only reduce the number of pickups of your release but would also cause your company to lose the regard of some editors.

)OR MAT

rsible, non-slip mat
exible V-ribs on one
and a pattern of
knobs on the other.
of a special NIRU
ound that resists
e, oil, alkali, alco-
nd acid, new Cross
I matting may be
on floors of plants and laboratories to prevent
and falls. Samples are available on request.
C. **Musson Rubber Co.**
0 Archwood Ave, Akron, OH 44306
- **6706** ◢ identifies this—write it on your Reader Service For

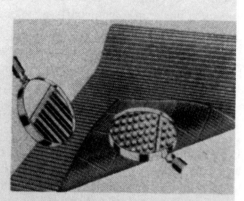

Fig. 3-4. Composite illustration made by combining photos of magnifying glasses and rubber mat.

Always make new-product prints with borders, not borderless. Editors need the white space for crop marks and scaling instructions for their art and production people. The more space the better. To play it safe, make all new-product photoprints glossy; most editors prefer them that way.

If, in viewing your picture, the editor or reader could have any doubt which is the top, type the word "TOP" and shoot it on Kodalith. Then strip that little piece on the top of the main negative.

SUMMARY

Keep it simple; show the product clearly, especially important details; insert action and human interest; show the product in use or being demonstrated; lean toward medium to high contrast; and go for color.

One more point: Study the new-product pages of the big new-product tabloids — *New Equipment Digest, Industrial Equipment News, Product Design & Development* and so on — and the verticals serving your company's fields. See what the editors are using, how large they print the new-product photos, which ones grab you, and how various photos reproduce. Also, try to think up ways to plan and shoot better pictures than what your competitors are sending to the editors.

Chapter 4
Why Releases Fail

Only one out of five releases mailed ever sees print, on the average. Why?

To find out, I conducted a mail survey of 28 editors of trade periodicals. The magazines chosen for the poll represent a broad cross section of industry and business, and vary widely in circulation, size, and format. Twenty-eight editors replied.

"Not very scientific," you may object. "Twenty-eight responses won't give a very accurate picture."

True, the poll was not scientific, but I was after general indicators, not numbers with decimals to the fourth place. More important, I was after spontaneous comments from the editors. As you'll see, they came through with some telling, valuable comments.

The one-page questionnaire contained six questions. Following is a summary of the replies:

1. How many new-product press releases do you receive each month, on the average?

   Average number: 382.2
   Highest number: 2,000
   Lowest number: 37

2. Of the releases received, how many do you edit and print each month, on the average?

   Average number: 66.3
   Highest number: 350   *(EE–Electrical Equipment)*
   Lowest number: 4   *(Automotive Cooling Journal)*

Percentages of releases used vs. releases received were:

Average percentage: 20.5%
Highest percentage: 62.5% *(American Building Supplies)*
Lowest percentage: 2.4% *(Materials Performance)*

3. What length of press release do you prefer?

	Number	*%*
Less than one page	7	25.0
One page	8	28.6
Two pages	1	3.6
Depends on significance of product complexity of message	12	42.8

4. For which reasons do you most often reject new-product press releases?

Since this was an "essay" question, the wording of the replies varied considerably. For tabulation, answers similar in meaning and wording were grouped. Here's a list of replies, in order of frequency.

	Number	*%*
a. Product not relevant to our field.	22	78.6
b. Release is poorly written: not clear, or not enough information; doesn't tell what product will do for reader.	11	39.3
c. Too much "puff."	9	32.1
d. Product is not new, or we have run this release before.	8	28.6
e. Too much copy; "nuggets" hard to find.	5	17.9
f. Product not newsworthy — obviously a minor development.	3	10.7
g. Poor photos.	3	10.7
h. Same company continually saturates us with releases, sometimes sending duplicates, even triplicates.	2	7.1
i. Sloppy, illegible typing or printing.	2	7.1
j. Cover letter attempts to entice or pressure, with hints of advertising.	2	7.1

	Number	%
k. No photo or other illustration.	2	7.1
l. "Dum-dum agency omitted their client's name, address, phone number."	1	3.6
m. Release originates from agency noted for representing old products as new.	1	3.6
n. Similar releases from two or more direct-mail sellers of same product.	1	3.6
o. Company never advertises in our magazine.	1	3.6
p. Company has no distribution setup.	1	3.6

5. What are your most frequent complaints about the illustrations sent with new-product press releases?

	Number	%
a. Too "busy" for amount of space we can give to it; won't stand reduction.	8	28.6
b. Picture lacks clarity, delineation between product and background.	7	25.0
c. Poor focus, exposure, or printing.	6	21.4
d. Models dominate photo(s); by the time photo is reduced, product can scarcely be seen.	5	17.9
e. Odd-shaped pictures — they take up too much space, can't be cropped well.	3	10.7
f. "Sexist" — superfluous use of women or stupid, forced picture idea with model.	3	10.7
g. Pictures with type in them — usually copies of composite art or catalog covers; type can't be read anyway.	2	7.1
h. "Too many photos with pretty girls but ugly products."	2	7.1
i. "Hard-sell" photographic tactics, including nudes.	2	7.1
j. Product is not shown in use or environment for which intended.	2	7.1

	Number	*%*
k. Dull "catalog shot." (Company should use more imagination, think up picture that grabs.)	2	7.1
l. Company sends catalog, wants me to cut out picture and use!	1	3.6
m. No reference-point in photo; which way is up?	1	3.6
n. Can't tell what product is or how it's used.	1	3.6
o. Doesn't show key, internal parts or design of product. (We prefer cutaways.)	1	3.6
p. Picture shows packaging or display, but not product or its use.	1	3.6
q. Lack of borders for crop marks.	1	3.6
r. Marking on back of print shows through.	1	3.6
s. Ball-point writing on back of print; leaves "tracks" on emulsion.	1	3.6
t. Color snapshots, color Polaroid prints, photostats — we don't want 'em.	1	3.6

6. Any additional comments?

The figures and replies to our first five questions were instructive, but this last question elicited some of the most pungent and telling comments. Evidently we touched a number of raw nerves. Following are some of the answers given to Question 6.

"I believe the trade-press or PR groups should provide all marketers with a standard product-release format. If magazine circulation departments can attain comparability standards, editorial can, too." — John Rehfield, *Construction Equipment.* "If industrial PR people would get the name of their company president out of releases, they'd be doing everyone a favor. The product is the thing which is most important, not that 'President John J. Jones announces that the company is going to market a new thingamabob.' While PR people may feel they are scoring points with the old man, they sure aren't with most editors." — Stanley A. Rodman, *Automotive Cooling Journal.*

"More time in preparation would bring better results." – Bruce W. Smith, *Grain Age.*

"There are a few really good ones, but lots of bad ones." – H.B. Barks, *Electrical Apparatus.*

"All too frequently, the original writer of the release fails to grasp the basics of the product he's trying to describe, and/or its importance to the market he's trying to reach. If he can't, we as editors frequently can't." – Sid Wrightsman, *American Building Supplies.*

"Never ask for a rate-card in the new-product release, and never ask for a copy of the magazine or a tear-sheet." – Robert J. Deierlein, *Diesel Equipment Superintendent.*

"Seems like a lot of people will send anything – with little thought behind it." – Thomas T. Hoke, *Materials Performance.*

"The growing number of errors in PR releases we receive is alarming!" – Robert A. Massaro, *Industrial Maintenance and Plant Operation.*

It's evident that the publicist who learns and bothers to write a tight, high-tell, low-sell release; thinks up imaginative photos that reduce well; and builds a lean, totally relevant mailing list – that publicist will score well in the trade press.

Chapter 5
The Case History

First, a definition. The case history is a story in which the writer tells of a problem that a person or company had and how that person or company analyzed the problem and solved it through the smart application of a product, method, material, service, or other means.

Many newsworthy case-history situations arise from the successful application of products and related services, such as assistance in selection, layout or system design, and installation. These are basically engineering stories and are bought by engineering and production magazines as well as by many company periodicals.

You'll find, though, that not all problems are engineering problems; not all case histories are "technical." Editors of business magazines want case histories dealing with problems and solutions in virtually any aspect of business, including marketing, employee relations, warehousing, and distribution.

You may come across other categories, depending on which industry you're working in. The point is, wherever a business person, engineer, or production manager encounters a problem or challenge, and finds a solution; wherever he finds a way to cut costs, boost profits, or improve efficiency; there you have the makings for a case history.

Ideally, the format of a case history follows a formula:

Lead — the introduction to a situation, statement of a problem, or statement of a solution.
Description of the problem, in detail.
Analysis of the problem by the story's "heroes," attempts at solution, and alternatives considered.

Description of the solution and how it was applied.

The happy results.

Notice that the case history is quite specific and sharply focused. It deals with one problem only, but explores that single situation in detail.

In this respect, the case history differs from the "installation profile," which deals with many aspects of a company's activities and may cover the products and services of many suppliers.

Another type of story closely related to the case history is the "satisfied user" report, a format favored by editors of some company periodicals. Usually, it is more broad and loose than the case history, and lacks the latter's sharp focus.

EXAMPLES

To give you a better idea of the case-history format, I've capsulized three case-history stories published in trade and company periodicals. In each instance, the capsule begins with either the actual headline used or a statement that gives the story's gist. Following the summary is a reference to the source.

1. *Underground pipe leaks pinpointed.* "Locating leaks in buried piping systems by means of the 'dig-and-search' method is not the most efficient way to get to the problem." Three plumbers, employees of the New York City Housing Authority, won $100 apiece for their prize-winning, innovative solution.

This involves the use of an inflatable rubber plug, positioned in the pipe from above ground, and opposed by water at 20 psi. Plug is moved until pressure gauge shows sudden drop in water pressure. Leak can then be pinpointed to within a few feet, saving much digging time. (*Compressed Air Magazine.*)

2. *$1,000 a year — previously down the chute — now saved.* "The Jamacha Sand Plant, Inc., of El Cajon, California, was experiencing a costly problem on their steel discharge chutes. Every two or three months, they could count on replacing the main chute, due to the abrasive wear of sharp sand and gravel particles."

After trying 3/4" steel liners, they switched to an abrasion-resistant rubber sheeting. After six years, that original set of rubber liners is still going strong. Estimated savings in parts, labor and production: $1,000 a year. (*Gates Industrial News,* The Gates Rubber Co.)

3. *"No-dress" wheel extends up-time.* At the Johnson Products Division, Sealed Power Corp., a one-minute shutdown of their through-feed, centerless grinding line means 6,600 engine pistons forfeited.

Switching from standard grinding wheels to a new "no-dress" type of wheel not only cut down time dramatically, but extended wheel life by 33 percent. (*Production Magazine.*)

If covering product-application case histories is to your advantage, then you'll want to get close to your company's salespeople or clients. They're on the front lines where the dollars change hands; they know which of their customers want publicity and which do not; and more often than not, they crave publicity themselves.

For every lead you get from an editor, you'll get 25 from salespeople, dealers, and/or distributors. Moreover, these salespeople will go out of their way to open doors for you, make arrangements, have the equipment or facility spiffed up for photos, and so on.

Just be sure that you tell them exactly what you want, and keep them informed as the story progresses.

COVERING THE STORY

As mentioned, the case history has a typical anatomy, which has developed out of its very nature. In fact, you'll seldom go wrong by covering and writing the story by formula.

Regardless of the business or industry involved, you should obtain the answers to these general questions:

What was the general situation — company, store, production line, etc. — in which the problem occurred?

What were the specifics of the problem?

What initial steps did the protagonist take to analyze and solve the problem, and what were some of the alternative courses of action considered?

What were the specifics of the solution? Indicate actions taken and equipment, materials, services, or methods used. Be sure to give names, titles, and affiliations of people who played a role.

What have been the results of applying the solution? Specify the benefits as precisely as possible; avoid vague generalities.

What does the protagonist intend to do from this point on? More of the same?

Get the answers to these basic questions, and you'll have the story. Of course, specific details will vary widely from one industry to the next and from one situation to the next.

THE PHOTOS

Long and adequate books have been written on photojournalism, so we won't spend much time discussing case-history photos (see Figs. 5-1 and 5-2). Just a few pointers:

- Show people doing things. Don't show only the hardware.
- If you need to pose a picture, make the pose seem natural. Get the subject to loosen up; shoot a few practice frames, and the pose will flow into a seemingly candid attitude.
- Shoot black and white, primarily. Don't burn up color film unless you see a likely market for it, or unless you see a possible cover-shot.
- If you do use color, shoot transparencies rather than negative film. Most editors prefer transparencies over prints.
- If possible, shoot the pictures on 120 or 220 (2 1/4″ by 2 1/4″) film, rather than on 35 mm. The contact proofs show more to the unaided eye than do those skinny little 35-mm strips. To examine a 35-mm contact proof, the editor must use a loupe or other magnifier. That's more work — perhaps an irritant, perhaps an adverse influence on the editor's decision to use or not use the material.

CLEARANCES

You can avoid having your nose bashed and wasting a lot of your time if you'll remember to follow these procedures:

- Get the lead from the dealer, distributor, salesperson or whomever. Gather enough facts to sell the story idea.
- Query the editor. Sell the story idea and ask for a go-ahead.

- Obtain approval from the customer and your salespeople to cover the story, and make preliminary arrangements.
- When the editor says "go," follow his instructions. You may be asked to bring a company salesperson or a particular member of the customer company into the interview. Perhaps these people will have to be included in one or more photos, too.
- After you've conducted your interviews and shot photos, tell the salesperson, dealer, and any customer representatives involved that they will receive copies of the story, photos, and captions for their review.
- Some company editors prefer that writers obtain story and photo approvals from the people involved and get their signatures before submitting the material. In this case, route just one set of manuscript and photos for approval. First on the routing list should be the customer, the "hero" of the story. Then come the dealer and the salesperson.

WRITING THE STORY

Much of what you've already read gives clues on how to write a case history. We won't waste time repeating those clues. Following are a few additional tips, though, that you may find helpful:

The case history is, strictly speaking, a problem/solution story. Stages in its development are: Situation, problem, analysis, solution, and happy outcome. As you see, these developments unfold in a chronological order. So, in most instances, you can apply a narrative treatment.

Though many editors refer to these stories as articles, you can often give them a news flavor. Headline and lead can state the outcome of the solution, then fill in with details on situation, problem, analysis, and solution. Look at these newsy case-history headlines:

"Tension/tension cylinders solve fatigue-testing problem for L-1011 airframe."
"Air-operated clamping device makes perfect drawers – every time."
"New invention saves time, money for oyster farmers."
"All-air controls eliminate shock hazard on fruit-packing machines."

Grabbers, aren't they? All written for case histories.

hanger which had to be assembled, taking more time. And the hangers would often snap when workers were tugging on the filler to get it to hang."

Circle 404

New material simplifies packaging, cuts costs

Ex-Cell-O Corporation's Plastic Components Div. in Athens, TN has found a pallet replacing application for a new structural fiber-beam packaging material trademarked "Fiberplank." It is made on machinery from Fibertech, Inc., Monroe, LA.

Ex-Cell-O makes plastic foam parts for some of the nation's leading manufacturers of computers and copying equipment. The division ships its precision molded cabinets and parts, weighing from 1 to 76 lb, to customers all over the U.S.; a typical load weighs 150 to 200 lb. Three truckloads leave the plant on an average day.

Charles W. Morris, purchasing manager, says that the Fiberplank shapes are easy to handle and require little storage space since each piece of slotted paperbeam nests into another. He also notes that the material holds and protects ⅝ in.-wide strapping in its slots.

Before using the paperbeam, the company used wood pallets which had to be channeled to receive strapping. With the paperbeam, the company was able to reduce packaging material by one-third, and Morris found Fiberplank to be approximately 27 percent less expensive than wood pallets or solid fiberboard.

Two pieces of slotted paperbeam are stapled from the inside to the bottom of a corrugated case and secured with plastic strapping in the slots. The paperbeam can support 400 lb per linear ft.

The laminated, formed and slotted paperbeam is available in 4 to 144-inch lengths. It can be ordered to a specific length or cut on standard woodworking equipment.

Ex-Cello-O ships more than $250,000 worth of pallets a year

from its fast-growing facility, so there is significant savings potential when pallets are replaced by slotted paperbeam.

Circle 405

Storage efficiency frees up space for manufacturing

Expanded sales at FMC Corp.'s Airline Equipment Div., San Jose, CA, created a problem which was solved by the construction of a new warehouse.

Airline Equipment's products include cargo loaders, trailers, deicers and transporters which are sold primarily to commercial airlines around the world.

Their problem was finding places to store a growing inventory of bulky and heavy manufactured and purchased items. For lack of storage space, most of their manufactured items ended up outdoors on pallets on the ground.

In order to take fullest advantage of available cube in their new warehouse, FMC chose a seismic design Sturdi-Bilt multi-level standard selective pallet rack mezzanine system supplied by Unarco Materials Storage. The rack is single deep and provides maximum access from front and rear to its 1300 pallet openings. The rack occupies 11,880 sq ft of the

Fig. 5-1. Product case histories published two columns wide in the "Cost Cutting Ideas" department of *Material Handling Engineering*. Illustrations submitted with case-history releases should be able to stand reduction to single-column width.

Cost Cutting Ideas

13,000-sq-ft warehouse.

Stored items include engines, transmissions, boxed goods and numerous heavy fabricated components and assemblies too heavy and bulky for storing on conventional shelves. Inventory turns over three to four times a year.

Unit loads are slotted by random location. Slower-moving items are stocked on the upper rack levels, faster-moving items are stored at lower levels.

Pick lists are sorted by work order and then by location and part number. This allows an order picker to pass through the warehouse once and pick from available stock without having to backtrack.

Some of the immediate benefits cited by Airline Equipment Division include adequate space indoors with identified storage locations and greatly improved housekeeping. Most important, the consolidation of stores freed an acre of space for the use of manufacturing.

Circle 406

Energy and dollars saved by multi-vapor lamps

Johnson & Johnson installed General Electric 325-watt Watt-Miser I-Line Multi-Vapor lamps in their 168,000-sq-ft warehouse in Menlo Park, CA. One result has been a $4800 yearly savings in energy costs based on 5¢ per kilowatt hour and 4680 operating hours per year.

"Electrical energy costs are constantly rising, up 36 percent in the past year to 6.4¢ per KWH now," David Sauter, supervisor-Staff Services, reports. "We monitor en-

ergy use on a monthly basis and look for ways to offset the increase in costs while continuing to meet company lighting specifications for a safe work environment.

"The decision was made to turn

off half the lamps in the warehouse areas and replace the remaining 400-watt mercury vapor lamps with energy efficient 325-watt metal halide lamps."

The warehouse lighting system incorporates 80 phosphor-coated Watt-Miser lamps mounted in existing luminaires. The lamps are mounted 30 ft above the floor on 20 x 40-ft centers in a newer 118,000-sq-ft area and 17 ft above the floor on 20 x 40-ft centers in an older 50,000-sq-ft area. They provide 18 horizontal footcandles in the 14-ft-wide aisles and 10 vertical footcandles 5 ft above the surface. The old mercury lighting system was delivering less than 10 footcandles.

The single-phase, 120-volt system in the old area and the three-phase, 480-volt system in the newer area are both operated by a single manual control system.

"We looked at turning off up to 50 percent of the mercury lights in the warehouse as a way to cut electrical energy use," Bill Worrix, maintenance department foreman, explained. "However, studies showed that this approach would reduce light levels below those specified by the company's Environmental Health Program, and this was unacceptable."

Circle 407

Fig. 5-1. (continued)

instances where an extremely
heavy pallet of paint is received, it is

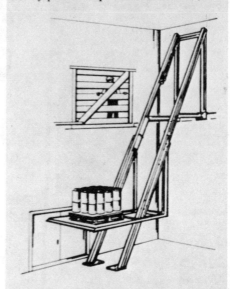

broken down before lifting. "This
does not impose a handicap," says

it was considerable. Baskets of steel
gears and other heavy parts which

go into power steering equipment
were too heavy to be loaded by

Fig. 5-2. Case-history illustrations that reproduce well even at a relatively narrow (14-pica) column width. Simple drawings work well at this width.

These boxes are preferred because of their cushioning proper-

ties, strength when stacked, and
ruggedness for bulk shipping and

Fig. 5-2. (continued)

A case history is essentially a business or engineering story. You submit case histories to editors of business, industrial, technical, and company periodicals. Readers of these periodicals expect not entertainment or opinion but facts that will help their readers to do a better job, make more money, cut costs, save energy, reduce pollution, etc.

The point is, get to the point of the story as quickly as possible. Grab the reader with a statement of dollars saved, percentage increase in sales, number of extra sales, percentage of cost reduction, or some other benefit.

Another good way to grab the reader in the lead is to open with a description of the problem. If it's a common type of problem, the reader will identify. If the problem has an unusual twist, the reader may become intrigued.

Whether you stop the reader with benefits or problem, keep your writing factual and businesslike. Don't mistake cleverness for intrigue. Consider yourself primarily a reporter, not an artiste. Let your writer's art be so plain, clear, and simple that it shows off the content of the story, not your own artfulness.

Before you start writing, make certain that you know how much detail the editor wants concerning any products, materials, or services that play roles in the story.

Should you include model numbers, sizes, colors, ratings and other specifications? Read the magazine; if in doubt, ask the editor. Tailor the story to suit the needs of the editor and the readers.

For a commercial periodical — one put out by a business publisher — maintain a reporter's objective stance. When writing for a company periodical, include testimonials and play up the company's products or services.

Once again, though: Read the magazine. Some company editors like copy that almost drips with "sell," but others prefer a more detached, low-key approach.

Chapter 6
Seventeen Ways to Stretch the Case History Budget

Publication of case-history releases and articles is one excellent way to help your company or client solve a number of marketing problems. Placed in the appropriate media, with careful timing, case histories can pull inquiries and can demonstrate problem-solving abilities, technical acumen, experience in targeted markets, acceptance by well-known companies, and scope of products and services.

Moreover, through continued placement of case-history articles — along with technical articles and news releases — in selected "vertical" periodicals, you can penetrate or explore some of the smaller, narrower markets inexpensively. This enables you to reserve your ad money for the periodicals most important to your marketing efforts.

There are other good reasons for publishing case-history articles; we won't try to cover all of them. The point is that if you're using case-history articles to any extent, you know that (1) they work and (2) in terms of cost per exposure, cost per column inch, and credibility, case histories are a bargain.

Even if you've been employing case-history articles for some time, however, it's quite possible that you may not be realizing all their potential value. Each of us, no matter how adept, falls into restricted habits of thinking and doing, and all of us are subjected to pressures that limit the time and inclination for creative experimentation.

Basically, the trick is to make yourself think in terms of case-history *material*. Regard the facts and illustrations as elements that, like Tinker Toys, you can use and reuse in creating many communicative forms.

Following are 17 tips for getting the greatest possible value out of your company's case-history budget. Applied with judgment and imagination, these pointers can help you to accomplish more with each case-history dollar.

1. Make each trip count. If the customer is located a fair distance from the office of the person(s) covering the story — far enough to make the trip more than an over-and-back, one-day affair — try to line up two or more stories to cover on the same junket. That way, you can spread the travel costs among the various projects and reduce the cost per project.

2. Consider the reporter/photographer (R/P). If you need a constant flow of case histories — perhaps for your company's advertisements and house organs as well as for trade-magazine articles — consider employing the services of an R/P who knows your field well.

Have the R/P mail back raw field reports, negatives, proof sheets, and transparencies. Then you, your staff writers, or your agents can shape the material into as many forms as required.

This method has worked well for an Illinois company that builds equipment and systems for asphalt paving. The company's advertising and PR people require great numbers of case-history reports and photos for trade-magazine articles, an external house organ, ads, capabilities brochures, slide presentations, and other forms of communication.

To obtain the case-history material, they occasionally send out staff writers and photographers, but for the most part they rely upon a professional industrial R/P. He knows the asphalt construction field inside out and services several noncompeting equipment manufacturers.

Before making a "loop" from his Ohio home — say, through the Southeast — the R/P lines up case histories to cover for each of his clients. Then, as he covers each story on the loop, he mails the tape recordings and exposed rolls of film to his secretary back in Ohio.

She transcribes the tapes, typing them up as field reports, and has the film processed. Negative film is contact proofed; transparencies are sleeved. She then mails the reports and film materials to the proper client.

This system has proved extremely efficient and economical, not only for the Illinois company mentioned but also for the R/P's other clients. Travel costs are prorated among all the case histories and clients.

You may want your reporter to write up the story as a trade-magazine article, and perhaps place it, too. If you anticipate multiple uses for the information and photos, however, you'll probably find it less expensive to order raw field reports.

3. Inform, inform. Take the time to explain your objectives to reporters, writers, photographers, and everyone else who'll get involved in covering the case history. Tell them exactly what you want, and why, and how. A small expenditure of time on briefing will prevent mixups, mistakes, arguments, cancellations, delays, re-writes — all of them costly.

Equally important, don't forget to bring your company salespeople and distributors or dealers into the act. Most of them want and appreciate publicity; all of them resent not being told about case-history coverage involving their customers.

Get the salespeople on your side, and they'll "grease the ways" for you and your agents. Cross them, though, or ignore them, and you can be in for big headaches, along with higher costs.

4. Check with the editor. Before you, your staff writer, or your agent even begins to write a major case-history feature article, pick one periodical as the Number One target and call the editor.

Describe the story you have, tell him how the material pertains to his field, and point out how the article would benefit his readers.

Then, assuming you've sold the editor, ask him what he wants: length, slant, pictures, etc. In other words, find out how to tailor the package to his needs — and do it.

All too often, a writer will sit down with the reporter's notes or tapes, dash off a "general" case-history article, and then try to peddle it. That may seem to be the easiest and quickest way to go, but often it proves the most expensive.

A good editor wants case histories tailored to his periodical's style, format, story length, etc. Material that doesn't readily fit may be returned for revision, or rejected. The results: More time, more phone calls and letters, more rewrites, and higher costs.

5. Be sure you have clearances. Many leads to case histories come from salespeople, dealers, or distributors who are doing business with a friendly and cooperative person within the customer organization.

That person may have any one of a hundred functions: project director, maintenance supervisor, purchasing agent, chief engineer, etc.

When making arrangements to visit a customer's plant, lab, or job site, make sure that:

- Your salesperson has actually obtained permission from his contact to visit the installation site, interview people, and take photos
- The salesperson's contact has obtained permission from *his* superiors, on up the chain of command as far as necessary
- The salesperson, his contact, and the contact's superiors understand exactly what you want, how you intend to use the material, and how you plan to go about obtaining the necessary information and pictures.

During the process of setting up the project and obtaining permission, make it very clear that you will release nothing for publication until it has been checked, corrected, and released by the people responsible. Repeat this in conversations and correspondence until you're certain that all the people involved have heard and understood.

I've seen a number of potentially good case-history stories killed because not all the people with PR responsibilities were informed or had given permission for coverage. The further along you take a case-history project, the more expensive a kill becomes.

6. Work with client's PR and ad people. Determine whether or not the customer organization has a manager of public relations or advertising. If they do, be sure that he (1) is aware of your case-history project; (2) gives or obtains approvals for coverage; (3) gets involved, if he so desires; and (4) checks and releases the story draft, photos, and captions.

Get the PR or ad manager on your side early in the project. He can make the field work go quickly and easily by obtaining prior permission (which you might not get on your own), scheduling for interviews, having equipment cleaned up and ready for photographs, etc.

Then too, many company PR and ad managers have their own staff or contract photographers. Some managers insist that these photographers do all the shooting; in other cases, the photographer's services are available to you upon request.

Either way, take full advantage of the situation. You'll build good will and save money on film, processing, and prints.

7. Check first on art. Before preparing drawings, diagrams, graphs, or other line art to illustrate a case-history article, determine the periodical's preferences regarding artwork.

Most periodicals like to receive original, camera-ready ink drawings or sharp, well-exposed Kodalith copy prints. A few major trade magazines, however, prefer quick but accurate pencil sketches. Their own staff artists then render the drawings in accordance with the magazine's established art style.

So for line art, check with the editor. One phone call may save considerable time, bother, and expense.

8. Make notes and recordings. Regardless of who covers the story, direct him to tape-record interviews *and* to take copious notes. Doing so will assure you of a more accurate, complete first draft; preclude the need for embarrassing, time-consuming call-backs; and, at the bottom line, save money.

"How to interview" is a subject about which books have been written. Rather than trying to cover that whole subject here, I'll give just a few basic pointers that will help your interviewers to make good recordings:

• Before leaving for the customer's plant or job site, check the recorder batteries, perhaps with a multimeter. If in doubt, insert fresh batteries.

• Carry an extra set of batteries, just in case.

• Also before leaving, check the tapes. Use cassettes with tapes for 90 minutes of recording time or less. Long tapes tend to hang up or break more easily than short ones.

• If possible, use a recorder with automatic recording-volume control. If the recorder has manual control, adjust the volume to the interviewee's voice and to the distance from microphone to interviewee.

• Make certain that the interview site — office, conference room, or whatever — is as free as possible of background noises that might drown out portions of the recorded conversation. Listen for noises from sources such as air conditioners, compressors, large electric motors, hydraulic pumps, typewriters, and faulty ballasts on fluorescent-light fixtures.

Should you find that there's too much background noise at the site initially chosen, ask the interviewee if the two of you can move to a quieter place.

• At the beginning of an interview, record the conversation for a few minutes. Then rewind to the beginning of the tape, and play back the recorded portion. This will enable you to make certain that your record button is working and to check for proper volume and for background noises.

• Transcribe tapes as soon as possible after recording them. That way you'll be able to remember, edit, and interpret more details than if you let the tapes sit. You'll also find it easier to make accurate, direct quotes.

Following the preceding tips will help you to obtain more and better data, avoid missed or ruined recordings, and thus conserve your case-history dollars.

9. Route one copy for approvals. When obtaining clearances on article drafts, photos, art, and captions, route one set to the people who must give OK's. Unless directed otherwise, route the set first to the customer, then to the distributor or dealer, field salesperson, sales manager, and others involved.

I recommend this procedure because once the user of the product or service has made the changes he wants and initialed the copy, the other people down the clearance chain will be less inclined to make arbitrary, subjective changes.

Unless you're pressed for time, don't send duplicate sets simultaneously to all the people in the chain. Rarely will the opinions of one person jibe with those of the next. Reconciling differences in opinion will require some painful, compromising rewrites, plus additional correspondence, calls, etc. You'll end up trying to please everybody but satisfying nobody.

Should you have a tight deadline to meet, though, you may be forced to make simultaneous submissions for clearance. In this situation, go with the opinions of the customer — the user of the products or services — and perhaps with those of the distributor or dealer who serves the account. Their opinions usually carry enough weight to get you through any quibbling by the others.

10. Shotgun the article as a release. After a case-history article has been accepted and published as an exclusive by one periodical, condense the article to two pages or less and trim the number of illustrations to one or two. Send out copies of the story, shotgun-fashion, as a case-history release to the vertical periodicals serving your markets.

This technique can enable you to get two, three, even five times as much editorial space as you got from the original story. Just make sure you don't send the material to competing vehicles. Type "Exclusive in Your Field" at the top of the first page; that will let the editors know you've sent the material to publications in other fields, but not to competitors.

Some case histories don't lend themselves to this treatment, but most bear within themselves at least one good news angle. Make the most of it; stretch your case-history dollar.

Releases to the business and general-news media won't sell many products, but they will help you to reach and impress potential stockholders, lenders, and employees. Publication or broadcast of case-history material also gives your employees a boost.

The cost? Negligible.

11. Save everything. For each case history covered, make a permanent file, indexed by job number and customer name. Hang on to everything pertaining to the job: approved copy, model releases, condensations, negatives, spare prints, transparencies, notes, correspondence – everything.

Doing so may spare you a lot of anguish and expense later on, should a customer or distributor come back after the article appears in print and holler, "I didn't see or approve that story!" Showing him his initials or signature on the clearance draft will squelch the noise quickly, and perhaps save the cost of legal defense. Sad, but it happens.

12. Look for other uses. Put the case history material to as many uses as you can dream up. Here's a preliminary list of ideas:

Articles, news stories, or photo/captions for your company's internal, external, and/or sales house organs.

Advertisements and commercials.

Product brochures, bulletins, etc.

Application bulletins or "user reports," keyed to markets and product lines.

Article reprints, for use as mailers, handouts, and salespeople's "talk pieces."

Company "capabilities" brochures.

Annual and quarterly financial reports.

Technical literature – manuals, bulletins, etc.

Slide presentations for salespeople, trainees, customers, prospects, distributors, dealers, reps, community leaders, trade groups, professional groups, security analysts, stockholders, students, etc.

Trade-show and seminar displays.

Displays for plant lobbies, museums, schools, colleges, etc.

Textbooks and directories.

Magazine publishers' yearbooks, handbooks, and roundup articles.

Calendars, memo books, other premiums.

Each time you find another use for your case histories, you stretch your initial investment a little further. The trade-magazine ad or article is only the beginning.

13. Cover some stories by mail and phone. Your more important case histories should be covered in person and on site by a reporter/photographer or by an agent plus a photographer. For less-important, routine case histories, though, you or your agent can do an adequate job by mail and telephone.

Make up a standard questionnaire form, containing all the routine questions that should be asked: name and address of customer, products or services involved, product specs, how the product or service is (was) used, problems solved, people involved, etc.

Send a copy of the questionnaire to the distributor or dealer who serves the account. Tell him what you're after, and why. Ask him to get the information from his customer, when convenient, and work out a method for getting photos.

Often the customer will be happy to supply the photos gratis. If not, your distributor or dealer can engage a local photographer – and bill your company, of course.

This technique works fine for routine case-history coverage, and enables you to get more stories and photos per dollar.

14. Co-op with customers. Explore the possibilities of co-op history projects with your customers. Such ventures will not only save money

for you but also build the customer's good will and loyalty toward your company.

A good example of how this technique works occurred a few years ago. The organizations involved were the port authority for a large West Coast city and a company that builds and designs conveyor systems.

The port had just completed installation and start-up of a huge new materials-handling system for unloading bulk materials – grain, sand-gravel, etc. – from ships, storing them on open or enclosed stockpiles, and reclaiming them for loading onto trucks, railroad cars, and barges.

The manufacturing and engineering company had supplied the system design and components, plus general contracting, start-up, and checkout services.

When our company PR director approached the port's PR director and suggested a joint venture in publicity, the latter was delighted. He had done some publicity for the local news media, but because of pressing duties hadn't had time to produce publicity for the trade press, wire services, or other media.

We came up with a deal that neither of us could refuse. Our man did the reporting and photography, and we wrote and placed the articles and photo/captions. We concentrated on magazines serving the material-handling, shipping, and trucking and railroad industries, plus one of the national wire services.

After totaling up our charges, we split the bill down the middle. Half went to our client, the other half to the port authority. The media gave us tremendous exposure (it was a spectacular system), and all concerned came out heroes.

15. Reward the reporters. Offer incentives to field salespeople, dealers, and distributors to submit field reports and usable snapshots of interesting product or service applications. Provide them with standardized case-history questionnaires, and urge them to submit 35-mm or 126-size negatives rather than Polaroid or wallet-size prints. Full 8 x 10's from the customer are even better, of course.

Much of the case-history material obtained this way will be suitable for house-organ articles or photo/captions, but not for trade periodicals. Once in a while, though – perhaps one time out of ten – a salesperson will send in material that can lead to a really fine story. You can then get back to him and his customer, and develop the story fully.

At first glance, this method appears wasteful; you're paying for ten submissions but getting only one with potential for trade-press publicity. Look at it this way, though: You're getting ten house-organ features at a low cost per feature, plus the lead to a good article that you might not have found otherwise.

As you probably know, one of the problems in trying to maintain a flow of first-class case-history articles is uncovering the leads to those articles. Salespeople have enough reports, record-keeping, and other nonselling chores to perform; they're not much inclined to increase their "unproductive" time by becoming reporters. Some sort of remuneration is necessary to make the reporting function worthwhile for them.

One company — a manufacturer of fittings and valves for chemical-processing and nuclear-power-plant piping systems — has been using a dollar-incentive system successfully for three years. This company goes after case-history material for trade-periodical articles and for features in its bimonthly house organ. The latter is directed toward customers as well as distributors and field salespeople.

When the house organ was launched, the editor ran into the classic problem: getting the people in the field to submit story leads, secure permission from customers, and so on.

It was the company's sales manager who came up with the solution. "Carrots work better than clubs," he opined. "We'll pay $25 for each product-application report, and $25 more for usable pictures."

Within a week after the news of this offer hit the field, the editor had half a dozen story leads, including one that ultimately netted over two pages in a trade magazine. And the hopper now contains a comfortable backlog of case-history leads, reports, and photos.

16. Let the photographer shoot. Tell the photographer who's covering the story, "If in doubt, shoot it." Give him free rein to shoot the subjects from many different angles, with and without people in the scene, high-angle and low, wide-angle and normal.

So often I have found that it was the last shot on the roll, or the frame shot off-handedly, out of whimsy, that turned out to be the best.

Shooting many views will increase the odds of getting exactly what you want for the article. And having a large selection will decrease the chance that you may have to send a photographer back to take one or two vital shots he missed.

17. Plan film formats. Think ahead, and list all possible uses for photos of the product application: not only trade-magazine releases and articles, but all other formats as well.

Then consult with the photographer in determining which types of cameras and film he should use. For articles, usually the main requirement is for good black-and-white prints, relatively low in grain. Next, consider the possibilities for full-color editorial illustrations and for that prize of prizes, the front cover. And last, make provisions for color 35-mm slides.

Another wrinkle: The PR director of one company recently began getting into super-8 movies, and wants product applications shot on color movie film as well as on prints and transparencies. The company makes machinery with lots of moving parts — an ideal subject for dynamic motion pictures.

To accommodate her, the agent has been carrying a compact super-8 camera along with the still cameras. He now shoots quite a bit of available-light footage, sometimes with sound-on-film recording.

So you see, there are many angles to consider when choosing types of cameras and film for case-history photography. Plan ahead, and spare yourself the expense of a second trip.

Incidentally, don't forget to obtain signatures on model-release forms from the people photographed. Once in a great while, someone will cause trouble, or try to make a fast buck, by complaining about having been photographed "without knowledge or permission." You'll find it's much easier and less expensive in the long run to obtain signed releases than it is to go to court.

Try some of the techniques mentioned, as they apply to your own situation, and you'll find you're getting more and better results from your case histories. Further, you'll be helping and pleasing more of your company's salespeople, distributors, and dealers.

The potential benefits are well worth the effort.

Chapter 7

The Contributed, Bylined
Feature Article

Writing and contributing bylined feature articles to appropriate magazines can generate some important benefits for you and your company or clients. These benefits include:

- Gaining and maintaining visibility. Publication of a contributed, bylined feature article — a "CBFA" — is an event that can gain much attention.
- Establishing the author and his company as experts in their field. Publishing articles seems not only to reflect expertise but also to confer it on the sources.
- Furthering the careers of those who receive the bylines.
- Enhancing the careers of those who write and place the articles. Help someone to get published, and you gain a lasting friend.

At this point, I'd better define the contributed, bylined feature article, or CBFA. "Contributed" signifies that the article is not written by the magazine's staff but comes from an outside source. Some magazines pay a modest honorarium for articles, but even so, the editors regard such articles as contributed. "Bylined" means someone receives credit as the source of the article — e.g., "by John Jones, Chief Engineer, Maximum Corporation." Some staff-written articles are not bylined, but nearly all contributed articles receive bylines. Occasionally this may take the form of a credit line such as "by the staff engineers of the Maximum Corporation." "Feature" means that the article receives prominent play in the magazine issue. The editor "features" the material. In contrast, some short contributed articles may be used as filler, receiving less prominence than a feature. And of course, "article" distinguishes the material from other types of material, such as news stories, news features, editorials, photo features, and others.

That brings up the question, "What is the purpose of a CBFA?" In the industrial fields, the main purpose is usually to instruct or inform. The scope of the CBFA may be narrow and deep, or it may be quite broad. What gives the CBFA its special value to readers is the combination of the qualifications of the bylined source, the depth to which the source can expertly plumb the subject matter, and the breadth of the source's experience and vision.

A company president, for example, may be able to shed valuable light on the causes for common problems in productivity. A chief engineer may be able to set forth much useful, timely information on how to design, select, install, operate, or maintain a specific type of equipment. In any event, the editor will base his decision on whether or not to publish the article partly on the qualifications of the bylined source.

An assistant product manager in a small company making one size and model of tractor would not be a likely source for an article on how to select tractors. On the other hand, the vice-president of marketing for a large company making many types and sizes of tractors would be considered a well-qualified source. Another good source for this kind of article might be the president of a large dealership that carries several tractor brands, types, and sizes.

To instruct or inform is one valid reason for a CBFA, but not the only one. CBFA's may also seek to persuade the readers toward one side or another of an issue. Sometimes the intent to persuade, conscious or not, may be subtly masked by omission of certain facts or types of information, or by emphasis on others.

Who writes CBFA's? Occasionally they come directly from executives, managers, engineers, or technicians who like to write. The authors may receive some help from others such as PR staffers or editors, but the authors do the bulk of the writing — and certainly most of the thinking — themselves.

Often, though, CBFA's are ghostwritten by professional writers, such as company PR staffers, agency PR writers, freelance journalists, or technical writers. The source — the one to receive the byline — outlines the content and thrust of the article. He provides interviews, literature, letters, drawings, and other raw material to the ghostwriter.

Ideally, the PR manager or agent then approaches an editor and tries to sell the *idea* of the article. If the editor gives a go-ahead, the ghost works up a first draft and turns it over to the source for changes and corrections. The changing and correcting continue until the source, ghost, and editor are all satisfied. Chapter 8 gives a procedure for ghostwriting technical CBFA's.

HOW CBFA'S GET STARTED

Consider the total number of industrial, trade, business, and technical periodicals being published. Multiply that number by the average number of CBFA's used by each periodical in a year. The volume of CBFA's moving through and sitting in our Postal Service network must be — well, at least three bags full.

Who conceives the ideas for all those CBFA's? I've seen them start in many ways. A few present genuine creative challenges to the PR people involved. Here's one hypothetical instance:

You're the PR manager in the 51-year-old, medium-sized Wattsavolt Electric Company, which makes and markets electrical connectors. Some of your product lines are new and easy to publicize, but others have recently celebrated their golden anniversary.

One day, Ernest, the general sales manager, approaches you and says, "Joanne, our Model 1-B connectors could stand some publicity. It's a mature product line" (he snickers), "and it hasn't been moving well. How about you and I doing a bylined technical article and giving old 1-B some hype?"

You gulp, but you accept the challenge. A creative person never says "can't be done," right?

How can you handle this challenge? One obvious way would be to make a counterproposal: "Let's go after case histories. Let's tell about installations in which the first 1-B's ever made are still functioning perfectly. The testimonials would be fabulous."

Your idea has merit, but you feel it's a cop-out. You hunker down and think. You run into pillars, doors, and short people because you think while you walk. You gather facts about 1-B: what it is, how it's used, how it differs from other connectors, its advantages and limitations. You review everything that has been written in your company about 1-B, and you check your article reprints and tear sheets from years back. Some appear to have been printed on parchment.

You let all this raw data simmer in your kettle, and before long an idea begins to take shape. Your plan goes something like this: "Type 1-B connectors were designed to do a specific kind of job. They do that job well — as well as some competitive makes, better than others.

"Now, suppose we take our focus off the product and look instead at the applications. Type 1-B's are used to join certain standard sizes of electrical cables in wet or humid environments, including outdoors. The connectors come in a full range of sizes, covering most conceivable applications where water must be excluded from the connection.

"Ernest, I suggest that we consider doing an article embodying one of these approaches: How to make waterproof connections, or ten pitfalls to avoid in making waterproof connections, or selecting and sizing cable and connectors for wet environments.

"The article would be generic — that's what editors want, not sales-talk — but all the illustrations would show 1-B's. We'd propose to the editor that we use not only catalog-type shots but also cutaways, cross sections, application photos, graphs, and tables. Type 1-B would play the starring role."

Luckily, Ernest sees the wisdom of your plan. You then do more creative planning, this time for your sales pitch to the editor of the leading magazine in your field. (More later on how to write query letters.)

Not all CBFA's start that way. Sometimes the PR practitioner gets the opportunity to dream up ideas. Sometimes advertising people see good opportunities. The same goes for product managers, dealers, field service poeple, even the company president.

The point is, no one person and no one occupation has a monopoly on good article ideas. Keep your mind open, your switch on, and your antenna all the way up.

Once in a while, an editor will get an idea for a CBFA. The topic is timely and important. He'd like to write the article himself but hasn't the time. Nobody else on the staff is qualified to write it. Besides, a byline such as that of your company's chief application engineer would give the article much weight, believability, and reprint value.

The editor calls you, outlines his proposal, and asks, "Would you like to do it? Can you?" At that point, try not to swallow your gum. Say pleasantly that you'll look into the matter and call him back. Then pray that you have enough time and budget to handle the project, and that a qualified source is willing and able to help.

WHERE TO FIND IDEAS

Sometimes good ideas for CBFA's will drop into your lap. Editors will call with their own proposals, and the people in your company or client organizations will proffer a certain number of sound, usable ideas. If you work in a climate where creativity is encouraged, you may even receive more article ideas than you can handle.

Suppose, though, that the ideas come only infrequently. Suppose further that you are aggressive and ambitious, and that you love the smell of ink: ink that's been printed on magazine pages to convey articles for and about your company or clients.

To complete the picture, let's further assume that your working situation fosters the conception, production, and placement of CBFA's. These conditions prevail:

• You have a mandate to gain favorable editorial exposure. Your boss or client has said, preferably in writing, that "we want visibility in the industries we serve."

• Your mandate also includes the directive to establish the expertise of the company and its personnel. Mere visibility can be achieved by other means, but building and maintaining a reputation for expertise is the forte of the CBFA.

• You have funds budgeted to cover research, writing, illustration, and placement of a reasonable number of CBFA's during the fiscal year.

• You have not been totally limited in advance to certain subjects. Your budget and mandate have been structured in a way that allows you some freedom to shoot at "targets of opportunity" as they pop up.

True, your marketing people must have a say in what you write about. The main reason for a company to spend hard-earned profits on CBFA's is to achieve marketing objectives. Your marketing people are smart enough, however, to lay down broad guidelines and pinpoint some specific communications goals, but to let you plan the implementation.

In other words, the marketing people may say, "We want to establish our expertise in these fields," and, "We ought to get something published on such-and-such a technology this year." At the same time, though, they allow you to play the major role in choosing the approach to the subject, the scope and tone of the article, and the list of target periodicals.

Pretty picture. It's what I consider an ideal situation for a creative, adventurous, capable PR person who wants to experience the thrill of seeing articles published and the satisfaction of helping a company to achieve its objectives.

Freedom imposes responsibilities, though. It's up to you in this situation to dig around and find the ideas. Then you must sell the ideas and implement them effectively.

Where can you find good, salable ideas for CBFA's?

We'd better define "good, salable idea." First, it's an idea that you can sell internally, to the people who will say yes or no within your own company or your client organization. You must be prepared to show how publication of the specific article package – manuscript, photos, graphs, etc. – will help to achieve a specific marketing communications goal.

Second, a "good, salable idea" for an article is one you can reasonably hope to sell to an editor. You may be able to visualize an eight-page editorial spread that would dazzle your management; one of your engineers may have a pet topic that he'd dearly love to see in print; but unless the idea is one you can make an editor want, it isn't "good and salable."

What can you sell to editors? What do they want?

Without exception, the article ideas editors not only want but crave are those that address current, important problems in their fields. The more universal the problem, the greater the need for articles that will help readers to find solutions.

Say that you have the freedom and you know in general terms what will sell. Where can you find the ideas?

Editors

Get to know the editors of the leading magazines in the fields served by your company or its clients. Talk to them by phone, visit them in their offices, and meet with them at trade shows and conferences. Establish a friendly rapport with the editors, and every so often ask them, "What are the hot topics? What are your advertisers and readers talking and worrying about?" The answers will provide clues to ideas for articles.

The Target Magazines

Read the magazines in which you want to place publicity. Observe what they run and don't run. Scan not only the features but also the departments, especially those containing news about legislation, standards, technical developments, and industry trends.

In addition, read the ads. They tell you much about the industry and the magazine's readers.

I recall seeing an ad for a new type of machine tool control. In the ad, the company made much of the fact that their controls utilize something called "bubble memory." This is a type of electronic memory, analogous to tapes and disks, wherein data are stored and transported in little pockets or "bubbles" of magnetism.

Two months later, a news item in one of the business magazines told of marketing trends in the control industry. As I recall, the writer said that the market for bubble memory apparently was flattening out. He expected that the relative share of the market for bubble memory would remain fairly constant from then on. The reason? "Bubble memory is great for some applications but not for others," he said.

Upon reading the news item, I remembered the ad, and an idea for a feature article popped into my head. "Bubble memory: is it for you?" Tell what it is, what it performs, what it does well and not so well. Give examples of applications, and so on.

One and one made three: ad, news item, article idea. The creative process might not have begun, though, unless I had seen and read both the ad and the news item.

Other Periodicals

You have just so many hours for reading, but try to stay current with one newspaper, one general news magazine, one general business magazine, and one industrial news magazine. In all these types of periodicals you will find facts and opinions that may trigger ideas for timely articles.

On occasion, pick up the vertical magazines in the fields you serve. Your opportunities for placing CBFA's are by no means limited to major horizontals. I've placed many short bylined features in verticals, and with good results. In the large horizontals they likely would have been handled as fillers or relegated to the middle or back of the book. In the verticals, these articles ran as features.

Editorial Calendars

Here's a tool that, in my experience, could be used to better advantage by the majority of PR practitioners. Editorial calendars are promotional tools put out by magazine publishers. Usually covering a full year, the calendars enable the magazine-space salespeople to show advertisers what's going to be featured in editorial, and when. The salespeople encourage their clients and prospects to buy ad space in issues featuring the types of products and services the clients and prospects provide.

Following are condensed excerpts from an editorial calendar published by *Material Handling Engineering.* Ideas for pertinent CBFA's appear in parentheses after the excerpts.

Feb. Storage drawer systems: concept and application. (How to design a storage drawer system for your assembly department, maintenance department, or toolroom. How to cost-justify a drawer system. Computerizing a drawer-based inventory system.)

Photosensors: the eyes of material handling. (The basic types of photosensors and how to select them. Inside photosensors – how they work. Maintenance and troubleshooting of photosensors.)

June. Power transmission in conveying. (The basic types of PT's now used in conveyor systems; pros and cons of each; how to select them. Comparison of energy consumption in the basic types. Complying with OSHA regulations for conveyor PT's.)

Dec. What's needed to move and ship small packages. (Selecting and sizing scales for a shipping room. Container closure: pros and cons of the basic methods.)

Mind you, I'm not saying that each of the article ideas listed is salable or that it will be in the future. I'm merely pointing out that reading publishers' editorial calendars can spark many ideas.

If you're a company PR manager and you don't have a file of calendars from the major periodicals in your field, see your ad manager or agency account executive. If you work freelance or with an agency, talk to agency media buyers, or write directly to the magazines.

Keep in mind, though, that editorial calendars do not list all features to be published. For one thing, the editors want to keep some aces up their sleeves for competitive reasons. For another, editors like to be able to adapt quickly to opportunities that arise unexpectedly.

Government

Stay alert for announcements of new regulations or standards such as those from the U.S. Department of Labor's Occupational Safety and Health Administration (OSHA) and the Environmental Protection Agency (EPA). Also watcn for announcements from other federal and state agencies pertinent to your markets.

For instance, if you sell to the mining industries, you'll want to keep tabs on the messages and dictates from the U.S. Bureau of Mines. If highway transportation is your field, stay tuned to the U.S. Department of Transportation.

A reference you'll find handy is the *United States Government Manual,* published biannually by the U.S. Government Printing Office. This fat, softbound volume gives you the names, addresses, and telephone numbers of thousands of valuable contacts in the federal government.

For the asking, you can be put onto mailing lists for news releases from various federal and state agencies.

Why pay all this attention to government? Because regulations affect all your customers and prospects. Complying with regulations has been a major planning and cost factor for many companies. "How to design or change your system to comply" identifies a vast lode of article ideas.

Technical Papers

Check those recently given and those coming up. Go back through the files and see which topics could be updated with a current slant.

A bit of advice on technical papers: Often the authors present these at conferences sponsored by technical or professional societies. Then the societies grab the papers and publish them in their journals or house organs.

When you spot a paper that may make a salable article, point out to the author that you'd like to adapt the paper and get some broad, national exposure with it. Encourage him to notify the society of this and to reserve the copyright. If you have time, you can obtain a copyright for the author. That way, he retains the say-so on who can publish it and in what form.

Company Managers and Staffers

Stay on friendly terms with managers, engineers, technicians, and others in the sales, product engineering, application engineering, training, and field service departments. Ask questions such as, "What's on your customers' minds? In which categories do they apparently lack information? What mistakes are they frequently making despite all the courses, literature, films, etc.? In which kinds of situations do they lean most heavily on the suppliers?"

I once worked with a sales manager who literally spewed ideas for articles. He was a published author himself, so we had a great rapport. He would conduct a seminar for distributors, customers, and sales trainees; at intervals during the sessions, he'd make notes concerning his students' knowledge gaps.

Later we'd get together, and he'd haul out his notes. "Users of our equipment need help in this area, and this, and this," he'd say. Each idea seemed to trigger five additional ideas. It was almost too much of a good thing, because the disparity between the possibilities for articles on the one hand, and our capacity and budget for publicity on the other, caused much frustration.

If you must have a problem, though, that's a nice kind to have.

Dealers, Distributors, and Field Salespeople

Where is the real world? It's not in your office, nor is it in the editors'. It's not in the offices of your sales manager or engineers, either.

Then where is it? Out where the machinery whines.

Nobody has more frequent contact with your customers in the real world than do your dealers, distributors, and salespeople. Go out and confer with these people. They love to talk anyway, and they're usually flattered when you ask them to share their experience and opinions.

Keep in mind, however, that each individual lives within a limited world. Salesman Smith may have 30 years of field experience, but this may have been quite limited in geography, product, technology, or industry applications. When you get article ideas from field people, therefore, make sure you check the ideas against the broader experience of the sales manager or chief application engineer.

Customers

Now you're really in the real world. Now you're walking, listening, taking notes, and shooting photos where people get mud on their shoes and oil on their hands.

Again, though, remember that although this world is quite real and intense − it makes strong, lasting impressions on you − it also lacks scope. A visit to one furniture plant, even with interviews of five knowledgeable, articulate people in that plant, will likely not tell you all you need to know in order to write something for the entire furniture industry. The plant in the next county does things differently, so its people face different problems.

Conferences, Seminars, and Trade Shows

Which topics are the hot ones? Which seem to raise the most questioning and discussion? Which topics cause voices to rise and wrinkles to appear on brows? Make notes and follow up.

At trade shows, can you spot any trends in product design or suggested applications? Where are computers showing up, and what are their functions? Is a certain kind of product or design more prominent at this show than it was at the last one?

Company Literature

Browse through your company's literature, watching for article ideas. Check catalogs, bulletins, brochures, mailers, manuals, and article reprints. Also review the scripts for movies, slide/tape presentations, and illustrated talks.

Pay special attention to the article reprints, service literature, and training-course material. Is there a topic that could be updated?

Thus far, I've listed 10 different sources for article ideas. I'll wager that you can come up with others. With a little practice, you'll be able to spot the gems, even those partly buried and coated with mud.

HOW TO SELL ARTICLE IDEAS

You have an idea for a bylined feature article. The topic is timely and important to many people in industry. You've discussed the idea with one or more company engineers who are experts on the subject; they agree that you should try to sell the article idea, and they're willing to help you in producing the manuscript and illustrations.

What next? Following is a suggested procedure, step by step.

1. Draft a preliminary outline or summary of the article. Tell what it would cover, the approach you'd take, who would receive the byline, and the types of illustrations you suggest.

2. Obtain permission, preferably in writing, to prepare and place the article. Start with your superior, then go up the chain of command as far as necessary. Touch base with the marketing director or vice-president of marketing. If the article is to cover a technical topic, check with the chief engineer (design or application) or the vice-president of engineering.

Why go to such lengths? Because so far all you have is agreement from a few people that your idea is a good one. In addition to that, you need permission from company brass to execute the project. Failure to obtain permission could cause much harm to you and your company.

I found during my years as a company publicist that permission to write and place bylined feature articles usually came easily. Once in a while, though, permission was denied. Reasons for denial could include:

• The topic of the proposed article is too sensitive for publicity. Perhaps the company has litigation in progress, or there is much controversy over the subject in government circles or the marketplace.

The company's executives don't want to put their hands into a dark hole. "Let's see how the situation looks in six months to a year," they may say.

• The company is about to announce a breakthrough that will obsolete the products or methods you would cover in the proposed article. The new development has been kept secret.

• The company plans to drop a product or method, withdraw from a market, or make a radical change in direction within a market. Again, the plans have been kept secret.

These are but three of many possible legitimate reasons for denial of permission. Don't become discouraged if occasionally one of your ideas dies in the ground. Remember, your function is to further the interests of the company.

3. Let's assume that you got permission to proceed. Your next step is to make a list of the magazines you think may publish the article. Put them in some initial order of priority. Ask yourself, "Where would the appearance of the article do the most toward accomplishing our marketing communications goal?"

4. Study the magazines on your list. In other words, know the markets for your article. Zero in on your first-choice magazine, obtain copies of several back issues, and scan them from cover to cover. Read everything, including the ads.

How do you determine which magazine ought to be first on your list? You need to consider a number of factors, including:

The makeup of the audience.
The kinds of material the editor presents in bylined feature articles.
The magazine's personality.
The magazine's reputation, including its stature versus that of others in the field.
Total circulation.

If you want to do a thorough job of assessing the magazine's readership, obtain a copy of the circulation audit statement. This tells you the titles and functions of the readers, the percentage of the total in each title category, the standard industry classifications (SIC's) served, and much more.

In my judgment, the magazine's personality and the composition of its audience are far more important than total circulation as criteria. Each magazine has a unique personality, reflecting the personalities of the editor, publisher, and parent company. One magazine may be light, breezy, and heavy on graphics: a "flip-through" magazine for fast, easy reading. Perhaps it stresses news angles. If the editor runs bylined feature articles, they're probably short and loaded with illustrations.

Another magazine serving the same field may by comparison look staid. The circulation figure may be lower. The tutorial articles are likely fewer in number, longer, and laced with charts, graphs, diagrams, equations, and other technical graphics. This is not a flip-through magazine but one that the reader may take home to read in quiet leisure.

Which magazine should you choose and aim at? Well, what do you want to accomplish? How many people in which job categories do you want to reach? Would you be satisfied with the fast impact of a short, light, profusely illustrated article, or would you gain more by the heavier, more lasting impact of a long, in-depth piece?

Perhaps you have one eye on the magazine, the other on planned uses for reprints. How many pages do you envision for the reprint? How much can you spend for the projected quantity? And what about four-color process versus one, two, or more standard colors in the reprint?

Take your time in this step. Don't make a reflexive jump to the alleged "number one in the field." Gather your facts, prepare your case. Be ready to win over the new product manager who insists that you place the article in Magazine X. (They ran his picture two months ago.)

Media selection is a complex task. For you, it may be even more complex than for agency media buyers. They are concerned mostly, it seems to me, with circulation figures, space rates, and special deals. You must consider many more variables, including that undefinable, the magazine's personality.

5. Draft a query letter addressed to the editor of your first-choice magazine, the "target." The term "query" comes from freelance magazine writers, who must be experts in selling themselves and their ideas by mail. Essentially the query is a sales letter or proposal.

In your query letter, you'll tell certain things to the editor, urge that he accept your proposal, and ask for his preferences. The letter should:

• Describe the problem that needs solving. In other words, give an objective or justification for the article. An example: "Despite much training and literature, many users have trouble in choosing and installing connectors for waterproof electrical connections."

• Name the topic of the proposed article and describe its scope. What will it cover; what will it not cover? The scope of "How to make waterproof electrical connections on outdoor equipment," for instance, is smaller and more specific than "The basics of waterproof connections."

• Explain why you think the topic needs attention *now*, and why the topic is important to many readers of this particular magazine. If you've done your homework, you'll be able to make a strong pitch.

• Tell who would be your primary source or sources, who would write the initial draft, and who would get the byline.

• Give details on the qualifications of the source to write about the subject. List degrees, length and nature of pertinent experience, and current activities relating to the topic. If the source has lectured or written on this or related topics, say so. Mention any related patents held by the source.

• Explain the nature and degree of the involvement of your company or client in the subject area.

• Mention any previously published articles you have authored or helped to prepare, and enclose tear sheets, reprints, or facsimiles. Doing so will help to establish that you and your source are not beginners. If you haven't been published before, don't bring up the matter.

• Let the editor know how much time you and the source will need to produce the manuscript and all the illustrations, if you can estimate it. This will affect his decision and aid him in scheduling the article.

• Describe the kind of illustrations you suggest for the article, including product photos, renderings, cutaways, or cross-sectional views (photos, renderings, or line art), application photos, and schematic drawings (as for circuits). Also mention suggested tables, graphs, and charts.

Can you offer any graphics that are especially useful, attractive, interesting, or different? Make a set of prints or sharp, clear facsimiles and send them along. You are selling an idea by mail, and the editor always has graphics on his mind. Show him the pictures you can offer; doing so helps to make the sale.

• If the competitive magazines have been publishing material on this topic, tell how your article will be better, bigger, more useful. Stress the uniqueness, timeliness, and special value of your approach, relating it to the immediacy of the problem and the readers' need for solutions. If yours would be the first article on the topic, say so.

• Assure the editor that you have cleared the project with executives of your company. It's embarrassing, costly, and sometimes hazardous to jobs when a company official orders a typeset article killed or, worse yet, howls, "Stop the presses!"

• Thus far, you've been telling and selling. Now it's time for questions. Ask the editor: "May I proceed? If yes, how long should the article be? How many illustrations, and which kinds would you like? Do you want to set a deadline, and if so, what is it?"

Here's a sample query letter that I've made up as an illustration:

Mr. Ed. Baxter, Editor
OUTDOOR EQUIPMENT
(Address)

Dear Mr. Baxter:

Do you know that in spite of all the training sessions, manuals, and service bulletins on the subject, many users of heavy mobile equipment continue to experience costly problems with electrical connections? Our field service engineers and technicians report that they are spending over 50 percent of their time solving electrical problems.

I've read *Outdoor Equipment's* latest circulation audit statement. I know that a large percentage of your readers are equipment owners and operators. Many of them would benefit from timely tips on the topic. They know better than you and I the high cost of downtime.

We'd like to prepare a comprehensive, exclusive, technical feature article for you on the topic. A tentative title: "How to select, install, and replace waterproof electrical connectors." The text would give succinct, step-by-step instructions, pointing out pitfalls and common errors. We would include photos or drawings to illustrate, where desirable. A preliminary outline is enclosed.

We're well qualified to write on the topic because our company is the second-largest manufacturer of waterproof electrical connectors in the U.S. Wattsavolt makes just about every size and type of connector in use, except for a few specials.

The planning and first rough draft would be done by Charles Brown, our chief applications engineer. He holds an E.E. from Purdue University, has had 27 years of experience in the field, and has written eight technical papers on connectors. He deals with our field people every day, so he knows the details as well as the urgency and universality of the problem.

Mr. Brown would get the byline. I would work with him, polish the text, and oversee production of the illustrations. Our management knows of this proposal and has approved the project. Mr. Steve Orlicki, our vice-president of engineering, will review the editorial package before we submit it to you.

Regarding the enclosures: Recently we had a professional photographer shoot a sequence of black & white photos showing how to properly install waterproof connectors. A set of 5" x 7" prints is enclosed for your review. Each would be appropriately captioned and sequenced.

I think you will agree that the photos help to tell the story clearly and would provide valuable instruction for many of your readers. By the way, this set of photos has not been published anywhere as yet.

This would be the 12th bylined feature article our company has produced in three years. The last one ran in *Utility Maintenance* two months ago. I've enclosed a set of tear sheets.

As far as I can determine, no magazine has published an article on this topic in the past four years. If one had run, we would probably know about it and have copies in our reference files.

May we proceed? If yes, please indicate your preferences regarding length of article and types of illustrations. I have a copy of your style sheet and will tailor the ms. to your specs. Should you want to schedule the article in a particular issue, please give us a deadline. At this point, I think we'll need four months.

Thank you for your time and attention. I hope to hear from you soon.

Cordially,
(Signature)

Notice that the letter is friendly and direct. Notice, too, that it does not bring up the fact that Wattsavolt regularly advertises in *Outdoor Equipment*. The editor knows his advertisers; the writer is too wise to exert leverage.

Draft the preliminary working outline that will accompany the letter. You can simply expand and polish the outline you wrote to sell the idea and obtain approvals within your company.

Don't worry about sticking to all the details in this outline. The editor knows that it is preliminary and that you and your source must let the article go where it needs to go. After all, an article isn't a rock but a living thing. It grows like a tree, and you can't predict every bend and branch. Just don't change topics. Don't promise a spruce and then deliver a ginkgo.

Mail your query letter, outline, set of photos, and sample reprint to the editor. Be prepared to wait. If you haven't received a reply within four weeks, write or call.

If the editor says yes, you proceed. He may say no, however.

Why would an editor reject an article, even a great one? Maybe he or his competitor ran an article on the same topic a year ago, but you missed seeing it. Maybe he got a similar proposal from another company or agency and made a commitment to them. Maybe he's overloaded with bylined articles and isn't accepting proposals.

Whatever the reason for the rejection, the editor will tell you. He needs timely material and wants to maintain good relations with you and your company.

What is your next step? Go to the Number Two magazine on your list and repeat the process, including a thorough study of the magazine. Don't give up easily. Eventually you will get a yes.

Once you have worked with an editor, you'll find that selling ideas to him becomes easier. You'll be able to shorten your queries, or to phone and make the queries orally. If you deliver what you promise, and on time, he'll start phoning *you* with article ideas.

THE WRONG WAY

I've described the ideal working situation for the publicist who produces CBFA's, and we've gone through recommended procedures for obtaining clearances and selling article ideas. You may have noticed, though, that conditions in the real world sometimes fall short of the ideal. Sometimes, too, real conditions prevent or discourage you from following the best procedures. You may find yourself in this situation:

Igor the marketing manager comes to you and says, "Ralph, we need a technical article published on our line of plastic curtains for welding applications. It's a new line; our prospects don't know the properties of the curtains or how to specify them. We're the first on the market, and we offer several types of plastic material, so you'll have plenty to talk about."

Sounds good to you. A how-to topic usually sells well, you've found, and a news angle never hurts. Already you're playing with variations on the first headline that popped into your head: "The new plastic welding curtains — how to size and specify them."

"Great," you reply enthusiastically. "I'll start querying the editors and see what we can sell."

"No, not this time," Igor insists. "This one is tricky. We have a certain message we want to get across, in a certain way. Wording is critical.

"Better change your procedure this time, Ralph. You and the product manager get together and write something we can look at. Then you can place it. Keep me informed as the project proceeds.

And don't take too long." Igor whirls on the cleated heel of his purple plastic cowboy boot and stomps off.

That's that, you figure. A direct order. No discussion. Just do it.

The project has some urgency to it. At a critical moment, your brain short-circuited and you yielded. Next morning, you're interviewing the product manager, gathering raw material.

Two weeks later, after several revisions of the manuscript and much discussion about illustrations, you have produced a package that satisfies Igor, the product manager, and the vice-president of engineering. You weave in a few final revisions, and you're ready to start selling.

First you draft a short cover letter. It does some selling, but essentially it's a letter of transmittal. The article will explain itself.

You package the letter, manuscript, and illustrations neatly and securely, then mail the envelope to the Number One target magazine on your list. Within eight days – an unusually fast response, you muse – the entire package returns to you. Penned at the bottom of your letter is a note from the editor.

"Dear Ralph," it says. "Thanks for letting us see this material. You've done a good job, as usual, but I'm afraid that we can't use this article. We ran an article on welding curtains four months ago."

Oops. You forgot to check. Quickly you review back issues of your Number Two choice. No sign of any features on welding curtains. Off goes the package to Number Two.

Ten days later, back comes the package. This time the rejection is typed on a small green slip of paper. "We appreciate the chance to review your article," says the note, "but find it much too long a treatment of the subject. Besides, only a small percentage of our readers have any concern with welding. Please keep us in mind for future article ideas, though."

Friendly and polite, but still a rejection. You feel your spirits sagging. Now you're down to the third and last magazine on your initial list of targets.

After retyping several sheets that came back with coffee stains and spots of an undetermined oleaginous material (probably margarine) on them, you post the package to Number Three. As the mail clerk takes the package from your "Out" basket, you silently send a supplication skyward.

Three weeks go by, and no answer. Your hopes rise, fall, then rise again. "They're probably discussing it with interest," you reason. On the 22nd day, the peripatetic package reappears. Its bulky look now has a distasteful familiarity. Slowly, grimly, you cut open the package. Another hand-written note.

"Thank you for considering us," it says, "but I regret that we can't use the article as presented. We would want a much shorter text, more photos, and one or two additional charts. Would you care to prepare an article to our specifications? Please call and let me know."

Three swings, three strikes. Are you out? No, you can go back to Igor, the product manager, and the others. You can show them the last note and persuade them that you should talk to the editor, get his specs, and give him what he wants. Give him what he wants . . . .

"Why me?" you wonder. "What went wrong?"

Forgot to check back issues of Number One, you recall. What else? "I gave in quickly," you admit. "Should have stalled, gained time to prepare my argument."

The damage is done, though. You feel bad about the rejections, and you suspect that Igor and a few others believe the article was rejected because you did a poor job of writing. They don't know a good article from a bowl of borscht, so it's not surprising that they would land on the wrong reason.

There's a chance, too, that at least three editors now believe that either you are not too bright, or your company throws money around, or both.

Remember your pain, and keep in mind that every weekday, in editorial offices all around the country, editors are rejecting hundreds of unsolicited CBFA's, technical and otherwise. Why the editors reject these articles is covered in Chapter 9.

How can you persuade Igor that it's best to query first, then write to the editor's specifications? Here is one argument I have found effective:

"You're an expert in marketing, Igor, and you know the fundamentals of sound marketing better than I do. Stop me if my reasoning goes astray.

"Does our company send its product designers to the drawing boards, and our technicians into the lab, with instructions to develop anything they wish?" you continue. "Do we put a lot of time and money into a new product, then go out and see if anyone wants to buy it?

"No, of course not. We try to assess what the customer needs and wants. We find out details of the product features that will meet those needs and wants. Then we develop the product to specs based on demand in the marketplace.

"Well, an article is a new product," you say with an energetic gesture. You're warming up to this. "It requires planning, market research, development, and much refinement. We put a lot of time, effort, and money into each article.

"So, does it make sense to write the article that we want, then go out and see if an editor wants to buy it? Wouldn't it be more efficient to take our idea to the editor and sell the idea first? Then if he bites, shouldn't we let him set down the guidelines?

"Yes, the editor will write the specs a little differently than we would, but editors usually write loose specs. We'll get our message across; the editor will let us check the final draft for accuracy; and we'll receive much valuable exposure."

If that argument doesn't work, I suggest that you do some quiet querying as you begin the project. Then, when you get an acceptance from an editor, steer the project as best you can so the article meets the editor's wishes.

Insofar as possible, though, avoid the trap. Do no planning, research, or production until you've queried, sold the idea, and determined what the editor wants.

Chapter 8

Writing the Bylined Technical Article

Let's assume that you're an average industrial publicity practitioner. You're interested in science and technology, and you have some knowledge of the technologies practiced in your company or your client organizations. Your knowledge doesn't go nearly as deep, however, as that possessed by the company engineers, technicians, and managers.

Let's also assume that you occasionally receive requests from editors in your field for bylined technical articles (TA's), or that you see several ripe markets for such articles and you want to capitalize on the opportunities. (Table 8-1 lists some of the basic topic categories for bylined technical articles.)

How can you fill those requests or take advantage of those opportunities?

You could attempt to write the technical articles yourself. You're a skillful reporter, and you've had considerable training and experience in researching other kinds of feature articles such as case histories, profiles, and roundups. Why not take a crack at a TA?

I've tried it myself; I've seen the efforts of other PR practitioners who've tried it; and I've heard what many editors say on the matter. My advice is: Don't attempt to research and write a technical article unaided.

To be of value, a TA should have depth and scope. It should reflect the knowledge and carry the byline of someone who is well qualified to write on the subject. Unless you're an engineer/writer, you likely don't have the qualifications, nor would your byline carry much weight.

Table 8-1. Some Categories of Technical Articles.

1. Buyers' guide to X; survey of who offers what in the X product category
2. How X works — the design, construction, and operation of a device or generic type of device
3. Where, why, and how X is being used or could be used; survey of current applications; trends in application
4. Update on X — what's new, different, important in the field
5. How to size and specify X; procedure
6. How to justify X economically; procedure for the justification
7. Tips on how to plan or manage a project involving X
8. Tips on the correct way to install and operate X
9. What's new in options and accessories for generic X
10. Safety equipment and procedures for X
11. Current research and development (R&D) in the field of generic X
12. Current regulations and trends in standards for X
13. Capabilities and limitations or X vs. Y vs. Z
14. Some little-known uses or capabilities of X
15. New-found uses for X
16. Trends in the design of generic X
17. How to maintain and troubleshoot generic X
18. Ten common errors in the installation, startup, operation, or maintenance of X
19. Ten common oversights in the planning and management of projects involving X
20. Current practice in the automation of X

That doesn't mean you're stymied, though. You can use either of two methods:

1. Find a qualified agent or engineer/writer. He can work with one or more experts in your company to produce an article bearing their byline.

2. Collaborate with the experts yourself. You consult with one or more experts; then you either assist them in writing the article, serving as "midwife," or you act as ghostwriter and do most or all of the writing yourself.

When shopping for outside help, look for a writer, not an agency. The agency as a group can't do much for you in this activity. Only a talented, knowledgeable individual can deliver a first-class article.

Don't be overly impressed by the size or even the reputation of an agency. Do spend some time in reviewing the qualifications, including samples, of the individual writers within the agency.

If you work for a manufacturing or engineering company and you've been dealing with a full-service agency or public relations agency, you may already have access to a qualified writer. On the other hand, if the agency is small and doesn't offer complete publicity services, or if you're just beginning to develop a TA program, then you may want to look elsewhere for help.

Where to look? First, ask the editors of the top magazines serving your field. They may know someone – perhaps a freelance technical writer – who can produce and place TA's for you.

If the editors can't help, get in touch with the public relations directors of the trade, technical, and professional societies in your field. As a last resort, you can check the local Yellow Pages or advertise for help.

When considering a writer for an assignment, don't let geographical distance be too much of a deterrent. You want top-notch talent working for you. After all, you're going after space in the world's best periodicals.

Be prepared to pay for talent. You will get what you pay for, and the travel costs will be small in proportion to the value received. In the long run, the best talent is the easiest to work with and the least expensive.

Suppose, though, that your budget and schedule do not permit you to use outside help. You can still get the job done by collaborating with the expert or experts – we'll call them the "source" from here on – and ghostwriting the TA's yourself.

The source, who may be one or more engineers, managers, or technicians, provides the substance for the TA and a percentage of its form. You provide the balance of the form. You also sell the article idea to an editor, serve as liaison between source and editor, coordinate production of artwork, and see the project through to successful completion.

Before diving into a TA project, you need to assess the situation so as to determine the degree of your involvement. You will want to consider these factors:

• Does the source like to write? If yes, you may need to do only minimal editing on the manuscript.
• If the source likes to write, can he produce a readable, salable product? Does the source know the difference between a technical paper and an article? Will the source take suggestions, perhaps even extensive editing, from yourself and the editor?

If the source has a large ego, you may be in for a challenge — not only in writing and editing, but also in human relations. Your job will be easier, of course, if you and the source get along well with each other, and if the source respects your ability and judgment as a professional communicator.

• Is the source lukewarm or cool toward the project? Does he prefer to merely provide the technical information and let you do most or all of the writing? If so, you'll have the chance to tackle a genuine, full-blown job of ghostwriting. The task isn't easy, but it can be highly satisfying.

At this point, let's assume that you've obtained permission to do the article. You've sold the idea to an editor, using a rough initial outline. An expert (source) has agreed to work with you. The source likes to write, has had several bylined TA's published, and wants to do this one. He agrees to let you polish his manuscript, but wants the satisfaction of authorship.

I suggest that you lend this book to the source. Recommend in particular the following section, which covers writing style and the creative process for magazine articles.

ADVICE FOR THE SOURCE

When approaching a technical-article project, the first thing you (the source) need to do is define the objective. What is this article supposed to do for the reader? What's the point of it?

Defining the objective will determine not only the content but also the form of the article. For example, do you want to tell the reader all he needs to know in order to select a certain kind of product? If so, your article will necessarily give very broad coverage of a subject.

A hazard in writing this type of article is that it wants to come out reading like a chapter in an encyclopedia. To prevent this, try to maintain focus. Early on, tell the reader why the information you're giving him is important. From time to time in the article, remind the reader that what you're saying relates to his self-interest, for the reasons mentioned in the lead.

For instance, an article telling how to select electrical connectors for heavy outdoor equipment may lead off with statistics on the downtime caused by connector failure. Then, from time to time in the article, you can relate your bits of advice on connector selection to reduction of downtime. Repetition of key words helps to hold the article together.

Will your article attempt to tell and show the reader how to do something? In this case, you'll be writing a "how-to" or service article. Here you progress logically from step to step. At each you give reasons why and tell of pitfalls to avoid. Try not to digress for long from the narrative line.

Once you have determined precisely the objective of the article and the form it will take, start to gather notes, drawings, textbooks, and manuals on the subject. As you gather this raw material, ideas for sentences, illustrations, paragraphs, and sections will come to you in ever-greater numbers.

When you get an idea, put it down on paper at once. Like other kinds of opportunities, ideas often disappear forever if you don't bag them when you see them. Keep a small notebook or several sheets of paper with you at all times, just to capture fresh ideas.

Don't stop to evaluate the ideas as they come to you. During this gathering period, especially when ideas are swarming thick and fast, it is more important that you get lots of them than that all of the ideas are usable. You can take time to sort them out later.

After gathering just about all the raw material you'll need, make a new, more detailed outline. An outline is merely a skeleton on which the muscles, organs, and skin of your article will grow. Put the article's skeleton together carefully, making sure the foot-bone's connected to the ankle-bone, not to the neck-bone.

No matter what kind of article you tackle, you will derive its outline only from a clear, logical ordering of thoughts and facts. If you've done the best you can on the outline but still have serious doubts about it, have your publicity manager mail a copy to the editor. He'll be glad to evaluate it and offer suggestions. One minor improvement at this stage could save him hours of rearranging when he gets the final manuscript.

With your outline as a guide, start to arrange your raw material. Try to write a first draft of the whole article without stopping too long to polish individual sentences or paragraphs.

Once you get into the material, you may want to rearrange the subtopics, throw out some ideas and add others. Do this, but stick to the subject. Every sentence, photograph, paragraph, drawing — everything you say and show — must pertain to the subject. If something pertains to another subject, even a closely related one, throw it out.

As you weave your ideas into the first draft, ask yourself, "How can I best convey this: by words alone, pictures alone, or a combination of words and pictures?" If you're presenting a lot of figures, group them in a table. Too many figures in the text only slow the reader and irritate him. What's more, a table will show relationships among figures, relationships that the reader may otherwise miss.

Keep the average length of your sentences between 10 and 20 words. If you tend to write long, involved sentences, break some into shorter ones.

It is interesting to note that the sentences in popular digests average about 17 words, while those in magazines like *Atlantic Monthly* run close to 21 words. If your average is from 10 to 20 words, therefore, you're in safe territory. Should the average top 21, though, you had better do some revising. Otherwise your readers may find the going tough.

Vary sentence constructions (simple, compound, complex, compound-complex, etc.). If too many built-alike sentences follow one another, the resulting passage sounds monotonous and childish, even to the "eye's ear." Contrast these two examples:

"The motor driving the turbine is a squirrel-cage motor. It accelerates rapidly. The motor draws a peak current of about 100 A during acceleration. The current drops to between 15 and 20 A after the turbine is up to speed."

"The squirrel-cage motor driving the turbine accelerates rapidly. During acceleration, the current drawn by the motor peaks at about 100 A. Once the turbine has reached running speed, however, the current levels out at 15 to 20 A."

Mix both the lengths and structures of your sentences so that the overall effect is interesting yet smooth and natural. As a test, read the material aloud to yourself or to someone who will give you a frank opinion.

Avoid pompous, polysyllabic verboseness. Observe how these examples affect you differently:

"The switch is employed to initiate or terminate the operation of the blowing mechanism."

"The switch starts and stops the fan."

Sentences like the first sound stuffy, pompous, and academic, and are sure to repel a great percentage of your readers. Keep your wording simple and direct.

Use short, familiar, gutty Anglo-Saxon words instead of the long, unfamiliar, bloodless, Latin-root words. (Examples are given in Table 8-2.) The former have greater impact and create more vivid mental images. Hence they do a better job of conveying your ideas.

Prefer vigorous, active verbs over weak, passive ones. You'll find that in most instances where you've used the passive form, just a little rewording will enable you to use the active. Which of the following hits you harder?

"The roller on the limit switch is struck by the cam."

"The cam strikes the limit switch roller."

Keep your paragraphs short and unified. Because people have a limited attention span and need relief from concentration, they find it hard to read long paragraphs. So hold the average length of your paragraphs to between four and eight typewritten lines.

This doesn't mean, though, that every paragraph ought to be exactly six lines long. A succession of equal-length units strikes the reader's eye immediately and distracts him. Like sentence lengths, paragraph lengths should change in a seemingly random pattern.

If an idea is complicated and you think it requires a long paragraph for proper development, try to break the idea into sub-ideas, giving a shorter paragraph to each.

Table 8-2. Say it Briefly, Simply, Forcefully.

INSTEAD OF SAYING THIS. . .	. . .WHY NOT SAY THIS?
abbreviate	shorten, cut
ameliorate	improve, better
approximately	about, roughly
cognizant	aware
endeavor	try
indeterminate	vague, unknown
optimum	best, ideal
paramount	top, chief, first
problematical	doubtful, unknown
quadrilateral	four-sided

Arrange the paragraphs in a logical sequence. Each idea must follow smoothly and naturally from the preceding one. A gap in continuity, or too abrupt a change of thought, will jolt the reader and throw him off your track. If he's thrown too far, he may just turn the page.

Occasionally, when trying to work out exactly the right wording or arrangement, you'll find that no matter how hard you try, it just won't jell. If that happens, put the problem aside for the time being. Go on to another section, or take a walk, or just abandon the problem until your next writing session.

This is a trick you can apply in all sorts of problem solving. It lets the subconscious mind do some of the work. Often you'll discover that when you return to the problem, its solution has become obvious.

Now go over your first draft and refine it. As you do so, be sure you are choosing a level of terminology to fit your audience. If you are writing for an engineering journal, you can use technical terminology to your heart's content. Readers of these journals may, in fact, resent oversimplified, nontechnical language and explanations that seem to talk down to them. Just make sure that the terms you do employ are understood throughout the profession and that they are not merely part of a jargon peculiar to one locale or narrow specialty.

Upon completing your first draft, put it aside for a few days. At this point you're infatuated with it, so you won't see its faults. Later they'll become more apparent. After the cooling-off period, go back over the entire article. Check all the major points listed in the preceding sections: sentence length, simplicity, vigor, and so forth. Now is the time to apply the fine sandpaper.

Rewrite your introductory paragraph, making it as short, forceful, and tantalizing as you can. This paragraph, known as the "lead," is one of the most important parts of your article. If the lead interests and captivates your reader, you can be sure he'll read at least part of the article. Of course, if you want him to stay with you to the end, the rest of the article must never cease to satisfy the great expectations you built in your lead.

Once you've polished and condensed the lead, go back over the article and look for excess. Are there any globs of detailed description or explanation that interest you but may not be essential to your main theme? Can you shorten anything — words, sentences, paragraphs, sections — without losing important thoughts or breaking continuity?

Pretend that every word printed will cost you a quarter. Then for every word you put back in your pocket, you save 25 cents.

Above all, remember: Cold, gutless, indirect prose full of pompous, obscure verbiage may impress the ignorant few who are easily impressed anyway, but it also repels most other people. There is nothing unprofessional about expressing yourself briefly, clearly, simply, forcefully, and "humanly."

HOW TO GHOSTWRITE THE TA

Now we'll assume the situation at the other extreme. The source hates to write, doesn't want to try even a first, rough draft. He is willing, though, to talk with you as often and as long as you wish. In addition, he will provide sketches, tables, graphs, and other material for illustrations. You must do much of the digging and all of the writing yourself.

In this situation, you function first as a reporter, then as a feature-article writer. Following are suggestions for a procedure.

1. Do your homework. Read all the raw material provided by the source, plus related textbooks, brochures, and manuals. Find a technical dictionary or glossary pertaining to your field and learn the basic terminology. Keep these references handy throughout the project.

2. Prepare in advance for your first fact-gathering interview with the source. Draft and use a list of questions, including these:

In one paragraph, what exactly is the topic? Summarize as succinctly as possible.

Why is this topic important? Describe the problem or challenge and its significance to the reader.

Why is this topic important *now?*

To whom is this topic important; that is, who may benefit from reading the article and applying the knowledge it contains?

What should the article do for the reader?

The answers to these five questions will give you ideas and material you need to write the headline, the deck or summary, and a paragraph that tells the reader why he should read the article. The last-named paragraph may become part of the lead.

If the parameters of the topic have been at all fuzzy to you or the source, arriving at the answers to these five questions will enable both of you to define the task precisely. Precision in defining both the topic and the objective of the article is extremely important. You and/or the source may be a skillful writer, but you will not produce a clear, sharply focused message unless you have thought the project through. In other words, clear writing proceeds only from clear thinking.

3. Interview the source, using both tape recorder and notebook. So that you and the source don't become fatigued, bored, and impatient, restrict this and other interviews to one hour or less.

Make sure that the source answers all the questions on your prepared list, but let him digress if he wants. Listen and watch for signs of enthusiasm, concern, and other emotional involvement in the subject. When you detect emotion, don't stop and divert the conversation to another part of the topic, but encourage the source to continue. People talk most forcefully and vividly on matters about which they have feelings as well as ideas.

4. Ask the source to provide you with all available reference material pertaining to the topic. Give him a reasonable but tight deadline — say, two or three days. Request copies of technical papers, proposals, lesson scripts, articles, textbooks, brochures, and any other form of material available.

In addition, ask for copies of any illustrations that will help you to understand the subject. These may end up as illustrative material for the article. Seek out not only photos and renderings but also graphs, tables, and diagrams. Retain any pencil sketches the source may draw during your interviews.

5. After you have gathered all available current references and have reviewed them, draft a rough but fairly detailed outline, including head and deck and lead paragraphs. List the points that may be expanded on in the body. You may start with your preliminary outline — the one you used in selling the article idea — but refine it and add

more detail. On the outline, note those points that may benefit from illustration.

6. Review this outline with the source. Note any changes in content, emphasis, or direction that the source may suggest. If you disagree with his suggestions, speak up and arrive at resolutions of the disputed points.

Don't leave the interview with questions unanswered. Above all, don't terminate the interview until you both feel you have understood each other and arrived at an agreement. If you leave disputed points unresolved, they will hamper you later when you are alone and writing the article.

7. Proceed with the first draft, working from the outline. Write quickly and freely; leave the prose loose and rough. Don't worry about precision, grammar, or punctuation too soon.

Each writer has his own way of working. I'm not suggesting that you change your method overnight. I have found, though, after having authored hundreds of articles, that if I strive for perfection in the first draft, the writing proceeds too slowly. Too, if I go from longhand draft into clean-typed copy too soon, I'm reluctant to make changes.

The end result turns out better if I let the manuscript sit around in rough longhand or rough-typed form until the last minute. Between the time of the first draft, sometimes written in white heat, and the final typing, I scribble in all sorts of additions, deletions, transpositions, and other improvements. To an untrained eye, the rough draft appears to be growing rougher and sloppier each time I touch it. Actually, though, it is growing finer, tighter, better thought out, better crafted.

8. Take another inventory of illustrations. Set in motion whatever gears must turn to produce line art, photos, typewritten tables, or other graphics you want.

9. Make facsimiles of the rough or finished illustrations and draft captions for them.

10. Type a neat copy of the article and captions. Here neatness counts, because it helps to sell you and your ideas to the source and to anyone else who may read the material. Sloppy, marked-up copy signals the reviewers that perhaps your thinking, too, has been hasty and slipshod. If they receive this signal, they may be inclined to make arbitrary changes they otherwise would not have made.

11. Submit the package — copies of the typed article manuscript, captions, and illustrations — to the source. Retain a duplicate set. Ask the source to review your draft for technical accuracy and to make any changes he feels are necessary.

Be prepared for the worst. You have written the article; this is your piece of work. On the other hand, the source has not seen the article until now, and it will carry his byline. He must bear responsibility for every word and every picture. Besides, he knows the subject far better than you do. So trust the source's judgment and give him the benefit of the doubt.

I have had some technical articles come back from the sources virtually untouched. A few, though, have returned cut, rearranged, and annotated beyond recognition. In these cases, I hadn't understood the subject well enough; I hadn't done my homework.

12. Revise the material, following the source's suggestions regarding content. Disregard suggestions that in your opinion pertain only to style. In particular, do not make changes that would render the article more obtuse, dull, weak, or difficult to read. Let the source correct for technical accuracy, but retain your integrity as the expert communicator.

TAILOR FOR THE MAGAZINE

At this stage, you are polishing the article in light of the source's desires and your own feel for what makes an interesting, tight, well-paced article. Before having the second draft clean-typed, consider the style of the magazine and tailor your prose to that style.

Acquire copies of two or three back issues of the magazine. Examine the bylined technical articles carefully, making notes on the following elements of style:

• The main headline. Does the editor prefer short, tag-type heads, sentence heads, or question heads? Is there a discernible pattern?

• The deck. This is the copy some magazines place between the main head and the body of the article. If the target magazine uses decks, are they short or long? Do they amplify the head? Do they stand on their own, teasing the reader into the body, or do they provide summaries of the article's contents?

Analyze the decks, noting length, tone, and function. Along with the head and lead, the deck is one of the most critical parts of the article. It is here that many readers decide whether or not they want to make a commitment of their time, attention, and mental effort. The deck can persuade them to take the plunge.

• The lead. This may be one paragraph or a series of paragraphs, but its purpose is always the same: to further intrigue the reader and draw him into the body.

Which styles of leads does the editor seem to prefer? Some editors lean toward the statement, either startling or summary. Others like question-leads that seek to establish immediate, personal identity with the reader. Still other editors like the narrative intrigue of the anecdote-lead, or the general-to-particular drawdown of the funnel-lead.

If you see a pattern, draft your lead accordingly.

• Language. Look at elements such as the use of personal pronouns, rhetorical questions, and slang. Pay particular attention to the technical level of the language.

• Abbreviations, capitalization, the use of acronyms, metrics.

• Subheads. Are they separate or run in, teasers or tags? Does the editor prefer subdivisions identified by numbers and letters, or is the structure less rigid? What about bullets for series of related items?

Some magazines publish their own detailed style sheets. Ask for copies.

• Captions. Long, short, or varied in length? Do the captions repeat information in the body, or do they provide new information? Do the captions stand on their own or merely tantalize the reader to go back into the article?

• Length of paragraphs. Do the paragraphs tend to run long or short? Keep in mind that a six-line paragraph in a page set in two-column format will accommodate more words and sentences than will a six-liner in a three-column format.

• Callouts in illustrations. Some editors like numbered callouts, with the labels keyed and stacked next to or below the illustrations. Other editors insist on having the labels placed in and around the graphic elements, at the ends of the arrows.

• The closing. As a rule, the end of the article should bring the reader back down to earth with a satisfying thump. You will find, though, that some editors — particularly those in highly technical fields — prefer the summary closing. In this type of ending, the writer briefly reviews the main points made in the article.

You may run across other elements to consider, but we've covered the main ones. After making notes on the editor's apparent preferences, go back through your draft and tailor it to match those preferences.

"Why should I bother going to such lengths?" you may ask. "After all, isn't the editor being paid to edit?"

Yes, but most of the editors I've known don't really enjoy polishing and reworking copy written by other people. The majority of editors get into the business, I think, because they are writers, creative people. They'd much rather spend the bulk of their time researching stories and then creating their own lively prose.

So you see, when you tailor your copy to the magazine's style, you're doing the editor a favor. You're allowing him more time in which he can do what he likes to do best. As a result, you're building good will for yourself and your company.

And why do you need this editor's good will? Because most likely you will want to submit other articles, plus news releases, case histories, and other material in the future. If the editor has a positive feeling toward you and your company, the material you submit will receive favorable, even preferred treatment.

Another point: If the editor sees that you have carefully tailored the material to the magazine, his reaction will probably be, "This writer and this company are really on the ball. I'll bet this is good material."

In other words, your effort to tailor the material helps to sell it. The editor will more quickly accept tailored material, and he will be less inclined to make changes than if he were editing untailored material.

THE FINAL STEPS

You've woven in the source's changes, refined the article to your own standards and tastes, and tailored it to the style of the target magazine. Next come some important final steps.

1. Double-check the manuscript, including the captions, for spellings, numerals, and equations. Force yourself to go slowly and to check back to the original sources.

2. Key the illustrations to the typewritten captions. On photoprints, write the key numbers or letters on the back surface, down near the bottom edge. If there's the slightest chance that the editor won't be able to tell which way is up in a photo, write "TOP" on the border on the top front of the print, and also on the back at the top.

Perhaps you've been told that a caption should always be typed on a separate sheet of paper, then taped to the back of the print and folded over the face. Here's another procedure that makes less work for the magazine's editors, production manager, and art director:

Type a short, identifying caption, including your company's or client's name and a key number, on a slip of paper. Tape or rubber-cement this to the back of the print. The slip will help to identify the print as it makes its way to the printer.

Type the full caption, the one intended for typesetting, on a full-sized sheet. If you're sending more than one illustration and caption, gang the captions, leaving four spaces between. Don't forget to key the captions.

This way, the editor can review and edit all captions as a group. He doesn't have to risk tearing the print. The production manager can size and specify type for all the captions at one time. And the typesetter will have an easier time with them.

3. Show your revision to the source. If you've ignored some of his suggestions — suggestions that would detract from the form of the article — tell him why. Don't yield too easily to demands for arbitrary changes.

It's easy for me, an outsider, to offer such advice. Only you know the political situation in which you work. I offer the advice nonetheless because if you yield too easily on matters of form or style, you will soon become regarded as a pushover. Some engineers and managers may try to ram through all manner of dull, convoluted, barely intelligible prose. For the company's sake and for your own, you must take responsibility for the form of the article. Besides, you want to be able to look at yourself in the mirror.

Now the material is ready for packaging. Place your manuscript, photos, and drawings between two pieces of corrugated board or foam measuring 8 1/2" x 11" or larger. Fasten the assembly with tape or rubber bands, slip it into a large envelope, and send it on its way.

Expect to wait 10 to 30 days for an acknowledgment from the editor. If at the end of a month you haven't heard from him, give him a friendly call. Remember that he has many other projects on his mind. Don't assume that he has been ignoring your article, or that he has spent all his waking hours perusing it.

Expect your article to come back with the editor's suggestions for changes. Unless they would generate inaccuracies or misconceptions, regard the changes as mandated. You are a seller, and your customer is telling you exactly what he wants. Further, he knows articles, he knows his industry, and he knows his readers. Remind yourself and the source not to be unyielding.

Review the editor's changes, show them to the source, make any final notations, and return the package to the editor with a thank-you note. Then wait as patiently as you can to see your work in print.

Two final bits: Ask the editor when the article will appear, but don't pester him with numerous phone calls about it. And don't expect or ask to see either galley or page proofs. Once the copy has been set in type, that's it.

Chapter 9
Why Articles Bounce

One veteran editor, a friend of many years, tells me that he would go to almost any length to get contributed, bylined feature articles (CBFA's) for his magazine. "Nothing beats the impact of an authority's byline on an article concerning a timely topic," he says, "yet we don't get nearly as many article ideas or manuscripts as we could use. Evidently the managers, engineers, and public relations people in our field don't realize the value they and their company could derive from feature articles published. I will travel, rewrite, cajole, wheedle — anything to get solid material from experts."

On the other hand, another editor reports with chagrin that he has all but given up on CBFA's. "Out of 100 CBFA's which we receive unsolicited, we must reject about 99," he observes. "The 100th invariably needs a lot of work to make it worth printing. There seems to be a dearth of qualified writers working in public relations for our field."

These two widely divergent views led me to wonder: Is there a pattern in this business of CBFA's? How big is the market for CBFA's? Surely industrial magazines — or some of them, at any rate — receive significant numbers of unsolicited CBFA's; what percentage of them bounce, and why? And what advice would editors offer to company and agency people who want to enjoy the benefits of published CBFA's?

To obtain answers to these and related questions, I conducted a mail survey of the editors of 17 leading industrial magazines. Some are horizontals, serving people in many industries. Other magazines included in the survey are large verticals. Still others are what could be called "diagonals," serving many people in some industries, fewer in others.

Following is a report on my little survey. First, though, a few words of explanation about the terms "mean average" and "median average" in the report.

A "mean average" is derived by adding all the figures reported, then dividing by the number of responses. In this survey the responses totaled 17.

A "median average" is derived by stacking all the reported figures in a column, with the largest on top, then the second-largest, and so on in descending order. The smallest figure ends up at the bottom. Then you pick the figure in the middle of the column; if the total number of responses is an even number, you pick the two in the middle of the column, add them, and divide by two.

Usually a median average will give you a truer picture of the statistical reality in the sample polled. A few abnormally large figures at one end or small figures at the other can knock the mean average cockeyed. For instance, if there were two millionaires living in a blue-collar neighborhood having a total of 100 families, a mean-average report would tell you that the average income is $39,600. You know, though, that if family incomes here range from $17,000 to $23,000, a figure of $20,000 would be closer to the truth. For a more immediate example, see the answer to Question No. 2 in my survey.

1. Do you publish contributed, bylined feature articles (CBFA's) in your magazine?

	Number	%
Yes	16	94.1
No	1	5.9

Comment: The one magazine reporting "no" is *Production,* which is entirely staff written. There are probably other magazines with a similar policy. This fact emphasizes the need for you to query before preparing and submitting an article.

2. If your (the editor's) answer to Question No. 1 was "yes," about how many CBFA's do you publish in an average year?

Grand total for 17 magazines: 1011
Largest number: 300
Smallest number: 0
Mean average: 63.2
Median average: 30.0

Comment: As I recall, there are about 3500 business, trade, technical, and industrial periodicals published in the U.S. and Canada. (The figure came from *Bacon's Publicity Checker.*) If we delete the periodicals that are newsletters, and make an estimate of how many of those remaining do not accept publicity, we get a working figure of 2500.

If that figure is close enough for working purposes, and if the median average of 30 articles per year is valid universally, the total market each year for CBFA's in the U.S. and Canada is 75,000.

I suspect, though, that a more valid median average would fall in the range of 5 to 10 — based on my experience in the field. You see, in my survey I polled *Oil & Gas Journal,* which reported using 300 CBFA's a year, and *Plant Engineering,* which reportedly uses some 212 CBFA's a year. These high figures likely elevated both the mean and median averages in my little survey.

Still, assuming that a figure of 7.5 is nearer the true median for the universe, the total annual market is a respectable 18,750. That's a lot of ink for the companies placing CBFA's. How many did you place last year?

3. Do you actively solicit CBFA's?

	Number	%
Yes	13	76.5
No	4	23.5

Comment: Of the editors polled, more than three out of four are actively seeking contributed articles. Your chances of selling a timely, authoritative, well-written article are excellent. But query first.

4. Do you receive enough good CBFA's to fill your needs?

	Number	%
Yes	12	70.6
No	5	29.4

5. Of the CBFA's which you receive unsolicited — received over the transom from PR people, company execs, etc. — what percentage must you reject?

Largest percentage: 100% *(Production)*
Smallest percentage: 20%
Mean average: 68.7%
Median average: 75.0%

6. What are the most common reasons for which you reject unsolicited CBFA's?

	Number	*%*
a. Subject irrelevant, or not sufficiently relevant, to our audience.	14	82.4
b. Too much commercial puff.	6	35.3
c. Lack of solid technical meat; too shallow.	3	17.6
d. Article poorly written.	2	11.8
e. Subject is not timely.	1	5.9
f. Subject is dull.	1	5.9
g. Article not offered as an exclusive.	1	5.9
h. Not enough space in the magazine to run the good CBFA's received.	1	5.9
i. We use no contributed articles.	1	5.9
j. Article is too broad, doesn't focus sharply on one important aspect of the subject.	1	5.9
k. Article pertains to the products of only one company; we want generic information.	1	5.9
l. Subject doesn't fall into our carefully planned editorial schedule.	1	5.9
m. Article is too short for the topic, which deserves a fuller treatment.	1	5.9
n. Article was obviously written to please the boss or client, not to provide useful information to our readers.	1	5.9

	Number	%

o. Article is in conflict with another already scheduled or recently printed. — 1 — 5.9

p. Writer used wrong approach to subject; e.g., case history rather than tutorial. — 1 — 5.9

Comment: You can see from the preceding that editors reject unsolicited CBFA's for a variety of reasons. The one most often cited was "not relevant to our field," which means many publicity folk do not research their markets properly. (If you're forced by the boss or client to prepare the article to please insiders, before even making a query, reread Chapter 7.)

7. Would you advise PR people to call or write first with a proposal (query) before producing and submitting the article and pix? In other words, would it be better to first sell the *idea* of the article?

	Number	%
Yes	16	94.1
No	1	5.9
Don't bother	1	5.9

Comment: This question elicited a high percentage of "yes" answers and several "absolutely's." Many answers were followed by heatedly scratched exclamation marks. The "don't bother" reply came from, as you have likely guessed, *Production*. The "no" came from an editor who doesn't have much faith in the capabilities of writers who are not editors. He has been burned often by PR people who can't deliver what they offer. This editor would rather see the completed manuscript and pictures, whether preceded by a query or not.

8. Any other advice to writers on how to "score" in your magazine with CBFA's?

This open-ended question drew many interesting and valuable comments; most of them follow. I gave the editors the option of remaining anonymous, so some comments appear without attribution. The sequence is random.

"Usually the contributed, bylined feature articles coming directly from savvy manufacturers and consultants are the best. Those from agencies tend to be the poorest, probably because the writers don't know enough about the subject. The name of the agency or company seems to have little bearing on the quality of the article. It's the individual writer — his knowledge and skill — that makes the difference." — Gene Schwind, *Material Handling Engineering.*

"People who want to write for us should be aware of the nature of our readers and their needs, which in turn determine ours." — Jack Miske, *Foundry Management & Technology.*

"Outlines usually don't work, except to serve as a list of things for the author to say. The bulk of the article often ends up under what was category II, B, 3, c in the outline submitted. I like to see the completed manuscript and illustrations, and then work with the writer." — Ed Kompass, *Control Engineering.*

"Read the magazine!" — Don Taylor, *Ocean Industry.*

"It's easy. Simply provide good ideas, good research, good writing and good illustrations."

"I strongly suggest a personal visit to our offices, so the writer and our editors can explore the magazine's thinking." — Lindley Higgins, *Marine Engineering/Log.*

"Make the article pertain directly to our industry; call to discuss the idea; and hold down on plugs for the company and its products." — Richard Huhta, *Rock Products.*

"Know the publication you intend to write for... Quite frankly, I get tired of sifting through submitted material to see if there is anything of value, and most often finding promotional pitches in disguise." — Robert Kelly, *Assembly Engineering.*

"Read the magazine. Then call."

"Study the magazine! Identify the target audience and write for that, not for the company sales department. Let the expert with the product knowledge do the writing — not a writer who doesn't know the subject." — Gene Kinney, *Oil & Gas Journal.*

"I really get turned on by people who send in well-written, appropriate material, typed to width (36 characters for us), in our style and format. A good ratio of pix to copy helps us, too; then we don't have to stretch copy or squeeze a lot of pix into a small space." — Randy Gold, *Precision Metal Magazine.*

"Contact the appropriate editor in advance; give him or her as complete as possible an outline of what you want to do. Take heed of his or her suggestions, and stick to the agreed plan as closely as possible. Also, ask for a copy of the 'Author's Guide' which we provide." — Leo Spector, *Plant Engineering.*

"Cut out all the promotional puff; know what you're writing about; give details instead of bland generalities."

Final comments: You realize, I'm sure, that this survey was not scientific but was intended to draw out some useful guidelines and comments. Take the percentages as general indicators only. And, before you plunge into a CBFA project, study the magazine — and query first.

Chapter 10

Ten Ways to Stretch the Technical-Article Budget

If your company or client is engaged in industrial manufacturing, consulting engineering, construction, research and development, or some other technical field, chances are you already know the benefits of the published technical article. Along with the presentation of papers at conferences and seminars, placing articles in trade, industrial, and technical magazines is an excellent way to establish the reputation of a company and its members for expertise in their particular field.

What you may not know, however, are some of the well-proved methods for economizing in the conception, research, writing, and production phases of a technical article. With the money saved, you can produce and place additional articles, or divert the money to other forms of communication.

Following are ten tips for squeezing more use out of your technical-article dollars.

1. Motivate the experts. Encourage your company's engineers, technicians, and managers to write articles for trade, technical, and professional periodicals. Their experience and opinions are highly valuable, and are much sought by editors.

Some people take naturally to writing and enjoy the prestige that results from getting published. Others, perhaps the majority, find article-writing difficult and distasteful. Still others could write well and easily but prefer to keep a low profile.

Your challenge, therefore, is threefold:

• Encourage those who are willing and eager to write, without abusing their generosity and without allowing their article output to dominate excessively the company's total article output. Such dominance can create some nasty political problems for you as well as for the prolific writers.

• Motivate those who find writing difficult, or who haven't seen the benefits. You can create this motivation in several ways.

One method used by many organizations is a company-sanctioned monetary reward for publication of articles. A typical system involves the payment of a fixed amount — say, $50 — for each full page printed in the periodical. It's better not to offer X dollars per page of manuscript, as that only encourages wordiness.

Other methods used for motivating authors include publicity in the local news media and company house organs; an "authors' bulletin board" displaying tear sheets of printed articles, authors' portraits, and brief biographical sketches; and the reprinting and distribution of annual anthologies of articles published by company members.

• Motivate your "pheasants": those intelligent, colorful, but bashful birds who prefer to remain in the brush. In my experience, these birds are the most difficult to reach. They're often well qualified to write on matters of importance, but prefer not to. In some cases, they're fearful of appearing to be hungry for personal glory; others may be reluctant to take a chance on making a mistake or voicing a controversial opinion in print.

On several occasions I've witnessed an effective technique for obtaining valuable, well-written articles from pheasants. Here's how it goes:

First, you watch for an occasion on which a pheasant has been given the assignment of presenting a paper at a technical conference or seminar. To fulfill this, he'll produce at least a script, and perhaps a printed paper for handout.

Then, you point out the ease and benefits of modifying the paper and offering it for publication. You indicate that such-and-such an editor has expressed interest in the article (you've sold the editor beforehand) and offer to assist in editing for publication, preparing the drawings and graphs, etc.

Once the potential author has given the paper orally, he will have de-bugged it rather thoroughly. Comments on his presentation by his peers help him to remove any remaining flaws. He's then fairly confident that publication would be reasonably safe.

Another device you might try is to have the editor deal directly with the potential author. Some technical people are disdainful of PR and advertising folk within their own company or its agency but hold considerable respect for editors of prestigious periodicals. Sell the editor on the article idea, and then let him sell the author on writing it.

Encouraging your company's technical people to write, and helping them to produce the final package, will enable you to place more and better material. Doing so will also leave more dollars for those articles your company people can't or won't write.

2. Tie in with training. Integrate the technical-article portion of your publicity program with your company's training program. You'll find that in some cases research for one type of communication can also be used for the other, and the costs can be shared. This will save money for both you and the training director.

An instance of how this integration can work beneficially occurred a few years ago within a Cleveland industrial manufacturing company. For some years, the publicity manager (PM) and training director (TD) had been going their separate ways, without much dialogue.

Once in a while the PM would pick up an article idea from the TD, or the latter would latch onto a recently published article and adapt it for one of his courses. That was about the extent of their mutual activity, though.

Then one day the two got together and entered into a discussion of their individual programs and objectives. With no little surprise, they found they had many areas of common interest. Subject matter for several of the articles the PM had in work would be useful in a new course the TD was planning, they discovered. At the same time, much of the material being researched by the TD and his staff could be converted into highly salable technical articles. In some cases there was duplication of effort.

After that, the PM and TD met at least once a week for informal planning, review, and brainstorming. They jointly assigned many research and writing projects, either to a training staffer or to a qualified agent or freelancer. Who got which assignment depended on the knowledge and experience of the people involved.

This company's training and publicity programs benefited from the cooperative efforts of the two managers. For one thing, since research is one of the major cost factors in producing technical communications material, the overall costs for both the articles and the training texts decreased, even while total volume increased. There was no longer duplication of effort.

Secondly, where mutually useful projects are involved, the publicity and training departments saved significant sums in artwork production costs. Line drawings, cutaways, and other types of art were prepared and reproduced in such a way that they could be used for illustration of an article and a training text, with little or no adaptation. Similarly, when either the PM or TD planned a photography project — whether in a plant, lab, or studio, or out in the field — he checked with his opposite number. Together, they listed all desirable variations in photo subject matter, composition, angles, etc. Usually they instructed the photographer to shoot slides for slidefilms, plus black-and-white negatives and large color transparencies for article illustrations, textbook illustrations, and possible cover shots. Since travel time and setup are among the largest cost factors in many photography projects, the PM and TD were able to minimize their photo expenses through well-planned, joint photo assignments.

Thirdly, due to a synergistic effect, the number of good ideas for articles seemed to triple. Besides liking and trusting one another, the PM and TD were imaginative individuals. When they got together, ideas flew about and fused into new ideas, like molecules in a chemical reaction. This proliferation of new ideas was enhanced by the fact that while the two people had some common contacts in field sales, marketing, engineering, and other company departments, at the same time each had contacts — and therefore sources of ideas — that the other didn't have. For instance, the TD conversed with many more salespeople and distributors than did the PM, while the latter regularly chatted with editors, manufacturing managers, and others whom the TD never saw. A much greater number and diversity of idea sources were therefore available to both the PM and TD.

And finally there's the matter of direction. Thanks to his frequent discourses with the TD, the PM had a much better feel not only for training objectives but also for the company's overall marketing communications objectives. Discussions with the TD helped the PM to better understand which way the company wanted to go and why. This heightened understanding enabled the PM to give sharper, clearer direction to his publicity activities. He steered his ship on a straighter course with less wasted motion. In terms of results, therefore, he operated more efficiently and realized more value from each publicity dollar.

The point is, don't try to function in a sealed compartment. Exchange ideas often and freely, not only up and down the chain of command and within your own department but sideways as well. You and your peers in training — and also in sales, advertising, and sales promotion — can assist one another in many ways. Everyone benefits.

3. Recycle existing material. Sift through your company's printed and audiovisual material. Much of it can be updated, expanded, combined, or otherwise adapted into fine, salable technical articles.

Places to look include technical papers and reports, training and sales films, instruction manuals and bulletins, product literature, product-selection charts, and so on. Look not only at current literature but also at material that has become outdated and is no longer in use.

By refurbishing material already on hand, you can produce many useful articles with a minimum investment in research. Often you can also use much of the text and illustrative material.

Just one example: A few years ago, a client of mine — a manufacturer of couplings for air hoses — asked me to update a product brochure, adding information on new models and design changes. Upon receiving a copy of the old brochure, I found that it gave its readers a bonus: a well-illustrated section telling how to install and utilize the couplings for greatest economy and safety.

Here was a good opportunity for an article, and it was already partially written and illustrated! I checked with an editor; "Of course we'd like the article!" he shouted over the phone. "You needn't have asked." Seems that articles that touch on safety have always been welcomed, but are even more welcome nowadays thanks to OSHA.

Then I worked up a quote for the product manager and called him. "Sure, go ahead," he replied. "At that price, how can we refuse?"

As you may have surmised, the figure I quoted was low for a technical article. I was able to quote a low figure, yet still make a decent profit on the project, because most of the information and pictures were right there before us.

I whipped the article out within the week, and two months later got a full two-page spread in our Number One target magazine. Everyone involved benefited — the editor, his readers, our agency, the product manager, and his company. And all because someone knew how to recognize an opportunity for an article in existing material.

4. Update recurrent topics. Build a file of reprints and tear sheets of articles bylined by members of your company and published in the past. Go back as far in the company's history as you can. In addition, build a file of articles bylined by members of competitive companies.

Every once in a while review these files. Look for opportunities to produce similar articles that will bring the reader up to date on the subject. Often you'll find you can use much of the previously published material simply by revising it, giving it a contemporary slant, and adding the latest facts and figures.

Some of the types of subject matter that lend themselves well to this treatment are:

• "State of the art." What has changed in the art? Any recent developments that warrant discussion?

• Cost of operation, maintenance, etc. No doubt the numbers have changed upward. And what about major changes in cost factors: oil, gas, electricity, labor? Is there a story here?

• How to select, install, operate, maintain, troubleshoot, etc. What's new that would warrant an update? Any major developments in regulations, product designs, materials, techniques, or usage patterns?

Those are just three categories. Surely you'll find others — if you look. Doing so will pay off in many good articles, at low cost per.

5. Look ahead to a book. When planning a technical-article program and budgeting for it, watch for the possibility of a book.

As you may have observed, companies that publish and distribute a manual or textbook on the technology of their field benefit greatly in terms of the book's promotional value. If a book is truly useful, your customers and prospects will use it. Moreover, people assume, rightly or not, that the person who wrote the book and the company that published it are the experts in the field.

Does someone in your company already have a hankering to publish a technical book? If not, perhaps you could work up an outline and try to sell the book idea to management.

Why all this about a book? Because, for one thing, with a little adaptation, much of the material to be researched, written, and illustrated for the book can be published in article form first. And for another, the costs for research, writing, photography, and drawings can be split between the publicity budget and the budget covering the book.

One word of caution: Make certain you've placed all the articles before the book is published. Once a piece of material has appeared as a chapter or section of a book, it's difficult to sell that same material as an article without incurring considerable expenses for rewrites, new illustrations, etc.

I recall one instance in which the project began as a series of articles. Then someone got the idea for a book, and the book project moved along so quickly that the publicity manager forgot about article possibilities. After the book appeared, he had several editors tell him, "Wish you had given us that material first; we could have given you a series."

6. Shotgun a condensed version. Feature-length "how-to" technical articles lend themselves well to a procedure called "shotgunning." Here's how it works:

After the full-length article has been published as an exclusive, condense the copy to three or four pages. Also, go through the illustrations and eliminate those that are not absolutely essential to the condensed story.

Then make a list of all the vertical markets in which your company is now selling, plus those in which it would like to sell. Go through your directory of periodicals; jot down the full name, title, and address of the editor of the top periodical servicing each of the vertical markets selected.

Next, have the condensed article and its illustrations reproduced. Quantities are determined by the number of the periodicals on your list, plus a couple of extra sets.

Write one standard cover letter, but address each copy individually. In the letter, point out that you are offering the article as an "exclusive in your field." This lets the editor know that you're offering the same material to other editors in noncompeting fields and that no other editor in his field is getting the material.

Incidentally, you'll find that a few editors don't like this technique. They want everything as a 100% exclusive. Most editors don't mind, however. In fact, since verticals are so often understaffed, their editors sincerely appreciate receiving good how-to material.

Just take care not to mail the condensed version to a horizontal, or to competing editors within one vertical market. Either of those mistakes will cause you to lose valuable editor-friends.

A former client of mine who manufactures controls and lubrication devices for compressed-air lines has enjoyed the benefits of the shotgun technique for many years. In one instance, for example, I placed a full-length feature on "how to plumb compressed-air lines" in one of the big horizontal magazines serving managers of industrial plants. The editor gave it two and a half pages.

I then boiled the copy down from seven to three manuscript pages, reduced the number of illustrations to one − a schematic diagram − and shotgunned the shortie to 15 noncompeting verticals.

Of the 15, 7 printed the article, giving my client an additional 10 1/2 pages. So for the price of the original article, plus a few hundred dollars for the condensation and art reproduction, my client got a total of 13 valuable editorial pages.

In cases where the editor of a vertical rejects the shortie, you simply mail it to another vertical serving the same market. If you stay with it long enough and don't run out of time, money, or patience, you may be able to score in all your target markets. This technique does three good things for you and your company:

Enables you to reach prospects in many vertical markets at a low cost per impression

Leaves more advertising dollars for the large horizontal periodicals serving your major markets

Helps you to stretch your technical-article dollars

7. Adapt for house organs. Does your company publish periodicals going to sales personnel − salespeople, distributors, dealers, reps, etc. − and/or to customers and prospects? If so, adapt some of the technical articles produced for trade publications and run them in the house organs.

This yields two important benefits. First, it increases the likelihood that your sales personnel and/or customers and prospects will see the material. Few of them read as many periodicals as you do. Second, running technical articles in your house organs enables you to get more value from your initial investment.

8. Reprint and merchandise. As soon as possible after a full-length technical article has been published, order reprints from the publisher or obtain permission for your company to reprint it.

If the article is of major consequence to the people in your markets, consider spending a little extra, and reprint the material as a booklet with a nice-looking cover. Then make the reprint available in quantity to people throughout your company's marketing and sales staffs and to distributors, dealers, reps, and warehouses. They can put the reprint to good use as a talk-piece and image-builder.

9. Offer reprints as premiums. Offer the more important reprints by announcing their availability in news releases. In addition, use reprints as incentive premiums in ads and direct mail, as handouts at trade shows, and as stuffers.

Don't forget possible uses in other departments of your company, such as training, financial relations, and export.

10. Save on line art. Before you prepare inked drawings, diagrams, cutaways, graphs, or other line art to illustrate a technical article, check with the editor.

Most periodicals like you to send camera-ready ink drawings, or at least sharp Kodalith copy prints. On the other hand, some of the major trade periodicals — for instance, *Machine Design* and *Production Engineering* — prefer quick but accurate pencil drawings. Their own staff artists follow a prescribed style when rendering the drawings.

So, before you put a lot of dollars into line art, make a phone call. It costs less.

Chapter 11

The Roundup Article

The roundup article (RA) is an article in which facts, opinions, and/or forecasts on a topic have been gathered from a number of qualified sources. Other names sometimes given to this genre are survey or informational article.

Written by one or more members of the magazine staff, or by freelance journalists paid by the magazine, RA's give thorough coverage of their topics. These articles are generic and nonproprietary by nature; that is, they do not attempt to advance the products, opinions, or other causes of any one source.

RA's bear marked differences from contributed, bylined feature articles, which is bylined by one or more experts in a single organization or joint effort. RA's also differ substantially from case-history feature articles, which usually promote the expertise and products of a single company.

Which kinds of topics do RA's cover? Editors look for topics that are current, perhaps even urgent, and of interest and importance to a large percentage of their readers. Table 11-1 lists but a few of the many approaches to subject matter that can be taken in an RA. If an editor adopts one of the approaches listed, and wants to give broad, many-sided coverage, he must contact a number of sources and tap their varying experiences and viewpoints.

For instance, the chief application engineer in a company making a broad line of air compressors could probably write a thorough, accurate set of instructions on how to size compressor capacity to the job requirements. The procedure calls for accuracy and a scientific method.

Table 11-1. Some Types of Approaches Utilized in Roundup Articles.

1. What's new and important or exciting in:
   a. Products
   b. Techniques or processes
   c. Services
   d. Regulations or standards
   e. A given field or industry
2. Trends in:
   a. Design of generic X
   b. Usage of generic X
   c. Techniques
   d. Practices or interpretations
3. How to:
   a. Select and size
   b. Perform
   c. Apply
   d. Operate
   e. Maintain and troubleshoot
   f. Control
   g. Automate
4. Recurrent, chronic problems, and what to do about them, in:
   a. Performance
   b. Application
   c. Operation
   d. Maintenance
5. Buyers' guide to:
   a. Products
   b. Services
6. Inside the generic X: the design, construction, operation, and performance characteristics of X product or system
7. New-found uses for a generic type of product
8. Forecasts
9. Myths and misconceptions about generic X
10. Opinions on how to deal with problem or challenge X

On the other hand, neither that engineer nor any of his cohorts could likely provide the breadth of experience and diversity of opinion needed for topics such as "Trends in compressor usage" or "What's new in compressor rental and leasing." Each of us lives and works in a relatively small environment; no single person or company sees all of the possibilities in the industry. Once a roundup approach has been selected, therefore, the very nature of the beast requires the editor to survey a number of sources.

At first glance, it may appear that the RA doesn't offer much opportunity to the publicist. The experts in your company or client's company can't get a byline. The RA won't focus on your company's or client's products or services. If you're working in an agency, you can't make much of a project (or billing) out of participation in a roundup. Why get excited? Indeed, why bother?

Because the RA is a major event. It packages the latest facts, opinions, and graphics on a topic — material drawn from all across the industry — and presents them in a big, bold splash. If the magazine is a leader in its field, publication of the RA will help to mold opinions, and may even make news.

Moreover, since the RA is staff written, it carries an aura of objectivity, an aura stronger than even the most dispassionate article bylined by a company source. In some cases, the work of veteran editors may even be regarded as better informed and less biased than the work of qualified experts in the industry.

Look at it another way. Suppose a leading magazine comes out with a major, featured roundup. The topic is interesting and important to many people in one of the fields served by your company or client. For some reason, though, your company is not represented in the article.

Result? You have missed the opportunity to appear in the showcase, the latest word on an important topic. You may not perceive the loss immediately, but eventually the competitors who were represented in the RA will pull ahead, at least in terms of reader recognition.

Another possible result: The sales manager, marketing director, or company president (or all three) see that your company or client wasn't represented in the RA. *"Why weren't we in there?"* Perhaps you can already hear the din and feel the migraine.

How does an editor select his sources for an RA? How can you secure numerous mentions, generous quotes, and prominent use of your graph material in an RA? What can you do to anticipate and capitalize upon the opportunity of participating in an RA?

These and other questions will be answered in the sections that follow.

HOW THE RA COMES INTO BEING

In *Material Handling Engineering's* monthly editorial preview for September 1981, one of the five items said: "UPDATE ON INDUSTRIAL ROBOTS — Robotics is a technology that's moving fast. Here's a look at what robots can do for material-handling systems."

On the basis of that announcement, manufacturers of robots, as well as suppliers of associated equipment and services, would find it advantageous to place publicity in that issue. The greater the volume and diversity of material on robots in the issue, the greater its impact on prospective users of "steel-collar workers."

How do subjects come to be chosen for publication and entered in the editorial schedule? Generally speaking, two kinds of subjects qualify: subjects that are current, topical, and of interest and concern to a sizable percentage of the magazine's readers; and subjects the editors must periodically treat in order to ensure broad, complete coverage of the industry.

Almost every trade and industrial magazine has a list of "must-cover" subjects. The list changes over the years, of course, with advances in technology, shifts in practices, fluctuations in the economy, and other evolutionary phenomena.

For example, in 1960 the industrial robot was a relatively new type of machine. Few people outside the auto industry knew much about the robot. Back then, if you said "material handling," your listener's mind automatically conjured up lift trucks and conveyors — but not robots.

By 1980, however, the robot had come on strong and was being accepted for palletizing, stacking, sorting, and other traditional material-handling functions. Come the 1990's, the robot may be the centerpiece in material handling, much as the lift truck was in previous decades.

Selecting the Sources

Let's assume that the magazine's managers have chosen a subject for treatment in a given year. For the sake of consistency, we'll stay with robots.

The next task the editors have is that of narrowing the focus. A good article on robots can't tell all there is to tell on the subject; that calls for a book. The editors attempt to narrow down from a broad subject to a single, sharply focused topic.

What should readers need and want to know about robots — now? The editors evaluate many possible angles of approach. Let's say that the editor who makes the decisions chooses to cover the roles of robots in material handling today and the latest developments in computer software as they affect those roles. The editor either takes the assignment himself or assigns it to one or more of his staff editors. (From here on, the term "editor" means the person who is handling the project.)

The next task is that of gathering facts, opinions, forecasts, and illustrations. How does the editor select his sources for these materials?

I can't speak for all editors, of course. Each works in his own way. Moreover, an editor will handle Article B differently from the way he handled Article A, and Article C in yet another way. The procedure is not precise; it varies according to the time and budget available, the nature and importance of the project, the editor's previous experience in the subject area, his personal preferences in operating methods, and other factors.

What I can give you, though, is a general outline of the kinds of sources an editor considers. These include:

• Printed material. Upon receiving an article assignment, the editor will search out and study articles on the topic published previously by his own magazine, articles published by other magazines, scripts of talks and technical papers, textbooks, brochures, and other printed matter. Sources include manufacturers, publishers, and trade associations.

This material contains reference and historical data. Most editors don't stop with existing printed material unless they and their readers are willing to settle for a piece that reads like a high-school term paper. A professional editor will use the printed record partly as a source of facts and figures, but primarily for leads to the names and affiliations of:

• Living experts. Unless he is doing a historical article, the editor wants current, updated facts, plus original opinions and forecasts, from the experts.

Now the editor faces a number of decisions. Which experts should he consider as primary sources, which as secondary and tertiary? After all, there are experts, and then there are experts.

Back to my example, the article on robots in material handling. In 1981, there were some 17 companies in the U.S. either building domestic robots or importing foreign robots suitable for use in material-handling applications. There were also numerous robot distributors, consulting engineers, and academics qualified to talk on the topic. Add government researchers and people in private R&D labs, plus engineers and managers in companies already experienced in applying various kinds and sizes of robots, and you begin to grasp the potential complexity of the source-selection process.

But it isn't really that difficult in practice. The editor says to himself, "I have so much time and so much money for travel and expenses. I shall visit, say, three experts, call four or five others on the phone, and contact most or all of the others by mail."

Then comes the crucial part. The editor asks himself and his peers, "Who knows the most about the topic? Who is best qualified? Who will give a good interview?"

Again, I can't speak for all editors, but in my opinion there are three criteria for primary and seconday sources:

- He is already highly visible and recognized as an expert. He may have long service in the industry. He probably gives talks at seminars and conferences. He may be relatively green in the industry but may have handled some interesting, trailblazing projects.
- He is affiliated with a manufacturing or engineering company that is a major force in the industry. His affiliation lends weight and credibility to what he says.
- He has granted formal or informal interviews to the magazine's editors on past occasions. From these experiences, the editors know that he talks openly, forcefully, and from deep, precise knowledge. He gives hard facts and strong opinions. Perhaps he has a colorful way of expressing himself and his quotes make good copy. Further, he is not overly concerned about "getting burned" in print.

Of those three criteria, the most important are 1 and 3, in my opinion. Experts may qualify as secondary sources who meet criteria 1 and 2 but not 3, or 2 and 3 but not 1.

The editor may also elect to contact a number of tertiary sources. These are people who are not in large companies but who can contribute to the completeness of the roundup. For instance, if the editor wants to survey all manufacturers in a field, and perhaps construct a product selector chart, he will try to reach every manufacturer regardless of its size or the completeness of its product and service lines.

Another type of tertiary source is the person or company that specializes in one or more aspects of the field. Small manufacturers, suppliers of components or computer software, consultants, private labs, and government researchers sometimes fall into this category. Tertiary does not mean inferior, for these sources can provide information, opinions, and "color" not available from anyone else.

Indeed, the world is full of surprises. Primary sources sometimes yield material that is less than sparkling. The experts may arrive at interviews fatigued, preoccupied, bothered by indigestion, or just plain uninterested.

Tertiary sources often provide surprises, too. The editor will telephone or write, expecting a quick, matter-of-fact reply, but get material that is delightfully novel, colorful, or controversial. This material may assume an important role in the article, or it may end up as a self-contained box or sidebar.

How the Editor Proceeds

The broad subject has been decreed. Within the subject area, a narrow, sharply focused topic has been chosen. The editor has lined up his primary, secondary, and tertiary sources. What's next?

Speaking from my own experience and that of a few other editors, the next steps in production of an RA include:

• Drafting of a preliminary outline and a set of "working questions." These always change a little during the research phase. Each article project is a journey into unknown territory. The explorer slogs through swamps, moseys off on side trips, sometimes wanders into box canyons. Periodically he must back off and take a new set of compass readings. If he doesn't do that, or if he forgets his original goal, he may end up wandering aimlessly.

I've often been tempted to wander off course, chasing after interesting side-topics. Then, too, I've encountered sources who would try to evade my prepared questions and instead attempt to tell me what the article ought to be about. The editor needs to be determined as well as flexible.

• Travel to the offices, plants, and labs of the primary sources. The visits include personal interviews plus requests for graphic material. The editor often asks not only for photos but also for blueprints, graphs, charts, impromptu sketches, printed material: anything that will help to show as well as to tell. Some editors tote cameras and shoot their own photos.

• Telephone interviews with secondary and tertiary sources, and follow-up calls to primary sources. Here again the editor may request graphic materials. As when interviewing primary sources, the editor works from a set of prepared questions but lets the source expand upon side-topics if the material is pertinent and interesting.

• Letters and questionnaires to tertiary sources. Sometimes the editor will simply ask for facts, but often he also asks for opinions or advice for the reader. The open-ended questions may elicit written comments that trigger follow-up calls.

• Pulling it all together. At some point, the editor must cut off the research and move into the writing phase. He goes back through his initial outline, reviews all the raw material he has gathered, then revises and begins to expand upon the outline. From here on, the editor's procedure is much like that outlined in Chapter 8.

HOW TO SCORE IN RA'S

Thus far you've learned a little about how topics are chosen for RA's and how editors select their sources and proceed with article research and production. Now we're down to the meat of this chapter: how you, the publicist, can help your company or client to gain copious and prominent exposure in roundup articles.

Arranging Personal Interviews

Let's assume that an editor has chosen your company or client as a primary source for an RA. The editor knows that one or more people in your company have the needed expertise, but he doesn't know who they are. He asks you to suggest someone whom he could contact in order to set up a visit and an interview. How should you proceed?

1. Select an expert who knows the subject and has a prestigious title. He should also be one who speaks openly, forcefully, and freely, expresses opinions as well as facts, and isn't overly cautious.

You may know of a project manager or staff engineer in the company who is not only brilliant in the subject area but is also an eloquent conference-level speaker. If he doesn't carry a prestigious title, or at least one that sounds prestigious to outsiders, the editor probably won't want to quote him in the RA.

Remember, in this case the editor chose the company, not a person. If the editor attributes facts or quotes to someone in United General Consolidated, he wants the readers to know he talked to a person high up in UGC, someone really "in the know."

Should you feel nonetheless that the brilliant young project engineer could contribute something of value and perhaps deserves some editorial exposure, you could suggest to the editor that the engineer sit in on the interview and contribute. If the editor has enough time to spend at your facility, perhaps you could arrange two or more interviews. The politics may thicken a bit for you, but if two or more experts in your company are contributing lively opinions and interesting facts, your chances for quotes and attributions increase.

Generally speaking, the more generous you are with time, facts, opinions, and graphics, the greater will be the amount and quality of editorial exposure you gain. Conversely, if you and your people are stingy, the RA will reflect that stinginess.

2. Let the editor and source talk to each other directly; let them schedule the visit and interview to suit their mutual convenience. Sometimes when a PR person tries to serve as arranger, he only slows and complicates the procedure. Put the two people in contact with each other, and then get out of the way.

3. Either before or immediately after the editor and source have scheduled the interview, ask the editor, "What are you after? What are some of the questions you'll be asking?" Knowing what the editor wants, you and the source can zero in on the topic, collect materials, and perhaps even prepare answers in advance.

If the editor is taking a precisely defined approach to a technical topic — for instance, how to analyze a plant function for possible application of a given product — he knows exactly the kinds of information and opinions he needs. He can tell you precisely, and the source can respond in kind.

On the other hand, sometimes the editor doesn't know what he wants or needs. Sometimes he "goes fishing," looking for an interesting angle. When you ask him what he's after, he may reply with a vague, "I'm taking a broad-brush approach, so we'll wing it."

This happens when the initial assignment was broad and vague. Maybe the editor's boss said, "Let's do an update on what's new, interesting, and important in the field," and then left it up to the editor to cast here and there, find a suitable angle, and narrow the focus.

You and the source could become frustrated by the editor's vague specifications. You could react by saying, "If this guy doesn't know what he wants, we won't strain ourselves. We'll simply wait until he arrives, and then — as he said — we'll wing it."

You could, but you shouldn't. By being vague, the editor has opened a wide door for you. He has given you the opportunity to discuss what *you* want to discuss, and to cover a wide range of subtopics.

Make a list of all possible subtopics that could come under the broad, vague specs. Then gather as much reference material, promotional literature, and graphic material as you can. In other words, prepare to conduct a massive assault across a broad front. The more points you make, the greater the number of penetrations and possible pickups.

4. When you ask which kinds of information the editor wants, also ask about graphics. Does he want photos? Should they be application shots only, or could he use some closeup shots of details? What about tables, graphs, blueprints, cutaways, cross sections? Could the editor use color pictures?

The editor doesn't know what you have in stock or what you could prepare to his specs. He won't know until you tell him. At times he himself doesn't know what he wants, and will sincerely appreciate your suggestions. Provide him with drawings that illuminate key points and photos that jump off the page and grab the reader, and you'll surely score well.

From the editor's point of view, researching for facts and opinions is relatively easy. Finding good editorial graphic material is quite another matter, however. Later in this chapter, I'll point up the benefits of stocking good graphics and anticipating editors' requests.

5. Before the interview, brief the source. Go over the questions the editor said he would ask. Reassure the source that it is not only permissible but desirable that he open up and speak freely — without revealing proprietary information, of course.

Emphasize that your company and the trade press are really in the same business together. We all want to promote the welfare of the industry and the nation as a whole. For a magazine to knowingly try to do damage to a manufacturer or service company in its industry would be suicidal.

6. Have all the literature, photos, tables, drawings, and other ammunition ready so the editor can take them along. Don't promise later delivery of custom-shot photos or new drawings unless you are sure that they will arrive at the editor's office on time. As a rule, when editors give you deadlines, they're not padded.

During the Interview

What should be the role of the publicist or PR person during an interview between an editor and a company expert? To be available but unobtrusive, helpful without interrupting unnecessarily, anticipating the needs of both the editor and the source. The publicist plays a vital role here, but it is one of enabler, not star. If you have ever drafted a list of personal requisites for the skillful publicist, hopefully the list includes humility, or at least deliberate self-effacement when the occasion demands.

Following are more pointers concerning the interview:

- Start the interview on time.
- Arrange to have the interview in a room that's light, cool, well ventilated, quiet, and free of telephones. A blackboard and chalk sometimes prove useful for explaining points. So do notepads and pencils.
- Have all phone calls to the source intercepted, except for the most urgent.
- If possible and permissible, let the editor and source or sources conduct their interview in private. The presence of nonparticipants generates political considerations and degrades the quality of the interview.
- If company policy dictates that you must be present during interviews, stay off on the fringe. Don't interject unless you're asked for facts or opinions. Should points arise that you want to discuss with the editor, make notes and talk to him later.

Why not contribute, if you feel you know some useful facts? Because a good interview is an interplay, a lively personal exchange, that builds up momentum. Interruptions break the flow and slow the momentum.

• There may be occasions in which the source exhibits nervousness or reticence during the interview. He refuses to open up, and the editor must pry every phrase from him. Perhaps the source lacks experience in being interviewed, or has been burned in print. In this situation, the publicist can help to save the day by putting the source at ease and subtly drawing him out.

If you suspect in advance that a source will likely be cold and stiff during an interview, perhaps you can arrange to have the source plus one or two other people meet the editor for dinner on the previous evening. In the relaxed atmosphere of a meal, the source may come to feel comfortable with the editor as a person, and thus will be more at ease the next day during the formal interview.

Another ploy that works well is to have the source and editor go to lunch after the interview with people well known to the source. Once the tension of the interview has been left behind, he may loosen up and freely provide information and opinions.

• Keep in mind that you're arranging and facilitating an interview, not a sales presentation. The overt purpose of the interview is to allow an editor to ask questions, obtain graphic material, etc. Stiff-arm the sales manager who wants to "do a number" on the editor.

Once in a while — not often, thankfully — the editor walks into a company plant for an interview, only to have the PR person (or someone wearing the PR hat) say, "Here's what we'll do today." He then proceeds to outline a carefully prepared presentation or modified sales pitch, perhaps illustrated with slides or flipcharts. After the pitch comes a tour of "our modern plant and laboratories" (I'd love to tour an old-fashioned plant for a change) and a lunch with 12 major and minor plant managers. If the editor is lucky, the session will end with a 10-minute question-and-answer session.

Bad form. No editor cares for this sort of treatment, however well-intentioned. The editor is there to gather information, opinions, and graphics. Let him take the initiative, steer the interview, ask the questions. And that leads to further admonitions:

• Unless the editor asks for a specific kind of slide presentation or lecture, skip it. As mentioned before, ask the editor what he's after, and then give it to him as best you can. Frankly, he doesn't care what *you* want to do by way of a production; it's what *he* wants that counts.

• Same goes for the plant tour. Unless the story concerns certain operations or equipment in your plant, the tour only wastes everyone's time. Of course, if the editor says he'd like to see your plant, out of general interest, that's another matter.

• Stick to the planned schedule. Sometimes after an interview the editor needs to drive for an hour or two in strange territory, turn in a rental car, check in his luggage, and catch a plane. Other times, especially near the end of a long trip, he'd like to wrap himself around a leisurely meal and unwind. Stretching the visit beyond its planned boundary puts a strain on the editor and degrades not only the interview but the impression you and your company leave on him.

• Remember the creature comforts. An editor is a mind, of sorts, contained in an animal body. A cup of coffee, a pit stop, a cold drink, a quick snack in the cafeteria — these are all important and much appreciated.

Telephone Interviews

Provided he has time, the editor will set up telephone interviews much as he would personal visits and interviews. He'll call the source or PR person, explain his needs, and make an appointment for an interview of half an hour or so over the phone.

Many of the points made concerning personal interviews apply here, too:

• Make sure that you and the source are near the phone at the appointed time.

• Minimize background noise and preclude interruptions.

• Let the editor and source conduct the interview. Don't try to barge into the limelight.

• If you have set up a conference call, make sure the editor knows the names and titles of all the participants at your end of the wire.

• Encourage the source or sources to talk freely, express opinions as well as facts, and tell illustrative anecdotes.

• Determine in advance the editor's questions and the thrust of the article. Also determine in advance the nature of his needs concerning graphic material.

Follow-up After Interviews

Occasionally, during an interview, the editor, source, or publicist will think of a good idea for a piece of graphic material that will help to illustrate the RA. Perhaps you can immediately provide a print from stock, but often the drawing or graph must be drafted, the table compiled, or the photo shot.

On these occasions, ask the editor his final deadline for graphic material – it may be later than the manuscript deadline – and accept the date as fact. If you can meet the deadline, fine, but don't make rash promises. And don't ever back out of a commitment for graphics. A picture that doesn't arrive may leave a very large hole, one that's difficult to fill.

The same rule applies to facts, figures, formulas, and other material suggested during an interview. If you promise something, deliver, and on time.

Invariably a lively interview starts the participants' creative wheels to spinning. The wheels continue to spin after the editor has left. If you or the source think of a bit of information, an interesting sidelight, or an idea for an illustration later that day or the next, by all means get in touch with the editor and pass along your ideas. He will appreciate your help and interest.

Again, though, keep the deadlines in mind; don't promise something you can't deliver on time.

Handling Mailed Requests

Editors gather much of their information and graphic material for roundup articles by mail. Often the mailed requests are followed by telephone calls.

Typically, the mailed request consists of a cover letter containing questions, or a letter plus a structured questionnaire. In the letter, the editor introduces himself, describes the article project at hand, and tells what he wants. This usually includes graphic material as well as answers to questions. The editor also specifies a due date for the material.

Here's how to handle a mailed request such as that described:

- Obtain answers to the questions from a qualified expert. Don't attempt to answer all the questions yourself.
- Be generous with your answers. Cryptic answers will yield tiny pickups.
- Provide photos and other graphics that match the editor's specs as closely as possible. Whenever you can, send a selection of photos from which the editor can choose. If the magazine uses color, send color as well as black and white.
- If you don't understand what the editor wants, or the questions in the letter or questionnaire aren't clear, call the editor for clarification. He wants and may urgently need the data and opinions your company's experts can provide. Forget that nasty old myth that says, "Don't bother the editor." He and the magazine depend for their existence on communication, and that includes communication with you.
- Read between the lines. See if you can think of information, opinions, or graphics that relate to the stated topic of the RA but that the editor did not specify. Then call the editor and propose your ideas.

I've seen many RA's improved, enlivened, and rounded off nicely by tables, graphs, or material in sidebars, boxes, or short follow-ons. Many times this supplementary material was suggested and provided by alert, aggressive publicists.

Suppose, for instance, that an editor is doing research for an RA on selecting and sizing electric programmable controllers. He's plunging ahead, going from one source to the next. He's collecting useful, up-to-date information and opinions from qualified sources, but he has his blinders on.

You're a publicist in one of the source organizations, and you see what's happening. You realize that there are opportunities for editorial exposure here. You also realize that because the editor is looking only straight ahead, you will have to take the initiative.

What might you suggest? Here are three ideas for supplementary material for the RA; in some cases, you may be able to have your contribution bylined by a company source:

A sidebar, box, or follow-on that explains the basic design, construction, and operation of the programmable controller. There's a good chance, you realize, that not all of the magazine's readers understand what goes on inside the controller's black box.

Another block of material on the related topic "Networking – the next step up." This material would show and tell how machines governed by programmable controllers can be tied together or "networked" in a unified shop system, and how that system ties to plant and company computers. You'd include information on techniques of networking, schematic drawings, hardware, benefits, and other aspects.

A case history on how one company was able to reduce its parts inventory, maintenance time, and overall costs by converting from relays to programmable controllers.

What you're doing is capitalizing on the editor's narrow field of vision. Young, inexperienced editors don't know much about any part of the field. Editors with a few years under their belts may know a good deal about some aspects of the field but little about others. No editor, regardless of his experience and knowledge, has a monopoly on good ideas. And every editor needs and appreciates suggestions.

Use your imagination; then call the editor and discuss your ideas. He will appreciate your input.

ANTICIPATING OPPORTUNITIES

You can do an adequate job as a publicist by merely putting out routine releases, maintaining basic news and case history programs, and reacting to requests from editors. Operating in this fashion isn't much fun, though. It's dreadfully routine, and not very satisfying.

On the other hand, you can do a better job and have more fun by seeking out, anticipating, and capitalizing on opportunities. The essential characteristics, it seems to me, are an aggressive spirit and a nagging hunger for lots of favorable editorial exposure. An adequate budget helps.

How can you anticipate and capitalize on opportunities for exposure in RA's? Here are a few tips:

1. Maintain files. Start, build, and maintain a stock of application photos, product detail photos, cutaway drawings, cross-sectional

renderings, and other graphic material suitable for magazine articles. Include color as well as black and white. Maintain a file of color-negative copies of large original renderings — for example, overall views of large systems — plus one or two 8″ x 10″ color prints from each negative.

In my years as an industrial publicist, I often served as expediter between editors and company experts. For every one interview I arranged, I received at least 25 requests from editors for graphic materials. Since I had built a large, diversified file, I was usually able to mail the requested material on the same day the request came in. Incidentally, the files' contents consisted mainly of residue from case histories, news releases, and bylined technical articles, supplemented by "timeless" reference-type charts, tables, and drawings.

Frequently the requests came from editors who had their backs up against deadlines and needed help quickly. Were it not for the large, diversified files, I could not have met these panic requests. Invariably my ability to help the editors led to closer friendships, more editorial exposure, and higher-quality exposure. If the increased exposure didn't come in the panic-job RA, it came later in other articles.

2. Consult the calendars. Obtain copies of the annual editorial calendars published by magazines that serve the fields your company serves (see Fig. 11-1). Refer to the calendars often; look for opportunities for participation in roundups.

Timing is important. Find out how much lead time the editor needs for an RA and when he is actively thinking about and working on articles for a given month.

Lead time varies from one magazine to another. It may be as little as six weeks or as much as six months. Within a given staff, lead time also varies according to the type of article, amount of coverage to be given, number of sources to be contacted, and other variables.

If you call with your suggestions for a particular RA three months early, you may get a polite "Thanks," and the editor may make a note and file it. On the other hand, he may promptly forget your call and suggestions. If the RA hasn't been on his mind, he's not immediately concerned.

I recall one publicist who called and offered information, photos, drawings, and other goodies for an RA that had been wrapped up and turned over to Art & Production on the previous day. Had that

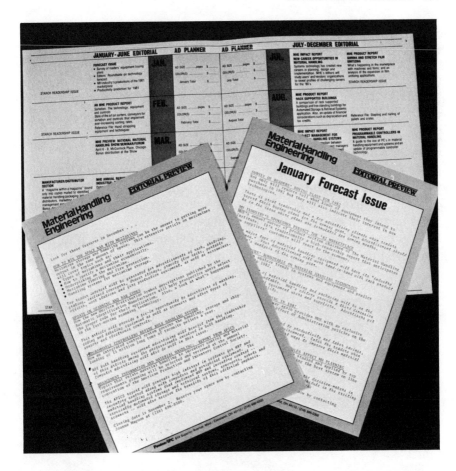

Fig. 11-1.   Editorial calendar, top, and monthly editorial previews published by *Material Handling Engineering*.   Life advertising managers, publicists would do well to read materials such as these published by industrial periodicals.

publicist called three or four weeks sooner, he could have scored heavily in the RA. His material, from what he said, was probably excellent, but his timing was bad.

Some magazines issue monthly editorial previews in addition to the annual calendar (see Fig. 11-1). The previews are much more complete and detailed than the calendar, giving you many more clues to opportunities for exposure. You must be able to react quickly to these clues, as lead time is short, but the potential exposure may be worth a scramble. As always, you must weigh potential benefits against cost and effort.

3. Remain visible. Keep in touch with key editors, by phone, and also visit them in their offices occasionally. "Out of sight, out of mind" may be a cliché, but like other clichés it remains in active usage because it contains truth. If the editor doesn't know you, he won't think of you; if he doesn't think of you, he probably won't call you with an invitation to participate in RA.

4. Do surveys. Periodically, do a survey — or have your PR agency or research consultants do it — of the problems faced by customers in your company's field. Compile the results and place an exclusive news feature in an appropriate periodical.

File the material. When you see that a magazine plans to do an RA pertaining to your field, haul out the report on the survey, and at the opportune time offer it to the editor.

Results from surveys make excellent components in RA's. Surveys always sound scientific; reporting on them adds substance to the article and automatically confers expertise on your company. And as you know by now, perceived expertise begets editorial exposure.

Chapter 12

Special Formats and Opportunities

Thus far we have looked at the major formats used in industrial publicity: press releases, case-history releases and feature articles, bylined feature articles, and roundup articles. In Chapters 13 and 14, we'll examine the press conference.

In addition to these major formats, there are many lesser-known formats you can employ in your publicity program. Each gives you opportunities to achieve the marketing communications goals of your company or client, at relatively low cost.

It has been my experience that most of these formats are underexploited by industrial publicists. You'll find that, partly because of the lack of competition, you'll be able to score easily and with little expenditure of time or effort.

Following are brief explanations of ten formats. Most are illustrated with photos; see Figs. 12-1 through 12-8.

FRONT-COVER ILLUSTRATIONS

Like consumer magazines, industrial magazines utilize original art (drawings, renderings, and the like), photos, or a combination of the two on their front covers (see Fig. 12-1). The magazines that use only artwork offer little chance for front-cover exposure for your company or client.

Most industrial magazines do not fall into that category, however. The majority alternate between artwork and photos, or employ photos

Fig. 12-1 Each of these four magazine covers utilizes color photos submitted by publicists.

exclusively, on their covers. Because of high production costs for full-color printing, the smaller, less-affluent periodicals print their covers in monochrome or in two- or three-color adaptations of monochrome photos. On the other hand, more and more of the industrial magazines with large advertising revenues are running their covers, as well as an ever-increasing percentage of their editorial pages, in full color.

Representation on the front covers can yield benefits to you and your company or clients. Landing a front cover is not easy, but it can be achieved through the application of certain techniques. We'll list these techniques and look at them one by one. First, though, a few words about how editors choose photos for front covers.

The cover photo usually pertains to the lead article or one of the major articles in the issue. This important article may be a roundup, installation profile, case history, bylined technical article, or news report. Often the type on the cover explains the relationship between the cover illustration and the subject of the featured article or report.

As a rule, the editor chooses the cover photo (or photos, in the case of a montage) from transparencies and prints gathered by staff editors or submitted on speculation by companies in the featured industry. A few magazines plan their cover photos and have them shot by local professional photographers.

Quite often selection of the cover photo is a last-minute decision. The editor waits until he sees all the photos submitted, then selects one or more from the batch. If it does not contain suitable candidates, the editor and his staffers may call people in the industry and ask for additional, last-minute submissions.

The cover illustration must not only pertain to the subject matter in the lead story, but must also contain strong visual appeal and technical excellence. The editor looks for a compelling photo, a "grabber," one with high impact. Further, the transparency or print must contain all or most of the elements essential to technical excellence: fine grain, proper exposure, good color balance, focus and depth of field appropriate to the subject portrayed, and so on.

If the lead story is an installation profile or case history, the cover photo will likely show equipment installed by one or more companies involved in the story. For general stories such as roundup articles and news roundups, editors like to use generic illustrations. Regardless of the type of story, however, editors usually prefer that their cover photos not be too commercial – in other words, that the photo or photos not blatantly plug specific companies or trademarked products.

Knowing that much about the factors affecting an editor's choice of cover illustrations, you can see the logic in the following suggestions:

- Invest in good photography. This includes not only illustrations for press releases but also application photos for case histories, installation profiles, photo features, and other editorial formats. The best of your shots may become candidates for front covers as well as illustrations for stories between the covers.
- Even though you think that coverage of a case history calls for black-and-white photos only, have the photographer shoot some color, too. File these photos for cover possibilities that may arise in the future.
- If possible, have some or all of your color case-history photos shot in medium- or large-format transparency film – that is, in the "2 1/4" x 2 1/4", 2 1/4" x 2 3/4", 4" x 5" or 8" x 10" formats." The large transparencies are more impressive than 35 mm, and editors can see what's in them without the aid of a magnifier, slide viewer, or projector.

Many magazine art and production staffers will accept good 35-mm transparencies but prefer to work with the larger formats because they permit easier, more accurate cropping. Then, too, some art and production people not only accept but prefer high-quality 8" x 10" color prints with borders. Make an effort to learn the preferences at the important magazines in your field.

- If limitations in budget or available photographic talent force you to have everything shot in 35 mm, single out the best of the slides and give them special treatment. Make color internegatives from them; from the internegatives, make 4" x 5" transparencies or 8" x 10" color prints for your stock-photo file.
- Build up a file of color and black-and-white photos that have potential for cover illustrations. Review your news-release and case-history photo files periodically, making special note of the numbers and locations of cover candidates. Be ready to respond quickly to requests from editors.

- A talented photographer has the knack of spotting opportunities for dramatic, arresting shots. Sometimes these shots pertain to the story being covered, sometimes not. Tell your photographers that when they are on assignment for you, they not only have permission but are encouraged to spend time and film on the "great shots" they see. Some of these nonreportorial photos could help you to land front covers.

- Anticipate editors' needs for front-cover illustrations by following the magazine editorial calendars and previews.

- When you submit material to an editor for a roundup article, offer the best photos you have in stock, and point out those you feel have possibilities for front-cover illustrations. In the haste and pressure of their work, editors occasionally miss seeing the potential in submitted photos. Your tips may prove beneficial to the editors as well as to yourself.

- Most editors don't want their cover illustrations to give gross, obvious plugs to individual companies or products. Instruct your photographers to shoot product-application photos in such a way that the company logotype or nameplate is visible and legible but not overly prominent.

- If you and others in your company or client organization like to gain exposure on front covers, be prepared to go to extra lengths in order to meet special requests from editors.

Suppose, for instance, that you know the company will get frequent and prominent mentions in a roundup article. You're also fairly certain that the editor plans to use three or four of your submitted photos as illustrations in the article.

Shortly before the editor's final deadline for the cover, he calls you and says he is still looking for something special to put on the front cover. He gives a general description of what he wants.

You review your file of stock photos but find nothing suitable. This is the moment of decision. Do you pass up the opportunity, or do you assign a photographer to spend half a day and several rolls of film shooting to the editor's loose and possibly vague specs?

The answer lies in the degree of your desire for a front cover. Do you want to reprint the roundup, and if so, would you derive significant benefits from having the magazine cover bear your company's photo? How much can you afford to spend on such an assignment? Can you deal with a photographer halfway across the country, or dispatch one from your own locale, and still meet the editor's deadline?

Anticipate this kind of situation, and be ready to make decisions quickly.

NEWS FEATURES

If you think in terms of short news stories but ignore longer, in-depth news features, you may be missing some fine opportunities for editorial exposure.

Most industrial periodicals use your short press releases as boiled-down items in regular departments. These bear titles such as "New products," "New literature," "Industry news," and "People on the move," to name a few.

In addition, though, many industrial periodicals, particularly the magazines, run longer news stories on significant events and developments in their fields. These stories typically report on topics such as major new-product introductions, especially those involving novel technical concepts, technical breakthroughs that are important to many of the periodicals' readers, results of important field tests, and other technical topics.

Figure 12-2 shows an example of a news feature printed in a major industrial magazine. To gain generous editorial exposure such as illustrated, you need the following:

- An important story that has not yet been told.
- A complete, detailed press release.
- A selection of illustrations from which the editor can choose. Include not only photos showing overall views but also close-up, detail shots. Consider the costs versus potential benefits in submitting reproductions of cutaway or cross-sectional renderings, circuit diagrams, and other types of artwork.

Publication of news features may result from a press conference (see Chapters 13 and 14) or from the mailing of a comprehensive press kit. Usually you'll want to restrict the mailing of these kits to the most important magazines and tabloids in your field. You can follow this mailing with a shotgun mailing of a shorter, less-detailed release to other periodicals.

You may find that in your industry there is one editor who insists on exclusives for first publication of major news stories. If this is the case, send him the press kit and offer the exclusive. After he has published the story, mail the complete kit to the other major periodicals in your field. You may not gain as large a total of column inches this way, but you'll get at least one big pickup, and you'll be covering the field.

Incidentally, stay alert for opportunities for color illustrations of major news stories. Color sells.

PHOTO-CAPTION RELEASES

Would your company or clients benefit from exposure in the business pages of daily and weekly newspapers? If so, you'll want to consider the use of photo-caption releases. Clippings of pickups resulting from two different photo-caption releases are shown in Fig. 12-3.

The essentials of a photo-caption release are a dramatic, well-composed photo with broad human interest and a caption that relates the photo to the interests of the periodicals' readers. The merit of the release rests almost entirely on the photo; the "story" need not be a big one, but it should be current.

If you're interested in using this format, your main concern will be to find one or more photographers who have the gift for seeing photo possibilities in your own and customers' plants, labs, and offices. Your photographers should have the freedom to roam and shoot pretty much at will, plus permission to briefly interrupt operations and set up photos they visualize.

A certain few companies are more adept and aggressive than others in the use of this format. Companies that come readily to mind are Goodyear, Eastman Kodak, Western Electric, and Bell Laboratories.

To test the procedures and effects of this format, you could start by imitating the styles (not the specific photos) of photo captions you spot in newspapers. At first, restrict mailings to newspapers in cities where your company or clients have plants or headquarters offices. Should you find that use of the format is producing desirable results at reasonable cost, you can then evaluate the costs and possible benefits

New brake system meets tough standards

THE NEW "PHASE III" BRAKE SYSTEM for large off-highway haulers, developed by B. F. Goodrich Co., was put through a series of downhill braking tests at the Cyprus Pima mine in Arizona on March 30. Following the tests, the British Columbia Ministry of Mines and Petroleum Resources certified the braking performance of a Euclid R-170 haulage truck equipped with the system. On the same day, the Phase III-equipped R-170 also passed tests for braking requirements of the Province of Alberta and for the Society of Automotive Engineers' proposed performance standard number SAE XJ-1224. Certification by these authorities is expected soon.

"Since the British Columbia and Alberta regulations are the world's most stringent, many nations that have not yet adopted their own regulations look upon certification by either of these two provinces as proof of high-performance braking," said Euclid vice president of marketing Ralph Keidel, "so the impact of certification by British Columbia and Alberta reaches beyond Western Canada, and indeed, far beyond the shores and boundaries of North America."

In 1977, British Columbia adopted a new braking regulation stipulating that a fully loaded truck must be brought to a stop from a speed of 35 mph within 500 ft on a 10% down grade using the wheel brakes alone. Prior to the new Canadian regulations, the wheel brakes were not considered the primary means of braking. They were designed to stop the truck only after the electric motor retarders had brought speed down to about 7 mph by means of dynamic braking. For the Phase III certification tests, the retarders were disconnected.

Other truck builders also are considering installing the Phase III system on their trucks, according to B. F. Goodrich product manager Dean Smith. Terex, Unit Rig, and Wabco trucks are being equipped for testing or are undergoing tests for certification, he said. If schedules hold up, the tests will be completed by the end of August.

At the AMC International Mining Show in Las Vegas on Oct. 9-12, Goodrich will display working models of the Phase III brakes and will show a 15-min movie of the R-170 certification tests. Several truck builders will also display the system on their trucks.

Components of the system

Major components of the Phase III system are a newly designed front wheel brake for large haulers with 49-in. or 51-in. rims, a motorized-wheel brake for the rear motor-driven wheels, and the parking brake. Another component, a new "inside-out" disk-type wheel brake, gives the owner the option of in-wheel, direct braking on the drive wheels rather than on the electric motor armatures.

The front wheel brake incorporates a new, patented thrustplate concept that facilitates lining changes and

extends lining life. It has 60% more lining area and 47% more lining volume than competitive disk brakes, according to Goodrich. An optional segmented disk permits dismounting and remounting of brake heads without removing the wheel. Internal porting minimizes fluid leaks.

The motorized-wheel brake, for mounting on the electric armature, has hardened molybdenum-steel disks balanced to within 2 in. per oz. Exclusive features include ⅛-in.-thick insulators on each piston, linings that can be changed by removal of one bolt, many parts in common with the older, widely used Phase I brake, choice of single or dual disk configurations, and choice of lining materials to suit the application.

The "inside-out" brake is offered for use on drive wheels as an alternative to the armature brake. It has larger disks than shaft brakes, providing greater heat dissipation. Rims can be removed without disturbing brake heads or disks, allowing easy access to motor brushes and armature. Many parts are identical to those of the Phase III wheel brake.

The Phase III system evolved from previous Goodrich brakes, mainly the Phase I. Says Philip A. Smith, chief engineer of the company's Engineered Systems Div.: "There's nothing radically new in any of the components."

How the tests were run

The March 30 tests took place on a dry, partly sunny day at a temperature of 76°F. The test procedure,

Euclid R-170 test vehicle is braked to a stop during certification tests at the Cyprus Pima mine in Arizona.

Fig. 12-2. Major news story in *Engineering & Mining Journal* that resulted from a publicist's efforts.

including the weigh-in and 17 stops in three series, took 3 hr. A strip-chart recorder was installed next to the seat occupied by the assistant driver of the test vehicle, to monitor and record truck speed continuously. The instrument also allowed the assistant driver to tell the driver exactly when to apply the brakes on each run. Hydraulic gauges installed in the brake linings measured brake pressure.

The "Paint-Mark" method determined accurately the distance covered from the point at which the driver applied the brakes to the point where the truck stopped. A .22-caliber brake-test detonator, pointing directly down, was mounted on the front bumper and was loaded with a shell carrying a light powder charge and a small amount of yellow paint. When the driver stepped on the brake, the detonator fired, leaving a well-defined yellow mark on the ground. When the truck stopped, test officials measured the distance from the yellow mark to the bumper-mounted detonator.

Empty weight of the truck was 102,200 lb on the front axle and 112,900 lb on the rear axle. With a payload of 175.4 tons, the weights were 168,900 lb on the front axle and 397,000 lb on the rear axle.

Testing began with a series of five stops for qualification under the SAE requirements. All stops were made well within the minimum requirement of 3 ft per sec deceleration (see figure).

To meet the British Columbia requirements, a series of five stops were made in 5-mph increments in speed, from 5 through 25.5 mph, to obtain data for a curve of speed vs. stopping distance. All stops were made well under the minimum deceleration rate. The final run was a "panic" stop from 35 mph on a 10% grade, with the truck required to stop within 500 ft. Actual stopping distance was 312 ft.

Tests for the Alberta requirements were made without an extended brake cooldown. Five stops, at 15-min intervals, were made from 28 mph down a 10% grade with a fully loaded vehicle. Rear brake pressure was reduced to 1,000 psi. Stopping distance averaged 238 ft, well within the required 280-ft distance.

Why B.C. instituted its braking requirements

Between 1967 and 1974, the number of large diesel-electric haulage trucks in British Columbia nearly tripled. During that period, the number of nonfatal accidents or dangerous occurrences at or near open-pit mines rose from 47, of which only eight involved mobile equipment, to 221, of which 103 involved mobile equipment. These statistics provided the motive for adopting the most demanding performance regulations in the world.

Besides requiring brake certification for each truck model sold in British Columbia, the regulations require annual downgrade brake testing of haul trucks at the mines. Any truck that fails to pass minimum performance standards must be pulled out of service. Required stopping distances for the tests are 160 ft on an 8% grade, 180 ft on a 9% grade, and 200 ft on a 10% grade. The requirements have generated a whole new line of brake hardware for large haulers.

For additional information on the Phase III brake system, write to Department 0745, Engineered Systems Div., B. F. Goodrich Co., 500 S. Main Street, Akron, Ohio 44318. Additional information on the Euclid R-170 is available from Ralph Keidel, Vice President of Euclid Inc., 22221 St. Clair Avenue, Cleveland, Ohio 44117. □

"Phase III" motorized-wheel brake and parking brake on Euclid R-170

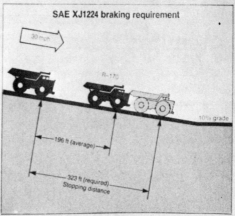

SAE XJ1224 braking requirement

30 mph

R-170

10% grade

196 ft (average)

323 ft (required)
Stopping distance

Fig. 12-2. (continued)

Winding down An inspector at the Rochester, N.Y., plant of Eastman Kodak Co. checks rolls of absorbent material used in instant color film before the rest of the film-making process goes on.

Fig. 12-3. Clipping of a newspaper pickup resulting from a photo-caption release.

of mailing releases to major dailies, wire services, and syndicates across the country, or even worldwide.

TECHNICAL RELEASES

A technical release (see Fig. 12-4) is a short, illustrated "how-to" article that offers handy hints on how to solve one narrowly defined, universal problem in plant, equipment, or procedures. The ideas offered in the story involve techniques or products available to anyone.

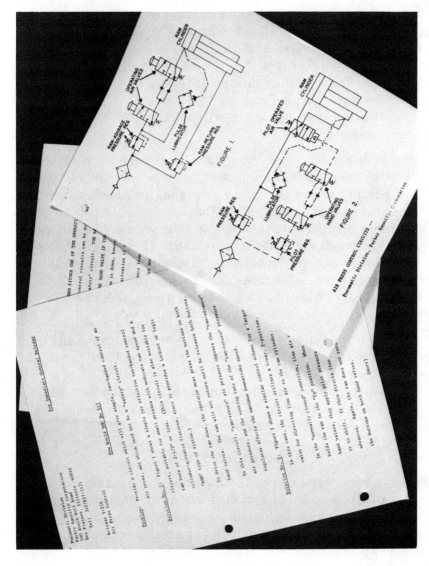

Fig. 12-4. Technical release consisting of a one-and-a-half-page write-up and a composite illustration containing two circuit diagrams.

Like a new-product release, a technical release may be sent to one periodical as an exclusive or shotgunned to many periodicals on a non-exclusive basis. Unlike a case history, a technical release deals with a generic type of problem, not with a problem encountered and solved in one customer company using one brand of product.

Illustrations for the technical release may include photos, drawings, renderings, or any other type. Since editors normally use the material in technical releases as filler, it is pointless to send color illustrations unless the editor requests them.

Following is a condensation of a technical release which I placed in several magazines:

> Does your plant handle explosive or corrosive fluids? If so, you must monitor pressures continuously, but regulations require that fluid passing through gages and valves in the instrument room be non-explosive and non-corrosive. The problem: How to keep the hazardous fluid from the instrument room yet measure and regulate fluid pressure with instruments inside. The solution: Install a piston-type accumulator between the monitoring circuit and the main fluid system. Hazardous fluid remains on one side of the floating piston, while the gage fluid − glycerine, for example − remains safe and uncontaminated on the other side.

This handy-hint story ended with credit to the engineers and company that originated the solution and the publicity. Pickups averaged one-half page per magazine.

Notice that the story does not tout one brand of product. Instead, it offers a solution that can be implemented through the use of any manufacturer's piston-type accumulator.

DESIGN-IDEA STORIES

The design-idea story (see Fig. 12-5) describes in detail the design, construction, and operation of a product, system, or process of potential interest to engineers and technicians. These readers may design original equipment for sale ("OEM" products), equipment for use in their own company's plants, or plant systems and facilities.

Some editors insist that the product or process described in a design-idea story be new. Other editors don't care about the age of the development but insist that it be one that has not previously been described at length in a periodical. The one requirement agreed on by all editors

IDEAS-FLUID POWER

Mechanical Linkages Sequence Pressure Generator

Simple flow-control system pays off in long service life.

LARS G. SODERHOLM, MIDWEST EDITOR

Valve-spool extensions are positioned through interconnecting linkages, springs, levers and locks in a relatively simple mechanical sequence control. A solenoid starts the cycle and pressure responses continue the sequence in advancing a ram, building high pressure and finally returning the ram to its starting position.

Control details of the "Hy-Power" hydraulic pressure generator were revealed by the Hannifin Press Div. of Parker-Hannifin, Des Plaines, Ill. Designed for reliability of operation, the unit depends on close tolerances to control leakage. Only three seals are used in critical areas.

There are four operating modes in the pressure-generating sequence. In its "neutral" position, the pump runs, but the primary valve returns the oil directly to the reservoir. In the "advance" position, the primary valve sends oil to the ram, which advances rapidly until it encounters the load. After working pressure has increased to approximately 1000 psi, the "power" stroke begins and the intensifier valve directs fluid to the booster cylinder. The cylinder's large area acts on a small area of working fluid, boosting the ram pressure to as much as 5000 psi. The "return" stroke of the ram is determined automatically by a preset pressure when the primary valve shifts to reverse the oil flow from the ram and reset the booster cylinder and other mechanical components of the control system.

To vote for this Design Idea, insert V07 on Reader-Service card.

Valve spools are positioned through interconnecting linkages, levers and locks.

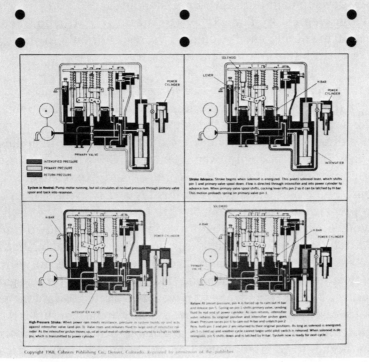

Fig. 12-5. Reprint of a design-idea story from *Design News*.

is that the development embody innovative engineering of interest to many people, particularly engineers and technicians.

Industrial magazines that regularly publish design-idea stories include *Machine Design, Design News,* and *Design Engineering.* You'll find it worth your while to review the magazines serving your company's or client's markets and determine which magazines now print — or could be talked into printing — design-idea stories.

After reviewing the magazines, you may find that apparently none publishes technical material aimed at engineers and technicians. That doesn't mean you are stymied, however. Approach the editor of the leading magazine in the field and point out that:

- The new product or method embodies interesting technical concepts;
- Design engineers, whether OEM or in-plant, will not buy and use the new development until they understand it; and
- Publishing a story that explains the design, construction, and operation of the development would be a service not only to your company or client but also to the entire industry.

As for preparation of design-idea stories: Some magazines send editors out to cover design-idea stories, while others ask that publicists prepare and submit the copy and graphic materials.

Since these stories go fairly deep into technical detail, their illustrations may include not only overall, external views but also closeup, detail photos plus cutaway, cross-sectional, and exploded-view illustrations. Some magazines that use this type of story have their staff artists prepare illustrations from blueprints submitted by the publicist.

If you convince an editor to run a design-idea story, study the magazine to determine an appropriate technical level. Material for *Machine Design,* for instance, goes mainly to engineers, so such a story should be written on a high technical plane. Material destined for a magazine read mainly by owners and managers would be slanted toward them. In the latter case, your prose would have a more general, consumer flavor, like that found in magazines such as *Popular Science* and *Discovery.*

Why bother to go after publication of design-idea stories? Because they build the company's reputation for expertise; they typically net a large amount of editorial exposure; and their reprints make fine mailers to technically oriented buying influences.

INSTALLATION PROFILES

The installation profile (IP) resembles the case history but is covered by a magazine staff editor or by a freelancer on assignment to the magazine (see Fig. 12-6). Publicists and freelancers on assignment to manufacturers do not normally cover IP's. The magazine bears the expense and writes the article to its own taste.

Further, an IP covers the entire installation or a major part of it, not just the application of one company's products or services. If the editor mentions vendors or brand names, he usually mentions all or most of the major suppliers involved.

Generally speaking, an IP occupies more pages than a case-history feature article, and involves an installation or problem/solution more significant than the average case-history subject. A magazine will invest time and money in doing an IP only if the installation is unique, technically innovative, or grand in scale.

If IP's are staff written and mention many vendors, why should you get interested in the format? For three reasons: (1) IP's not only occupy generous amounts of space but also receive a prominent position in the issue; (2) since they are staff written and mention many vendors, IP's have less of a commercial, promotional flavor, and so are more believable than case histories; and (3) the magazine pays the freight; you can gain large amounts of prominent, believable exposure at little expense.

Next time your company or client participates in a unique, large, or innovative project, notify the editor of the leading magazine in your field and offer to work with him. Be prepared to shoot photos – something you'd want to do anyway – and to prepare layout, flow, and control diagrams for use by the magazine.

Seldom will you have to start from scratch in preparing these diagrams. Your company's or client's engineering departments make large, detailed scale drawings that can readily be simplified and adapted for the magazine. In many cases all you need do is go through the drawings, select those that best illustrate the story, mark out superfluous details, and clarify the callouts or other nomenclature. Your illustrator can take it from there.

PHOTO FEATURES

As the name suggests, the photo feature (PF) consists mainly of photos and captions, with text playing a secondary role. This format serves

Floor-to-roof signatures

Total storage capacity in the racks is 4232 palletloads, two deep. At 30,000 signatures a pallet, that comes to a theoretical grand total of 127 million signatures.

come off the presses and folders, they're palletized and moved into short-term, WIP storage.

When all signatures and the covers for a magazine issue have been printed, they're brought together for assembly. The bindery stacks them in page order and binds them together. Finally the wraparound cover is glued on and the excess paper trimmed from the top, bottom and right side.

Part of Webb's problem stemmed from the nature of signatures. They're fragile; palletloads can't be stacked. Without some sort of vertical storage, the warehousemen must spread the materials horizontally to the walls, then crowd, then look elsewhere. Webb found itself strapped.

By mid-1976, the company had resorted to using other warehouses in the St. Paul area. Local cartage companies hauled palletloads halfway across town, put them into storage, then in a short time hauled them back to Webb for binding.

Gopher State's largest commercial printer solves pressing storage problems with new docks, racks and AS/RS. — by Joe Quinlan, associate editor

Have you ever flown on Northwest Orient, TWA or Frontier Airlines? If so, you've likely seen and read the in-flight magazines they put in the seat-back pockets on their jets.

These slick, colorful magazines — along with 23 other magazines, plus calendars, directories, government forms and other materials — come from the long-run, high-speed presses of The Webb Company, a remarkably multi-plant printer based in modern buildings on the Mississippi River at the edge of St. Paul, Minn.

Founded in 1882 as the Northwestern Fur Breeder, The Webb Co. grown rapidly and steady expansions of the St. went up in 1965. 1972 Webb has also acquired printing plants and press in Minneapolis, Minne St. Cloud, Minnesota.

From its modest beg two rented, third-floor ex-farmer Edward A. company has branched to tionwide sales which to million in 1980. Webb dividend growth rate ha

Drawing B — Plan view of the Webb facility after the 1978-79 expansion.

Ron Mrnak, first-shift operator of the AS/R system, at the CRT terminal.

The new shipping and receiving building added floor space for staging, and increased the number of docks from 6 to 11. The tan building which rises in the background is the new rack-supported warehouse.

the computer when a load is ready for pickup, indicate a completed task and prevent undesired load placement.

If only the back load in a cubicle is to be retrieved, the "Store/Triever" will pick up both front and back loads in the cubicle. The

unwanted load is transferred to the input station. The operator can then restore the unwanted load according to its original storage date.

Up to 17 dual retrieval commands can be entered at one time, thus building up a "queue" of retrieval work for the "Store/Triever" system. Retrievals will then be made in the order entered, unless the operator subsequently enters a "hot" command, giving a particular load priority over the queue.

In normal operation, the operator need enter only the item and quantity desired. The machines will then automatically retrieve loads on a first in, first out (FIFO) basis. Further, the machines will retrieve a sufficient number of palletloads to satisfy the quantity requirements.

Control hardware

The hardware in the Hartman "Flexitrol ICS" control system includes a Digital Model LSI 11/03 computer, Model LA-180 hard copy printer and Model VT-52 control console with cathode ray tube (CRT) display and associated keyboard.

Hartman has employed bulk core memory for storage of programs, data base and command queues. Since this memory is nonvolatile, a power failure will not cause loss of stored data or programs.

Also provided with the comput-

Fig. 12-6. Reprint of a five-page installation profile researched and written by a staff editor. The company that designed the installation provided the color photos and drawings.

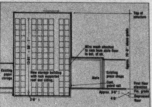

Drawing C — Elevation view of the new rack-supported warehouse containing the AS/R system.

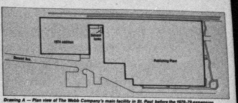

Drawing A — Plan view of The Webb Company's main facility in St. Paul before the 1978-79 expansion.

operation, you know the difficulties that can arise from bad weather, truck breakdowns and mistakes in communication. Tight, inflexible deadlines, combined with these difficulties, caused many a crisis.

Dockage in the 1974 warehouse proved inadequate, too. There weren't enough bays to handle the traffic, and the staging area was too small.

First, a study

In late 1977, Webb's management called in representatives of The Austin Company, consulting engineers and designers based in Cleveland, Ohio, to do a location study, review the existing facilities and make recommendations. The Austin team, headed by Project Engineer Robert Olson, aided by systems engineering staff consultants, came up with a number of

The two dual truck-drops are served by powered walkies, as shown here, and by forklift trucks.

er is a floppy disk drive. This enables the operator to copy the data base for security. Should the bulk core memory fail, the computer can work directly from the floppy disks.

The printer prints out all transactions performed by the system. As instructions are completed, the printer prints them in their order of occurrence, thus providing a paper transaction log.

At the console, the operator performs all entry and manipulation of data. He enters commands for control of the AS/R system machines, storage of stock information and extraction of reports at the keyboard, verifying his manual actions against display on the CRT.

Control software

Operation of the system is simple and concise because prompted questions and responses, displayed on the CRT, guide the operator at each step. New operators require only minimal training.

The keyboard serves as a link between the computer files and the AS/R machines. Contained in the computer software package which Hartman designed are:

1. Alphanumeric part number for each part.
2. Alphanumeric status code used to categorize loads of the same part number.
3. Quantity — up to 999,999.
4. Location address.

5. Optional load number used as a visual field aid in categorizing part numbers for reports.
6. Numeric aisle number.
7. Numeric load station identifier — used in store and retrieve commands.
8. Time of day.
9. Alphanumeric description.

In addition, when the operator is adding a new part number to the file, the computer will ask him whether or not the part is heat-sensitive. If "yes," the computer will automatically select a storage address that is suitable for such material.

This software package has a novel, three-phase process for selecting all storage addresses. The system will always try to store like part numbers together, front to back. In fact, at the time of load storage, the CRT asks the operator if he will have two like part numbers available. Should he say "yes," the system will automatically look for a completely empty cubicle. If none is open, the system will assign an address in front of a like part number.

The "Flexitrol ICS" control system has computed travel time to all empty locations, and selects the appropriate one with the lowest travel time. This feature speeds operation and lowers the costs of maintenance.

The software package provided for Webb has room for 3288 part numbers. If the memory is full but

the operator wants to add a part number, the computer automatically deletes an unused number and accepts the new one.

Benefits to date

As soon as the Hartman AS/RS and the new dock facility went into operation a little over a year ago, The Webb Company gained relief from the former problems, and began to enjoy some bonus benefits.

For one, the generous amount of vertical storage space in the racks enabled Webb to store all signatures in one place. The plant no longer needs to use outside warehouses or cartage. And there is still adequate cubicle space available for several years' growth.

In addition, the traffic jams in the aisles have been eliminated, and the additional docks have eased shipping and receiving. Stock control is now more accurate and current, storage and retrieval have been speeded up, and mistakes have decreased dramatically.

Then too, the printed signatures, formerly somewhat vulnerable when standing exposed on the floor, are now more secure in the racks. Spoilage has dropped to near zero.

Records have improved, too. "The operator must punch in all commands at the CRT terminal," Robichaud said, "and he is prompted at each step. This forces him to take his time and be accurate.

"In other words, the system imposes a discipline on the operator and all other people involved in source documents (load tickets) and data input. We therefore enjoy not only fast, precise operation but also very accurate on-hand and location information. These can either be displayed instantly on the CRT or printed out for management use.

"Mind you, I'm not inviting all our competitors to copy us," Robichaud concluded, "but I'll bet there are hundreds of large commercial printers in the U.S. who could benefit from a system like this."

After reviewing Austin's recommendations, Webb management assigned implementation of the project to Plant Engineer Bernard J. "Bernie" Robichaud. A veteran in plant engineering and project management, Robichaud had joined Webb in November, 1977.

He divided the project into two major portions: one, the rack-supported warehouse with AS/R machines plus the computer, accessories and software; and two, the concrete work and the balance of the structural work.

For the first, he sought bids from four major systems suppliers.

Webb's St. Paul facility before the 1978-79 expansion, Drawing B shows the facility as it now stands. The structures added in the expansion are shaded (in color). Total gain in floor space, including the rack-supported building which houses the AS/RS, was 25,800 square feet.

Addition of the shipping and receiving structure, shown at the left in Drawing B, brought 9000 more square feet for staging. The number of docks increased from 6 to 11.

Floor space of the rack-supported warehouse is 12,000 square feet.

The vertical distance measured floor to the top is 77 feet (see Drawing C).

...built and erected by ...gineering, the AS/R ...rack structure mea... high and 228 feet ...stance across, from ...ported wall to the oth...

...stem is 13 loads high ...ong. Standard pallet-...tures each measure ...g by 46 inches wide ...high. Average weight ...is 2000 pounds, the ...lly from 200 to 2500. ...imum design capaci-...e is 3000 pounds. ...rack structure, four ...utomatic sprinklers.

The total capacity in the 62,000-square-foot high rise is 4232 loads. About 75 percent of the stored loads consist of printed signatures. The balance includes finished products and supplies such as adhesives, wire and twine for the binders. A pallet carries about 40,000 of the 16-page signatures.

Each cubicle can hold two palletloads, one behind the other. In each of the two aisles between the cubicles (see photos and Drawing C), an electrically powered Hartman "Store/Triever" rides a floor-mounted crane rail, servicing the cubicles on either side. Retrieval time for any palletload in the system averages less than two minutes and never exceeds four minutes.

The AS/R machines have side-moving shuttles which can reach halfway into a cubicle to deposit or retrieve a single palletload — or can reach full depth to handle two loads at once or a single load in the rear of the cubicle.

Pickup and deposit for the system takes place at eight dual truck-drops. Operators service the drops with forklift trucks and powered walkie trucks.

Each dual truck-drop is dedicated: loading only on one side, unloading only on the other. This dedication helps to prevent congestion and confusion. The load/unload stations have sensors and interlock safety...

Reprinted from the May, 1981 issue of Material Handling Engineering. Copyright 1981 by Penton/IPC, Inc., a subsidiary of Pittway Corp.

Fig. 12-6. (continued)

Carousels team with modular robots

In a lab at White Data Systems, division of White Machine Company in San Diego, CA, a bottom-powered carousel and a "Mobot" industrial robot are demonstrating a promising technique in automated storage and retrieval.

Under the control of a minicomputer, the robot picks loaded tote boxes one at a time from bin shelves on the carousel and lowers them to a powered roller takeaway conveyor.

At a push of a button, the system reverses to load cycle. Then the robot picks loaded totes from the conveyor and deposits them in the proper carousel bin and shelf.

Cycle time in the demonstration setup is 20 seconds, including carousel travel time. This time can be cut to as little as 10 seconds by having the carousel and computer operate simultaneously.

"This type of system, or a variation of it, would be useful in many factory assembly operations," said Don Weiss, vice president of White Machine Co., headquartered in Kenilworth, NJ. "Electronics people have been the first to latch onto the idea, but al-

COVER PHOTO:
"Mobot" industrial robot picks loaded tote box from White carousel in demonstration setup. At left is Texas Instruments PC panel for Mobot. A Hewlett-Packard minicomputer controls operation of the entire system: carousel, Mobot and conveyor.

"Iron dummies" automate loading and unloading of "rotating shelves"; PC's and minicomputers control operation. — by Joe Quinlan, associate editor

most any plant assembling or doing repair work from small parts or kits could employ it profitably."

To date, two large companies have placed orders for White carousel/robot systems based on the equipment and techniques being demonstrated in San Diego.

One of these pioneering systems incorporates four carousels and two robots traveling on horizontal, floor-mounted rails (see sketch). One robot picks tote boxes from the front ends of the carousels, placing the boxes on a takeaway conveyor.

The other robot picks boxes from an infeed conveyor and loads them into designated shelf addresses on the opposite ends of the carousels.

The second system which White has sold is going into a large repair facility of a communications company. Here, eight robots will serve eight double-tiered carousels, with four robots serving each vertical column on the front end and four more at the rear.

Controlled automatically by computer, the high-throughput system will carry boxes of repair parts to work stations. Sensors will automatically signal the computer when a full box of parts is needed. Simple programming will enable the conveyors to take the correct parts to each work station, so operators never have to wait for parts.

The demo setup

The demonstration setup includes a standard, bottom-powered carousel with 14 wire bins, each six feet high. The shelves in each bin are spaced 12 inches apart vertically.

The robot is a "Mobot" supplied to White by the Mobot Corporation of San Diego. This particular robot — each Mobot is custom-built for the job from standard, modular components — consists basically of two members.

The upright member provides vertical travel by means of an electric motor and chain drive. Power comes from a 3/4-hp variable-speed d.c. motor. A counterweight compensates for the weight of the drive chain.

Horizontal motion comes from a 1-1/2-inch-bore, 24-inch-stroke pneumatic cylinder. This is actually canted at seven degrees from horizontal to coincide with the slope of the carousel bin shelves. The cylinder uses standard shop compressed air at 80 psi.

Fig. 12-7. Photo, feature, right, contains sequence illustrating operation of equipment described in a major news story.

well in situations where, in order to explain something, you would find it easier and more effective to show and tell than to merely tell. Examples of these situations include:

- How something was done – for instance, how a building, large machine or process-line was erected.
- How to do something – how to assemble, install, operate, check, overhaul, troubleshoot or modify a machine, component, system or process.
- How something works – the operation, step by step, of a machine, component or what have you.

Fig. 12-7. (continued)

A PF may stand alone as an independent article, or it may appear as part of a larger unit in the form of a box, sidebar, or follow-on (see Fig. 12-7). You'll find the PF an effective supplement to some in-depth press releases, "how-to" technical articles, and case histories. You may also want to consider preparing PF material for use by editors in certain staff written roundup articles and installation profiles.

COMPANY PERIODICALS

If your company or client publishes periodicals ("house organs") for customers, dealers, distributors, employees, or other publics, you probably write original material and adapt publicity material for use in them. Almost every kind of release and article you send to industrial periodicals can be adapted into useful, interesting copy for the audiences of your company periodicals.

Don't stop there, though. Look beyond your own company or clients to their suppliers and customers. Some of these companies may publish their own external periodicals — that is, periodicals going to customers and prospects — that would give your company valuable exposure.

Suppose, for instance, that a certain steel producer supplies steel going into a new line of products made by your company. Suppose further that the steel producer publishes an external monthly magazine. Chances are the monthly goes to many buying-influences that your company would like to reach with its message.

You could contact the editor of the steel producer's monthly and tell him about the application. He'll either assign someone to cover the story or ask you to provide copy, photos, and so on. For a modest investment, you can not only secure valuable editorial exposure but also help to cement relations between your company or client and a valued supplier.

The same opportunities and procedures exist with customers of your company or client. Say, for example, that your company recently sold a new type of prefabricated in-plant office structure to a customer who is renovating a plant. Determine whether or not the customer publishes periodicals. If yes, you can be fairly certain the editors will run one or more stories on the renovation.

So contact the editor and offer to provide technical details, photos, and drawings of the new office structure. Part of the package would be copy explaining the features, advantages, and benefits of the structure.

Keep in mind, by the way, that many companies publish several periodicals. Each has its own audience; equally important to you, each may have its own different editor who could use a packet of information and illustrations. Send a separate, duplicate packet to each editor.

MAGAZINE DEPARTMENTS AND COLUMNS

Much of this book pertains to the workhorses, the standard, well-known formats of industrial publicity: new-product and personnel press releases, case-history releases and feature articles, and bylined feature articles. Each of these familiar formats has not only a specific, well-understood goal, but also a predictable destination in the magazines.

New-product announcements end up in the "New products" department; releases about personnel changes go into departments entitled "Personnel changes," or "People on the move," or some such. Case-history releases are rewritten and condensed; then they're put into departments with titles such as "Cost-cutting ideas" or "Tips for profit and safety." Contributed case-history and bylined feature articles usually fit between the staff-written features and the "back of the book" departments.

You can restrict your thinking, planning, and production to these standard formats and departments, and you can fare well. Unless you dig further, however, you're missing many opportunities for editorial exposure.

Pick up copies of the top magazines serving your markets. Study the tables of contents; then page slowly through each issue. As you proceed, look for unfamiliar departments and columns, especially those containing stories other than new-product announcements, notices of personnel changes, and short case histories.

Notice that industrial magazines also contain departments bearing titles such as "Industry news," "News bulletins," "Contracts and sales," "Miscellany," and many other titles. In addition, some magazines run regular monthly columns bylined by staff editors.

Take a department entitled "Industry news," for example. It probably contains items concerning personnel changes, plus items about new plants, plant expansions, large contracts, new industry standards, government regulations, and many other kinds of topics.

Each department and column in a magazine holds opportunities for your publicity. To capitalize, take these steps:

1. Reread Table 2-1 in Chapter 2. The table bears the heading "What You Can Publicize."

2. Relate each item in the table to your current publicity program.

3. Review again each department and column in the periodicals serving your company's or client's markets. List the published items by generic topic: personnel change, plant expansion, contract, and so on. To that list, add generic topics you think could also logically go into certain departments or columns.

4. Expand the publicity program accordingly.

Now, assume you have a story that you would like to see in a certain department in the Number One magazine serving your field. Let's say the story concerns a speech given recently by the company president. In the speech, he made some very specific forecasts concerning technical trends in the industry. He's one of the industry's acknowledged leaders, and what he said contains genuine news value. You'd like to see the story printed in a department called "Trends and forecasts."

You could simply prepare a news release, mail it with a photo of the president to all pertinent periodicals, and hope for the best. That's like firing a shotgun at a distant target, however. What you want to use in this case is a high-powered rifle with a telescopic sight and just one sharp-nosed bullet. Here's what you do:

Call the Number One magazine and ask, "Who edits the department called 'Trends and forecasts'? May I speak with him?" When you reach the editor who handles this particular department, tell him about the story you have, offer an exclusive, and tell him the release and photo will be on their way by express mail today.

You've personalized your product, packaged it, and sold it one-on-one to an individual. You've emulated the salesperson who makes a friendly, persuasive, customized call on one prospect. His technique is far more concentrated and effective, per shot, than that of the mail-order company that mails thousands of standardized, impersonal pieces of mail.

The Number One magazine will likely give your story good play. After it appears, you are free to shotgun the same story to as many other periodicals and representatives of the electronic media as you wish. The promise of an exclusive has been honored.

You will find that the personal approach to editors works well with all types of publicity. Because of daily pressures and haste, a certain percentage of press releases become sidetracked or lost between the incoming-mail desk and the editors who can use the material in their departments. Insofar as is practical, address your really important stories to individual department editors and precede or follow the mailing with a telephone call.

Finally, an idea concerning a rare, valuable kind of opportunity: the contributed column. Let's say your company or client builds diesel engines, and employed at the company is a veteran troubleshooter named Anton Novak. He has had 31 years of experience with all kinds of diesels in every conceivable application. He knows what he's talking about, and he likes to give interviews.

Now look at the magazines serving your markets; pick one as your primary target. Would that magazine benefit by running a regular, contributed column with a heading such as "Diesel shoptalk" or "Anton's corner"? The column could offer practical, timely tips on diesel engine installation, maintenance, troubleshooting, and lubrication, couched in folksy, first-person prose. With the column head could be a photo or rendering of the real Anton Novak.

If the idea appeals to you, draft three sample installments and prepare the photos or drawings to be used as illustrations. Call the editor, tell him you have what you think is a terrific idea, and ask for an appointment at his office. Then go sell.

Should the editor of the Number One magazine turn down the idea for a column, suggest a 12-part series. If he rejects that idea too, take your ideas to the editors of Numbers Two, Three, and so on. Keep plugging until you get a "yes."

Too farfetched? No, it has been done in more than one magazine. Try it. The worst you can experience is a "no" reply.

TRADE-SHOW PUBLICITY

Virtually every industrial magazine covers trade shows pertaining directly or indirectly to the industry served (see Fig. 12-8). For instance, *Material Handling Engineering* does extensive reporting on the big material-handling conference and exposition held every two years. This magazine also prints shorter reports on trade shows and conferences pertaining to plant engineering and maintenance, automatic identification, bulk-materials handling, production and inventory control, packaging, factory automation, warehouse management, and robotics.

If your company or client participates in trade shows and related conferences, each show offers several types of opportunities for editorial exposure. Following are some suggestions for capitalizing on these opportunities:

1. Before the show. Most industrial magazines publish "show-preview" issues. Mailed shortly before and sometimes handed out during the shows, these issues typically contain calendars for show events and conference presentations, plus photos and descriptions of the equipment to be exhibited.

Review the editorial calendars of the magazines in your industry, looking particularly for notices of show coverage. Three or four months before the mailing date of a show-preview issue, send the editors press releases and photos on the equipment your company or client will exhibit. Find out which magazines print full-color illustrations in their issues, and send color photos accordingly.

If you are using the occasion of a show to introduce a new product, prepare a comprehensive press kit on the product. Weigh the pros and cons of holding a press conference at the show versus mailing the kits to editors before the show. (For more on press conferences, see Chapters 13 and 14.)

2. During the show. Producers of trade shows usually set up and staff press rooms. Typically, these rooms contain lounge chairs, hot coffee, and soft drinks, along with tables holding quantities of press releases, press kits, and brochures from show exhibitors.

Generally speaking, the quality of the materials offered to editors in trade-show press rooms is low. Not that the releases and brochures are poorly written, illustrated, or printed; it's simply that the materials offer *nothing new*. In most cases, the equipment being exhibited at the show is not new, and exhibitors merely proffer standard descriptions and stock brochures on the old equipment. Since it does not contain legitimate stories for the editors, this material represents a waste of the exhibitors' money and the editors' time.

What can you do if your company or client is exhibiting old equipment? Here are three ideas for providing fresh, legitimate stories that editors can use:

• Write and prepare two or three new case-history releases for distribution at the trade show. At the top of the first page of each release, put a release date coinciding with the opening day of the show. Include one or two black-and-white illustrations, and close the last page of each release with a note saying that you can provide additional pictures, including color.

• Preprint the complete texts of speeches or technical papers to be delivered by company members at the conference or show. Make these printed texts available to editors in the press room immediately before or during the actual presentations.

• Draft a statement by the company president, chief executive officer, or board chairperson concerning the future of the industry, the

Fig. 12-8. Pages from editorial coverage before (top) and after a national trade show.

significance of recent developments, or the direction and implications of industry trends. Date press releases on these statements to coincide with the opening of the show or conference.

Use some imagination to provide fresh material for the editors. If necessary, do something to generate news, as suggested in the preceding paragraph.

During the show and conference, have a photographer shoot a variety of photos, in color as well as black and white, of your company's or client's exhibits. The selection of shots should include some with visitors crowded around the equipment, perhaps during a demonstration. Also get shots of company members at the lectern delivering their talks or technical papers.

3. After the show. Following a major trade show and conference, the industry magazines usually publish illustrated reports. You can reap more editorial exposure than the average exhibitor by mailing the following kinds of materials to editors in your field:

• Captioned photos of products exhibited and demonstrated. The photos should include people as well as products. Send color photos to editors who can use them.
• Captioned photos of the company's entire exhibit − if it has marked visual appeal.
• Copies of complete texts of speeches and technical papers given by company members during the show or conference. In each packet include photos of the people delivering the talks.
• A report on the degree and quality of interest shown by visitors to your booth, the kinds of questions they asked, the problems apparently uppermost in their minds.
• A comparison between the last show and this one. Give a report on the numbers of visitors who signed up for literature at this show versus the last (give raw numbers or percentages), degree of interest in buying, changes in subjects of interest, and so on. The editor can use this kind of information in his report on the mood of the show, trends evidenced, and the show's relative success.
• Case-history and other releases distributed initially during the show.
• Press kits. If you held a press conference in conjunction with the show, mail kits to editors who did not attend but who could use the information.

In conclusion: Read a variety of magazines, looking for different types of formats you could employ. Search aggressively for opportunities. Discuss your ideas with editors. When the potential benefits seem to warrant it, play your hunches and submit offbeat material on speculation.

Chapter 13

The Press Conference

"Do I get invitations to a lot of press conferences? Joe, I could attend a conference every working day of the week, 52 weeks a year, in Chicago alone. Trouble is, only about one out of 100 is worth the time, bother, and expense. The other 99 stories could be communicated just as well by means of news releases and photos."

Speaking was a senior editor from one of the leading design engineering magazines. His skeptical attitude toward press conferences (PC's) is shared, I find, by many industrial editors. The results of a survey of 18 editors, reported in Chapter 14, reinforce this opinion.

Why Editors Go Anyway

If it's true that so many PC's present mundane stories and are a waste of the magazines' time and money, why do editors show up? It seems to me that some reasons are:

• The publicist or agent misrepresented the story. Using terms such as "unique," "hot," "breakthrough," and "first of its kind" in the invitation, he causes the editor to believe that the story will be important when it really isn't. Fortunately, this sort of deception is not common.

• The editor, influenced or even pressured by his magazine's sales manager or publisher, attends the PC because the company financing it is an advertiser or a hot prospect. If the magazine isn't represented at the PC, the advertiser may construe this as a slight. Money talks, and sometimes it's better to attend the PC than to risk offending the advertiser.

• Editors may sound skeptical, even cynical, about PC's, but editors' engines run on hope. There's always the chance that a story that sounds minor in the invitation may turn out to be significant.

Several times I have observed instances in which the company's publicists didn't see, much less understand, the full significance of the story. Lacking experience in industrial applications, they focused on the new product and its features but for some reason did not comprehend or communicate the impact of the new development in terms of potential benefit to the user: cost reduction, quality control, process simplification, and so on. Editors are sometimes able to spot these benefits and answer the ever-burning question, "So what?"

• The editor knows that he and other editors at the PC will get basically the same materials, but he figures he can look, question, and think enough to develop an original angle for the story. Attending the PC and talking to company experts facilitates this.

• Editors are − or should be − resourceful, inquisitive, and imaginative. Even the PC offering a humdrum story may yield ideas for feature articles. The tea may be vapid, the crumpets stale, and the oral presentations dull, but the editor can talk to the company engineers and managers present. He may be able to get these experts to open up, and their comments may trigger ideas for stories on industry trends, government regulations, and countless other subjects related in some way to the PC story. So although the story itself may be less than sparkling, conversation with the company experts can make the editor's expedition worthwhile.

Why Publicists Do It

Why do industrial publicists and their agents conduct so many PC's that proffer minor stories, and sometimes "unstories?" Here are some possible reasons:

• The publicist simply doesn't know that the story is minor. Lacking broad exposure in his industry, he hears his company sales manager throwing superlatives around and naively believes them. The publicist doesn't realize that what's hot to a sales manager may be cold, dull, and stale to an editor.

• The publicist, agents, sales managers, and others involved believe that a PC will always yield more editorial exposure than will the mailing of a news release or press kit. Their operating philosophy is, "Story be damned, it's personal contact that counts."

• The agency does a selling job on the company. A posh PC production can cost well into the thousands, yielding a nice, fat invoice.

• The publicist has been pressured by his sales manager into holding a PC. Perhaps accustomed to using bulldozer tactics, the sales manager thinks he can shove the stories into the magazines.

• The company president has an opinion on the national economy. He will use the opening moments of the PC — likely more than a few of those moments — to mouth his opinion, hoping for wide and generous pickup in the press.

• The company vice-president of marketing hasn't had many opportunities to rub elbows with editors. He wants to meet these influentials, impress them, and perhaps get his name mentioned prominently.

Great Potential Benefits, Though

Perhaps you think the preceding paragraphs sound cynical. Perhaps they are, to some extent. The PC format is much overused and often abused. Most PC's could be omitted and never missed.

At the same time, however, the PC — if properly planned and executed — is a powerful tool. The personal presentations, visual aids, and demonstrations can make a strong impression on the editors. They in turn have a chance to challenge claims, ask questions, and obtain clarification of key points.

In a way, the difference between a release-mailing and a PC is the same as the difference between direct-mail selling and personal selling. If you've had any exposure to sales, you know that this difference can be considerable.

Provided you have a significant story to tell, and you schedule and conduct the PC skillfully, then you can usually gain more and better editorial exposure from the PC than you could from a release-mailing.

Other potential benefits of the PC include:

• Personal contacts between publicist and editors. As I mentioned in a previous chapter, publicity is mainly a people business. Establishing and maintaining rapport with key editors in your field should be both a primary goal and a constant activity.

- Opportunity to meet and make friends with many editors at one time. Imagine how many trips you'd have to make in order to personally meet, say, 15 editors.
- Personal contact between the editors and your company's engineers, managers, and executives. When an editor meets and becomes friends with an engineer, for instance, that engineer becomes a potential source not only for the PC story but also for future bylined technical articles, case histories, roundup articles, and other material.
- Generation of ideas. The copious personal exchanges at a PC can trigger many ideas for feature articles. For example, during conversations with editors, your engineers and sales manager may recall interesting, successful applications of company products and services. If the editor becomes interested, these anecdotes may blossom into published case histories.
- Exposure of the full scope of your company's products and expertise to key editors. You can safely assume that no editor – repeat, not one – knows about all the products made, services offered, and industries reached by your company. The same goes for the range of applications for your company's products. Displays of products and application photos at the PC can begin to expose your company's capabilities and can spark editors' interest and ideas.
- Opportunity to provide adequate and special material. Each editor wants to feel he can get the whole story, with all details of significance to his readers. Moreover, he would like his report to be a little different from the reports that will run in other periodicals. The PC format enables each editor to ask questions, dig out details he wants, and obtain or request a photo, drawing, or graph especially for his periodical.

What Justifies a Press Conference

A PC can accomplish much for your company or client, but the important question is, *"Do you really need a press conference?"* Before launching plans for a PC, look very closely not only at the probable PC costs you may incur but primarily at the story itself. Determine the answers to these questions:

- Is the story truly significant? Ignoring the fact that the sales manager wants as much hype as possible – after all, that's his job – will the product, method, or service have a major impact in the market-place? How much importance will the development have to users, and to the industry as a whole? Does the development constitute an important advance in technology?

Example: A minor modification on a lift truck that has been available for 12 years may warrant a short news release and one photo or drawing, but not a long news release with several illustrations. The minor modification certainly wouldn't call for a press conference.

On the other hand, a new truck model added to an existing line may warrant a long, detailed release with several illustrations. But a PC? Not likely.

Suppose, however, that you are introducing a radically different kind of truck. It is made of welded tubular members rather than the usual plates. For its horsepower it weighs an average of 35% less than other trucks having equivalent power. Fuel consumption beats equivalent trucks by 32%. The new truck has some other innovations that will make the industry sit up and stare.

Does your introduction of this truck to the press and its readers call for a PC? I think so. Not only is the product new and interesting, but it also represents a technical breakthrough in several dimensions, including construction, weight, and fuel economy.

• Does the equipment, material, or method lend itself well to demonstrations and to comparisons with existing products or methods?

Suppose you are introducing a new type of adhesive. If it dries and cures rapidly, you may be able to dream up and conduct a dramatic demo — a variation on the old "lift a truck with a helicopter" ploy. On the other hand, if the adhesive requires eight hours of curing time . . . .

Let's go back to the example of the lift truck. It has a human operator, it moves around, it can pick things up and set them down. Weight and fuel consumption can be shown by means of instruments. The truck and its performance would offer outstanding opportunities for dramatic, effective demonstrations.

• Is the development not only significant but also so technically complex that it can't be adequately explained in a news release? Or is the development so exciting to the senses — visual, audio, tactile — that the only way you could possibly do justice to the story is to have editors come see, hear, and feel for themselves?

• Are you and the company representatives prepared to answer all legitimate questions about the new development, including questions on prices, adherence to safety standards, and the like? If you find yourself answering "No comment" to a number of hypothetical questions, perhaps you are not yet ready for the glaring exposure of a PC.

PLANNING AND PREPARING THE CONFERENCE

Let's assume you've determined that you have an important story to tell about a new product. It's complex and could best be conveyed by your company's or client's experts through illustrated talks and a demonstration. How do you plan and prepare for a press conference? What are the major elements you must consider?

Following is a list of those elements, along with some ideas and tips. After reviewing this list, you may want to develop your own PC planning checklist. You can tailor this to the particulars of your company, markets, and products or services. In tailoring the checklist, also consider the personalities, competitive alignments, and special requirements of the periodicals serving your field.

Location

Many editors of industrial periodicals express a preference for New York, Chicago, and Los Angeles as sites for press conferences. These cities have good air service, hotel accommodations, and local transportation. Further, New York and Chicago have large concentrations of industrial and technical periodicals.

Suppose, though, that you are announcing a large, heavy piece of equipment or a complex system. Or the product may have special requirements for power, ventilation, or motion. A hotel meeting room in Manhattan is no place to demonstrate such equipment.

You still have several options, including:

• Forgo demonstrating the actual equipment. Instead, show a movie, videotape, or slide/tape presentation. You can then hold the conference in one of the cities mentioned and draw a large percentage of the editors invited.

- Hold the conference and demonstration at your plant. If the plant is situated remote from a large city, you won't draw as many editors, but you can offset quantity of editors with quantity and quality of exposure. That is, a well-conducted PC with a dramatic demonstration will generate more and better exposure per magazine — both in copy and in illustrations — than would an audiovisual substitute.
- Save the announcement for an important trade show.   Set up the equipment in the exhibit hall, and hold your PC in a meeting room at the hall early in the morning on the show's first day. Make arrangements so that the editors can enter the hall, see the equipment, ask questions, and shoot photos before the mob arrives.

The Room

Requirements for the room in which you hold a PC are the same as for any room to be used for a sales meeting or training session. Check especially for these factors:

- Control over heat and ventilation. A room that's too warm, too cold, or full or smoke and stale air works against you.
- Adequate power outlets.
- Rheostat control over lighting. You want to be able to dim the lights for presentation of audiovisuals.
- Curtains, shades, or drapes that can be pulled to block out sunlight.
- Ambient noise. Don't settle for a room with only thin walls or dividers between it and the next room. Check, too, for the presence of noisy apparatus such as compressors, air conditioners, and hydraulic power units.
- Adequate space for displays, literature tables and other paraphernalia.

Time and Day

First choice of many editors is late morning on Tuesday, Wednesday, or Thursday. Monday is too busy for many editors, and travel on Mondays and Fridays is sometimes difficult.

For more on this topic, see Chapter 14.

Week and Month

As far as I can determine, most editors will attend PC's in any week of the month. It's always a good idea, though, to call a few editors before you do the scheduling. For each periodical, determine whether or not the editor or one of his staff can attend during the week and on the day you've tentatively chosen.

What about the month? Consider the weather as a major determining factor. Some editors limit their travel in the northern states during winter. Outdoor demonstrations during summer can become hot, wet experiences.

Consider vacation time, too. The staffs on industrial magazines are relatively small. When one or two editors are out on vacation, the others can't leave or prefer not to leave the office.

Who and How Many

Whom should you invite, and how many editors can you handle adequately?

Invite the editors of periodicals serving your primary markets and markets you want to penetrate. Few mistakes turn off an editor more totally than to have him travel many miles to attend a PC, at great expense in time, money, and effort, only to find that the story is only marginally interesting to his readers.

Invite only the editors of key periodicals. You can mail the press kit later to editors of other periodicals.

If the development would be of interest to people in the company's plant community — for example, if a new product will generate new jobs — consider inviting reporters and editors from the local media. The exposure will be good for employee morale, community relations, recruitment, and other aspects of public relations.

Limit the number of company personnel whom you invite to the PC, particularly the nonparticipants. You don't want to overwhelm the editors with a horde of passive but influential company onlookers.

As for quantity: A group of 10 to 20 works out best, I think. If the group is larger, many individual editors won't get a chance to talk to the company experts. Remember, personal interplay between editors and experts is one of the main strengths of the PC format.

What if, in drafting the invitation list, you can come up with only 5 to 10 names? Should you hold the PC anyway?

In my opinion, yes. Each editor will be able to spend that much more time with the experts, and each editor will go away with a well-detailed story.

The Invitation

Regard your letter to the editors as a sales letter. It must persuade the editor that he or one of his staff ought to attend your PC, but the copy must remain factual.

Moreover, the letter should contain all the information the editor will need in order to plan his trip. Include not only the why but also the where, when, how long, etc.

Here is a fictitious letter of invitation:

Dear Ed:

We cordially invite you or one of your staff to attend a press conference and demonstration at our factory and offices in Des Moines, Iowa, on Wednesday, May 2.

You'll find this affair worth attending, I believe, because we will announce and show for the first time an exciting new mixing plant for redi-mix concrete. Equipped with advanced, computer-based controls, our plant is smaller than the average redi-mix plant, yet can equal larger plants in output and top them in speed of mix-changes. In addition, the new plant consumes an estimated 20 percent less power than does an older plant of similar capacity.

We'll begin promptly at 10:00 AM with a meeting in our factory conference room. Using a new color videotape and operating scale model, company engineers will explain the plant's construction, operation, and control system.

At 11:00 AM, a bus will take us 12 miles to a commercial redi-mix company where one of the pilot models of the new plant has been running successfully for six months. You will be able to walk and climb around the equipment, view it in operation, and talk to the owner and operators as well as to our engineers. (If it rains on that day, we'll view an application movie instead.)

At 11:45, the bus will bring us back to the plant, where we'll have a quick lunch in the cafeteria. During and after lunch you'll be able to ask more questions of our engineers. Company sales and marketing executives will join us at lunch.

Official closing time will be 2:00 PM, but you are welcome to stay as long as you wish. If you'd like to see the new equipment being built, we'll take you on a tour of our fabricating, assembly, and test shops. (No photos allowed in the plant, though.)

Our press kit, by the way, will include a three-page news release, a copy of our new brochure on the equipment, and a selection of black & white photos plus one color shot. A company photographer will accompany us on the bus tour. He will shoot any special color or b&w photos you may request. We'll also be glad to show you our large selection of stock 4" x 5" color transparencies. This selection includes several dramatic shots which we feel would make excellent front-cover illustrations.

Cab service between our plant and the Des Moines airport (a seven-mile trip) is excellent. Should you want to fly in the night before, we'll reserve a room for you at a nearby motel.

One of our staff will call you soon to determine whether or not you can attend, answer any questions you may have, and help you with reservations.

Thanks, Ed. We hope to see you here on May 2.

Cordially,

P.S.: Enclosed is an 8" x 10" color print showing one of the control panels on our new mixing plant. Impressive, don't you think? You've never seen one like this because it's the first of its kind in the industry. Please come and see the rest for yourself.

Notice that the letter gives the editor good reason to go to Des Moines — the story is obviously important — and also provides adequate information regarding time, date, place, and other key details. An important point: Mail the invitations to arrive five to six weeks before the date of the PC. Magazines have limited travel budgets, and many editors like to gang several editorial visits — press conferences, plant case-history tours, interviews for roundup articles — into one trip. Then too, keep in mind that there are many other press conferences, meetings, seminars, and other assignments competing for the editors' time.

Selecting the Presenters

Usually it's best to have technical experts — design engineers, control system engineers, application engineers — explain with visual aids the construction, operation, functions, uses, performance characteristics, and comparative limitations of the product. In my experience, engineers tend by nature to stick to the facts, avoiding exaggerated claims.

Suppose, however, that the engineers who know the most about the new product are poor presenters? You don't want an awkward speaker creating a poor impression of your company.

Let the experts draft the scripts, but have an experienced speaker — say, the sales manager or two or three product managers — polish the scripts and give the presentation. At the same time, though, also have the engineers sit on a panel of experts at the PC. These technical whizzes can field questions during the question-and-answer period and can also converse with the editors afterward.

If you decide that the sales or marketing manager should give all or part of the presentation, insist that he keep control of his enthusiasm and not lapse into euphoric superlatives.

Some sales and marketing managers don't need to be told, and some engineers are skillful speakers. If you have such people in your company or client organization, you could consider the following sequence: First, an introduction by a public relations person; second, a short welcoming talk by the company president or other top exec; third, an explanation of the market situation by the sales or marketing manager; and fourth, explanations and a demonstration of the technical aspects by one or more engineers.

Accommodations

If some editors must stay overnight, an offer to reserve rooms in a nearby hotel or motel would be appreciated. Don't pay the bills for lodging or meals, however. Editors do not want to be beholden to their sources, preferring to pay their own way.

If you're holding the PC in a place remote from your company's plant, reserve lodging for yourself, your assistants, and the presenters as well as for the editors.

Assistance

A press conference is a complex project. The number of editors attending has little effect on the complexity; whether you're hosting five editors or 25, you must attend to hundreds of details. Careful planning, double-checking, and review of the details, including contingency measures, is one of the factors essential to a successful PC.

No matter how efficient and energetic you may think you are, you cannot handle all the details yourself. Resign yourself to the fact that you must appoint assistants and delegate responsibilities. Choose people who are good at detail work, and delegate tasks such as:

- Follow-up telephone calls to the invited editors.
- Production of the press kits.
- Material logistics — that is, making sure the right materials are at the right places at the right times.
- Reservations, meals, and refreshments.
- Coordination of tours and transportation, if needed.

Delegate these and other details so that you can spend most of your time as project director. This doesn't mean that you can forget about the details, of course. You'll want to check at appropriate times on the implementation of various phases in the project. Try to do so without making unnecessary changes and without "bugging" your helpers. And don't forget to give encouragement, appreciation, and due credit.

If you plan to hold the PC in a city remote from the plant, you may find it worthwhile to use the services of a professional meeting coordinator headquartered in the PC city. Experienced in handling sales meetings and seminars as well as PC's, these pros — sometimes employed by or affiliated with the hotels — know what it takes to conduct a meeting successfully. They can take directions over the phone and handle details concerning the PC meeting room, meals, refreshments, projection equipment, power requirements, and other aspects.

Elements in the Press Conference Format

What should the PC itself include? Once the editors begin to arrive at the meeting room, what happens?

Each PC has its own individual flavor and characteristics, but all PC's include certain essential, generic elements. In the usual sequence of occurrence, these are:

• Distribution of press kits and nametags. As each editor arrives, hand him a kit and tag and have him sign a guest book. If you've individualized the kits, take care to correctly match kit with editor.

• Introduction and welcome. This can be performed by the conference director or an executive of the host company. Introduce yourself, thank the editors for coming, and tell them what's going to happen at the PC. Inform them of time, duration, and other details concerning PC agenda items such as the illustrated talks, demonstration, question-and-answer period, lunch, and tours.

In addition, give the editors details on locations of telephones and rest rooms, instructions for calling a cab, overnight accommodations, provision for special photos, and the availability of stock illustrations.

• The story. Give the gist of the story, explaining that it is so important that you have called a press conference. Here is where you ignite the editors' interest and motivate them to pay careful attention.

• Who can use the product or service, and for what purposes. Cover the scope of known uses and suggest possible, untried uses.

• Important features and the benefits that accrue to the user because of these features. Always translate a feature — e.g., standardized threads — into a benefit — e.g., interchangeability worldwide. Never assume that editors translate features into benefits automatically.

- Significance of the development. What impact will it have on the activity or industry? Stick to known facts.
- What's unique about the development. If it's the first of its kind in a significant way, say so.
- How this development compares with similar products or services. What makes this one different and better, and under which circumstances?
- Description of the design and construction, in detail.
- Description of operation or function. Show and tell how it works and what it accomplishes.
- Function in the overall system, machine, or plant. Where does the development fit into the larger scheme?
- Advantages and limitations. You'll increase the credibility and usefulness of your story if you point out where and when *not* to use the development.
- Demonstration or audiovisual. Show the actual product or service in use. Never substitute a fake for the real product. If a demonstration is impractical — for example, because of the PC's location — show a movie, videotape, or slide/tape presentation, or present a well-illustrated talk on actual and perhaps theoretical applications.

A word of caution: When proposing theoretical applications, give your reasons for believing that the product or service would actually work in the given circumstances. Too much blue-sky theorizing without substantiation will generate skepticism in the editors.

- Question-and-answer period. Allow plenty of time for this period. Make sure your company engineers, managers, and other experts are accessible to the editors not only during the question-and-answer period but also during lunch, after the tour, etc.

Just in case the editors turn out to be deadheads and don't ask enough questions to fill a decent question-and-answer period, prepare some "oft-asked questions from prospects," and be ready to jump in with them.

- "Free-for-all." This is the time for the editors to see the product up close, touch it, perhaps operate it. In addition, this is when the editors can ask questions one-on-one with the experts, shoot or request special photos, and request additional drawings, charts, formulas, literature, and the like.

• The closing — the time at which the PC officially ends. Make it clear to the editors that although the PC is over, they are welcome to remain for a specified time if they wish. Once you have an editor interested, discussing the development and asking pertinent questions, don't shoo him off.

Notice that the anatomy of a PC is much like that of a sales meeting. Ideally, however, the PC should more nearly resemble a class conducted by a skillful teacher of physics. The PC may include plenty of "Look at this!" and "Did you hear that?" and other expressions of legitimate wonder, but no exaggerations, no undocumented superlatives, no baloney.

Theatrics, yes; puffery, no.

Lunch and Refreshments

Editors are people, like you. They appreciate not only big stories, skillful demonstrations, and a certain amount of exclusive information but also good food and drink. You can build editors' good will by feeding and watering them, but a few words of caution:

• If you start the PC period with a breakfast, keep it short, simple and not too greasy.

• Lunch after a PC is great, but never precede the PC with a long, heavy lunch. Nap time.

• Save the alcohol for after the PC. You want to be communicating with alert editors.

• Try to serve something original, even if it's only a different kind of dessert. Because they travel a good deal and eat many commercial meals on the road, editors become gourmets of a sort. They appreciate originality.

• Stick to your schedule. Start and stop the meals on time.

Rehearsals

The best way to work the bugs out of a PC and ensure that it will go smoothly is to rehearse all phases several times. Have each speaker give his illustrated talk in front of a small audience, using his actual slides, charts, or other aids. If possible, conduct the final rehearsal in the room where the PC will be conducted.

Demonstrations in particular require careful rehearsal. Watch for good coordination between the demonstrator's actions and the spoken commentary. "Dead spaces" should be broken up with commentary.

Showing a movie, tape, or other audiovisual material? Run through it three times exactly as you intend to present it. Include such actions as stringing extension cords, drawing shades, and dimming lights. Check coordination between the speaker(s), projector operator, and light attendant.

Taking the group on a short trip to another site? Check out the vehicle(s) and route and note how long the trip takes. Allow for boarding time and possible delays in traffic at railroad crossings and so on.

Planning for Emergencies

The best way to prevent emergencies and foul-ups in your PC is to rehearse adequately and triple-check all the details. Regardless of how much care you take, however, there are so many phases and details in a PC that your chances of putting on a flawless production are slim.

Assume that hitches will develop. Prepare yourself and your presenters to react quickly and, if possible, coolly. Look for situations in which problems could develop; anticipate them, and plan and rehearse emergency measures. For instance:

• What if one of your speakers takes his script and tray of slides home with him to rehearse, and on the day of the PC he arrives sans script or slides? He lives 30 miles away; there isn't time enough for him to race back home. What to do?

Answer: Direct your material logistics manager to keep duplicates of scripts and slide sets in his possession. Always make at least one dupe set of slides.

• Your new product is, say, a piece of electronic apparatus. In the middle of the demo, the equipment pops, sizzles, smokes, and quits. How do you handle this one?

Answer: Have a duplicate piece of equipment on standby, ready to be hooked up. If that's not practical, be prepared to switch to audiovisual presentation.

- On the night before the PC, one of your key speakers takes ill and can't possibly come to the conference. Well, clutch hitter, what do you do?

Answer: It's a good idea to delegate a stand-in for each key speaker and demonstrator. Make sure each of the stand-ins rehearses at least once.

- What if you've planned a bus tour, but when the time comes to depart, the darned thing won't run?

Answer: Have emergency drivers and their cars, station wagons, or vans ready to jump in.

And so it goes. You can make up your own list of "what if's" and plan contingency measures. Also, make a list of spares such as bulbs for the projector, a standby projection screen (in case the hotel's screen sticks up in the holder), and extra extension cords. Pay particular attention to vital equipment such as projectors, demonstration products and materials, and vehicles.

Visual and Audiovisual Aids

The arts of planning, producing, and using visual and audiovisual aids deserve more space than we have here. Just a few tips:

- Consult with the company training manager and sales manager. They're old hands in the design and use of slides, flipcharts, slide/tape presentations, and other aids.
- Look for basic texts in the field. Check the latest offerings from Eastman Kodak Co., 3M Co., and other makers of projection equipment and film. These companies publish excellent, illustrated manuals that are available either free or at low cost.
- Review not only the scripts prepared by your speakers but also their sketches and other rough art for slides, overhead transparencies, or charts. As you review the roughs, keep in mind that the basic requirements for effective visuals are legibility and simplicity.

Sometimes you may have to deal with engineer-presenters who want to show such things as reproductions of blueprints, complicated tables, or book pages loaded with lines, letters, and numbers. Offer to have an artist take the rough and produce a simpler, more legible, more colorful adaptation.

• At other times you will have to contend with artists who want to run the wording in, for horrible example, dark red reversed out of black. (Don't laugh; I saw it in a national conference, used by a company vice-president.) Reject the idea absolutely. Red on black looks sexy on the flat art, but it defies reading when projected.

• Sentences on a visual aid should be short. A punchy, telegraphic style like that on effective billboards works well. The total number of words and numbers should be small. Photos and drawings should of course be clear, simple, and easy to grasp in a few seconds.

• Remember that there is nothing visually stimulating in words and numbers by themselves. They're abstractions or symbols, and in order to derive meaning from them the viewer must think. Thinking is work, sometimes hard work, especially in a semidarkened room.

Minimize the mental effort the editors must expend. Hold the number of words, numbers, and formulas to a minimum. If a talk requires many such symbols, break up the sequence with visuals consisting of photos, drawings, cartoons, etc. And don't hesitate to change the pace with humor.

The Press Kit

What should you include in a press kit, and what should you omit?

A useful kit will include a copy of the PC agenda, a comprehensive news release, background data sheets, a descriptive printed bulletin or brochure on the development, the company's latest annual report or facilities and capabilities (F&C) brochure, selection of black-and-white photoprints, and perhaps one or two color photos. All this material can be packaged in a jacket or wallet having pockets.

• The news release. I used the term "comprehensive" because if the development is sufficiently important and complex to merit a press conference, telling your story may require quite a few words. Put as much information into the news release as needed to tell the story adequately.

Don't worry about how many sheets of paper you fill. I've seen excellent press-kit releases 10 to 12 pages long. I've also seen poor releases two pages long. The short releases were poor because they didn't tell enough; they forced the editors to dig through literature or make a phone call in order to obtain vital information. Brevity is *not* always a virtue.

• The background data sheets. These give information such as the history behind the development, details of construction and operation, estimated data on markets, performance graphs, and the like.

• Descriptive brochure. This can be the brochure or bulletin your advertising department produced for promotion of the product or service. If this piece contains artwork and sales-talk but no specs, drawings, selection guide, or other useful data, forget it.

No promotional literature available yet? Then perhaps you shouldn't be considering a PC or even a news release. How will your sales and advertising people answer the inquiries?

• Annual report or company facilities & capabilities brochure. Editors like to learn about the companies behind the developments.

• Black-and-white photoprints. Include a selection of overall views and close-ups of interesting details. If a graph or chart helps to tell the story, provide a line print. Major illustrations should be 8" x 10" or 8 1/2" x 11"; others can be 5" x 7" or even 4" x 5". All prints should have borders; these make it easier for the editor to make crop marks and write scaling instructions.

• Color photos. Provided your budget can stand the impact, include one of two 4" x 5" color transparencies in each kit packet. Even if the magazine doesn't run color on its editorial pages, there's always the front cover.

Want to economize? Personalize each kit; include color transparencies only in the kits going to editors of magazines that run editorial color.

Want to really score with the editors? Personalize the kits by giving each editor a different color shot. Let the editors know about this during the introduction to the PC.

• The jacket. Make it attractive but simple. An obviously extravagant jacket may cause the editors to wonder if the story is so flimsy that you need to hype it with expensive artwork, paper, die-cutting, etc.

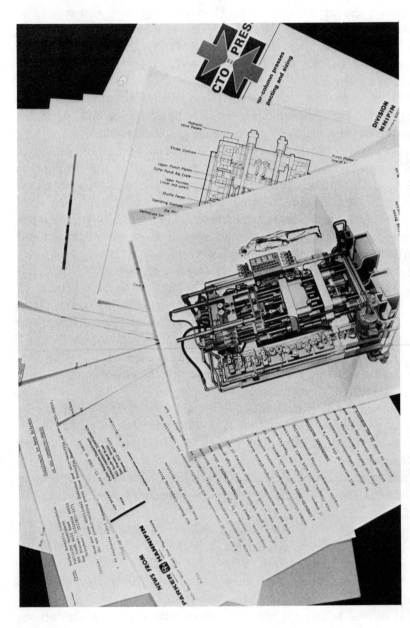

Fig. 13-1. Contents of a typical press kit pertaining to a new product. Included are a comprehensive release and background data write-up, left; continuous-tone and line illustrations, center; and a descriptive brochure, right. In this case, the materials were contained in a folder with a simple, die-cut flap.

So much for what to include in the press kit. Now, what should you omit? Biographies of the chairman, president, CEO, and other bigwigs. Flyers, mailers, and other puff pieces that do not convey useful information. The history of the company since colonial times — unless portions of that history have an important bearing on your story.

Special Photos

If the development is a photogenic product, process, or material, have a competent photographer present during the free-for-all. He can shoot special photos for the editors, to their specs. Provide for photography in color as well as black and white.

Some editors carry cameras and shoot their own photos, because doing so is one sure way to get exclusive shots. These editors will appreciate your thoughtfulness if you make available two or three photo floods with adjustable stands. Specify quartz floods or lamps that put out light at 3200 degrees Kelvin. Type B film is balanced for this color temperature.

If neither of these options seems practical or necessary, at least offer to have special photos shot for individual editors. Every editor wants to be able to run something different from what will appear in other periodicals, particularly the competitors'.

Plant Tours

Say you're conducting a PC at your company plant site. Should you schedule a plant tour as part of the affair?

If there's something in the plant or one of its laboratories that's either vital or highly pertinent to the story, yes. Otherwise, no.

I've seen situations in which the product or method did not lend itself to demonstration in a conference room. In some cases the product was too large; in another case, the new process (welding) required protective shielding and bulky support equipment. Following the illustrated talks in the conference room, editors and presenters trooped through the plant to a lab or shop where the new equipment was set up for test, debugging, and demonstration.

Usually, though, a tour through the plant reveals little information of value in a new-development story. Unless you have a specific, information-yielding function in the plant — such as a demo of a product or its application — it's better to forget the tour.

On the other hand, keep in mind that a certain small percentage of editors like to take plant tours even though they may not yield information for the story of the day. These editors want to pick up general information, specific odds and ends for other stories, or clues to application or "how-to" articles. For the sake of this minority, you could offer a plant tour as an option, to be held after the PC proper. If you decide to do so, inform the editors about it in your letter of invitation and in the introduction to the PC. Mention the starting time and length of the tour.

A few hints on conducting a plant tour:

- Start and end on time.
- Make sure that you and the demonstrators have rehearsed and prepared for the demo.
- Proceed in a group directly to the demo site at a reasonable pace. Allow time for a few questions en route, but don't dawdle.
- At the demo site, provide for the safety of the editors and make sure that every editor can see and hear the equipment and demonstrators before they begin the demo.

Regional Conferences

One of the options in conducting conferences is the regional or traveling PC. You and/or your agent plus one or two experts, perhaps lugging demonstration equipment with you, take the PC to the editors. You hold the PC at hotels or publishers' conference rooms in cities having concentrations of periodicals important to your markets.

For instance, if your company markets products in the general industrial field, you could schedule regional PC's for the Boston, New York, Philadelphia, Cleveland, and Chicago areas. If you sell into lumber and mining, perhaps you would add San Francisco — and so on. It's a matter of finding the locations of the key periodicals in your field and then deciding where you want to go and how much you can afford to spend on the tour.

The regional PC has some decidedly good and bad points. On the plus side, the tour enables you and the company experts to meet and chat with a large number of editors, probably many more than you could attract to a one-time, one-location PC. Provided you have a solid story to tell, the large number of contacts could yield sizable stacks of clippings and inquiries.

On the minus side, however, the regional PC suffers from these characteristics:

- High total cost.
- Large expenditure of time.
- Limited opportunities for demonstrations. How many product demo units could be packed and shipped in, say, a large trunk? Of course there's always the possibility of a working scale model, but good models cost dearly and are not "the real thing."
- Logistics problems. On a regional PC tour, you need to tote and keep track of personal luggage plus press kits, extra literature, projector, and slides, film, or tapes. And then there's the demo unit or working scale model with its cords, plugs, hoses, etc.

Does that rule out the regional PC? No, this option is still quite useful for initial get-acquainted meetings between editors and, for instance, a new marketing director or general manager. The regional PC also works well for stories that don't require a demonstration.

Make certain, though, that you have the basic requirement for a PC: an important story to tell.

PC's and Trade Shows

Holding a PC at a trade show offers advantages. Many editors will be attending and covering the show, and you may be able to pull a high percentage of them. Further, you may be setting up new equipment for the show anyway; you can demonstrate the new line for the editors by using the show model.

A few pointers on PC's at trade shows:

- Serve a breakfast or lunch in connection with the PC. Editors appreciate good meals at trade shows, where the ho-hum concession food, crowded cafeterias, and high prices often make meals a chore.

• If you're going to use equipment from the show for demonstration to the editors, here's a sequence that works well: First, breakfast; second, illustrated talks by experts; and third, demonstration in the exhibit hall.

• If possible, arrange to hold the demo early in the day, before the regular show attendees start arriving.

• Be aware that at major, national trade shows and conferences you may have to compete for editors' time. Make certain that you truly have a worthwhile story to tell before going too deep into plans, announcements, and expenses for a press conference.

If another exhibitor has a major story to tell and schedules a PC for the same hour as you do, most editors may choose to attend the other fellow's PC. Then, for lack of editors' interest, you may have to cancel your PC. The results: egg on your face and perhaps some needless waste of funds.

I recall one such incident at a big exposition and conference in Detroit. Three manufacturers, all aggressive in seeking editorial exposure, scheduled PC's for 7:15 AM on the same day, in different meeting rooms. Each offered breakfast, a press kit, "a chance to meet our executives," and other mild incentives. Only one of the three companies stated in their invitations, however, that it would make an announcement of major significance at the PC.

At least the other two companies were candid in not claiming to have big stories. One of these two noted that attending editors would be able to choose between "tomato juice or Bloody Marys, with or without Tabasco sauce." For lack of a story, the company offered tomato juice, vodka, and Tabasco.

Understandably, the company with the big story won out. Most editors must have chosen the PC despite the allure of the red beverages, because a week before PC day, the other two companies called the invited editors and told them that their respective PC's had been canceled.

As far as press relations are concerned, no harm was done. In fact, I'm sure that some editors found relief in the fact that they wouldn't need to arise before sunup to attend PC's that would make much ado about nothing. Still, a lot of planning, writing, clerical time, photography, and other expensive effort must have gone down the tube.

How can you avoid the predicament? There's no sure way, but you can take these steps: (1) Schedule a PC only if you have an important story to tell. (2) Stay in touch with friendly editors; ask them to keep you posted on who's calling PC's and what the invitations say. (3) When you draft your invitation, sell the story, not the tomato juice. Give editors a strong reason for attending.

• Before scheduling a PC at a trade show or conference, make sure there isn't another major event in your industry going on during the same week. The second event will draw a certain percentage of editors — perhaps enough to seriously jeopardize the success of your proposed PC.

Displays and Literature

Editors need and want to know more about your company, its products, and its expertise than what you present in the new-development story. Don't fatten the press kit with a lot of background miscellany, however; instead, use tables at the rear of the PC room for material such as the following:

• Blowup photos of product application (case history) photos, with complete captions.
• General company literature such as your facilities and capabilities brochure and a condensed general product catalog.
• An assortment of case-history bulletins.

The application photos and bulletins may trigger requests for case-history releases. Your general literature will not go to waste, for editors maintain reference files on companies and their products.

Your Press Conference Checklist

At this point, you have enough information to begin developing a PC checklist for your own company or clients. The list could include sections on:

• Invitations — the initial press relations activities.
• Accommodations and transportation for editors and your presenters, as required.

- Reservations for the PC conference room, furniture, screen, etc. Hotel personnel and professional meeting coordinators can assist you with these details.
- Materials — press kits, nametags, scripts, projection equipment, audiovisuals, demo equipment, and so on.
- Assignments — who's going to do what.
- Schedules — when the participants are supposed to do what. Include rehearsals, tours, and meals. Don't forget deadlines for first drafts of scripts and rough art.
- Scenario for the specific PC, including timetable.
- Follow-up assignments and actions.
- Budget and planned expenditures, including any agency fees.

CONDUCTING THE CONFERENCE

In my experience, success in a press conference comes from, first, having a big story to tell; second, telling it well; and third, careful planning, preparation, and attention to details. If you've planned carefully and rehearsed sufficiently, conducting the conference itself will seem almost anticlimactic, like another rehearsal.

Following are a few hints on conducting the PC. You'll be able to glean additional tips from the next chapter.

1. Distributing the press kits. As each editor arrives, greet him, give him his press kit and nametag, and ask him to sign the guest book.

2. As the first editors arrive, give them something to do besides examining the press kit. Encourage them to look at the new display you've set up, or at the demonstration equipment. Point out the snacks, which have been set out early.

3. Introduction, welcome, and review of PC agenda. Start the talks exactly on time. Encourage each speaker to keep to his rehearsed script and time limit.

4. As the talks proceed, keep tabs on lighting, heat, and ventilation. Also monitor sound volume and legibility of visual aids from the rear of the room.

5. If a hitch develops during a talk — for example, if a slide sticks in the projector — correct the fault promptly. If the fault hasn't been corrected within about five minutes, switch to your backup ("what-if") plan.

6. Same goes for demonstrations.

7. During the question-and-answer period, use a tape recorder or notebook to record the editors' questions. You'll find these records indispensable later in providing information and materials requested by the editors.

8. During the "free-for-all," individual editors will be asking questions and making requests one on one with you, your assistants, and your company engineers and execs. Each of you should make notes on these questions and requests. Don't forget to jot down the name of the editor in each case.

9. End the conference on time.

10. Thank the editors for attending.

FOLLOW-UP

Prompt, careful follow-up after a PC helps to ensure that you gain the most and best editorial exposure possible from a PC. Considering the time, effort, and expense you and your co-workers have put into the PC, why not realize maximum benefit?

• Questions. A few days after the PC, get in touch by phone with each editor who attended. Ask him: Any points to clear up or additional facts needed? Need any more photos, drawings, or other graphic material? Interested in a dramatic photo for the front cover? (If you don't ask, he may not realize you have good photos.)

• The notes. Refer to the notes taken during the PC. Send any information the editor has requested during the PC or since.

• Special photos. Send any special photos or other materials requested during the PC. If an editor asks for information or graphics, and you say you'll send it, the editor expects to receive it. Failing to deliver may turn the editor off and cost you some space.

SUMMARY

To close this chapter, let's look again at the basic requisites for a successful press conference:

1. Have a significant story to tell. The story should be important to the editors, their readers, and the industry as a whole, not just to your sales manager or top brass.

2. In planning and handling details, work from a complete check-list. Get help with the details.

3. Demonstrate the product, method, or service as realistically and dramatically as possible.

4. Schedule the PC with editors' convenience in mind.

5. When inviting editors, give them a good reason for coming.

6. Select presenters for their speaking ability, not merely for their technical expertise.

7. Rehearse, rehearse, REHEARSE!

8. Plan for goofs and emergencies. Cover as many "what-if's" as possible with contingency plans.

9. Keep the visual aids simple and legible.

10. Design your press kit to be complete but not burdened by material extraneous to the story.

11. Provide for special photos.

12. A few days after the conference, follow up by phone, and be prompt in providing the information and graphic materials requested.

Chapter 14

What Editors Say about Conferences

The material in the preceding chapter consists primarily of my own opinions. These stem from over two and a half decades in industrial publicity and magazine editing, and are tempered by information and opinions gleaned over the years from about half a dozen PR professionals and dozens of editors.

We're in a highly subjective area, though. Planning and conducting a press conference (PC) is an art, not a science; the art does not recognize many absolutes. So, in order to check out my own opinions and give you a variety of observations from people who really count, I conducted a small, unscientific mail survey of 18 editors of industrial periodicals. These included major new-product tabloids as well as magazines.

As with the two other surveys reported (Chapters 4 and 9), I gave the editors the option of remaining anonymous. Most of the editors polled for this survey took the option. Many replies quoted in this chapter therefore bear no attribution.

Following are the survey questions with quoted or tabulated answers. Some replies were not worth quoting and were omitted; you won't find 18 replies to each essay-type question. The comments in parentheses are mine.

1. When is a press conference more useful to you than a news release with one or more illustrations?

"Always. However, I prefer one-on-one visits by company personnel at our offices. More of our staff can attend, and we can ask specific questions without our competitors present."

"*FDM (Furniture Design & Manufacturing)* prefers not to participate in press conferences at all. Our industry is highly competitive, with three out of the five magazines very strong competitors. We have all found press conferences to be restrictive and usually uninformative.

"I prefer to be contacted with a story idea, for our follow-through, on an exclusive basis. A press conference usually results in none of the magazines featuring the material, because we all demand exclusives.

"It is best to offer the story to one magazine — otherwise the story usually ends up as a small news item." — Carol Carman, *FDM.*

(If you sell into the furniture design and manufacturing market, you certainly ought to know about Ms. Carman's preferences, and those of other editors in the field. Her remarks illustrate the point I made in Chapter 13: ". . .consider the personalities, competitive alignments, and special requirements of the periodicals serving your field." It could be that for your company a PC would in some cases be a complete waste.)

"When there are people available to answer questions after the basic announcement." — John Kirkley, *Datamation.*

"When the subject is issue-related, and the issue is controversial or complex." — Peter J. Sheridan, *Occupational Hazards.*

"When equipment is available for demonstration."

"When the product is technologically complex — requires Q&A session." — C.W. Beardsley, *Compressed Air.*

"When the news release is relatively non-technical and requires direct input from experts face to face; when the news release is broadcast widely and we want an exclusive story; if the development is worth the trouble; and when the subject is worth more than a news item and preliminary digging is called for." — Frank Yeaple, *Design Engineering.*

"Only when companies introduce MAJOR new products or technical developments."

"When a new principle is involved, when the equipment is complex, or when an actual hands-on demonstration better shows off the product. If several company representatives participate in the press conference, the approach is better than a news release." — Henry J. Holtz, *New Equipment Digest.*

"Seldom — we don't use product stories."

(Study the periodicals before you draft your list of editors to invite.)

"When the product is significant enough to merit treatment as a feature article." — Milt Ellenbogen, *EE Magazine.*

"When the product or system truly is newsworthy — not just an improvement."

"One, complex product requiring a demo to understand significance; two, product that represents a new market thrust or area for the manufacturer; or three, a new technology."

"This depends on the nature of the story. If it's big enough, would rather take own pictures and be able to ask questions, rather than use photos and canned statement that competition would also have." — Jack Trimble, *American Clean Car.*

"Only when I need a specific slant, where I need to ask the questions and shoot the photos."

"Rarely. If at all, it's useful when the info is too complicated or technical to put down on paper. Otherwise, it's just a chance to meet people.

"Note: Many editors of trade mags are required to attend conferences held by big advertisers, whether or not a story exists. We sarcastically call this 'showing the flag.' If I travel and don't get a story, it's a waste of time."

"A press conference is preferable to a news release. . .when it gives editors an opportunity to talk to and question officials of the company and learn things that may not be covered in a press release. If officials aren't going to answer questions — as has happened at some affairs I've attended — then it's a waste of time.

"If a new product is being introduced, editors should have a chance to see, touch and if possible use the product. If everything about a product can be conveyed in a photo and release, then a press conference is superfluous."

2. What kind of story would get you to travel, say, 500 miles to a press conference?

"It would have to be a major announcement by a company that we know was at the forefront of technology. We would also have to be given enough information, on a confidential basis, to prove that the trip was worthwhile."

"Major product announcement. Availability of an individual — an expert of some sort — not normally available for interview." — John Kirkley, *Datamation*.

"One that would mark a major development and be brimming with immediacy for our readers." — Peter J. Sheridan, *Occupational Hazards*.

"None." (That's worth knowing, too.)

"Only if it ties in with an editorial feature already scheduled." — C.W. Beardsley, *Compressed Air*.

"Several types: One, a design breakthrough of some sort, in our readers' direct interests; two, an opportunity to handle the equipment being introduced; three, an opportunity to combine the press conference with other visits in the same region; and four, an opportunity to meet all the key people in the company and to discuss engineering subjects in depth." — Frank Yeaple, *Design Engineering*.

"Hardly any, unless air fare is paid and a major advertiser is involved."

"A revolutionary product development. Bear in mind that I edit a product news magazine that does not use feature articles. If it is a good advertiser, the publisher might say 'go.'" — Henry J. Holtz, *New Equipment Digest*.

"Only if it fell into the theme of an upcoming issue — say, four months or so in the future."

"A breakthrough in a particular area of technology." — Milt Ellenbogen, *EE Magazine*.

"Really a breakthrough. Travel is expensive!"

"Very few. It would have to be a *super big* story and an *exclusive*. Even so, pictures and phone interviews would be almost as good." — Jack Trimble, *American Clean Car*.

"None if it's a general press conference. We prefer one-on-one conferences."

"Major innovation in industry technology."

"A news or feature story that would warrant one page or more of coverage."

"We require exclusive material for feature stories, so a press conference would only produce news items which are usually very small and represent only one of many facets of our editorial."

"A company that wants me to attend a press conference 500 miles away should have something important to say or to show. I'm skeptical of 'get-acquainted' press conferences with people I am already acquainted with. I also resist attending press conferences for a product that has already been publicized elsewhere, or for a speech that has been leaked to the daily newspapers in advance.

"Companies should save their press conference "chits' for truly significant occasions. My magazine gets many more invitations than we can accept; if we just attended a company's press conference two months ago, we'll be reluctant to go and see them again."

3. Which day of the week do you prefer for press conferences?

	Number	%
Monday	1	5.9
Tuesday	8	47.0
Wednesday	6	35.3
Thursday	7	41.2
Friday	1	5.9
Doesn't matter which day	8	47.0

(Some editors checked off more than one answer. Commented Hank Holtz of *New Equipment Digest*: "In town, the day doesn't make much difference. Out of town, midweek is best — Tues., Wed., Thurs. Travel on Monday morning and Friday afternoon is not good. Scheduling so that one-day trips are possible is best. If not possible, arriving late the day before and going home the next day after the PC is next best.")

4. Which week of the month do you prefer?

	Number		%
First	2		11.8
Second	1		5.9
Third	2		11.8
Fourth	2		11.8
Doesn't matter which week	12	or	70.6

(One editor commented, "Depends on my deadline.")

5. What time of day do you prefer for a press conference?

	Number	%
Morning	8	47.0
Noon (lunch) and following	7	41.2
Early afternoon	1	5.9
Late afternoon and cocktails	0	0
Doesn't matter	3	7.6

(One editor commented, "*Never* lunch followed by press conference. Most editors fall asleep." Another exclaimed, "NO!" to "Late afternoon and cocktails.")

6. Do you like to see demonstrations of new products, processes, and techniques?

	Number	%
Yes	12	70.6
Qualified yes	5	29.4
No	0	0

(The comments were:)

"Definitely, but real, not faked. We can tell if the 'product' is an empty box."

"If they're truly new."

"Yes! There's no better way of understanding the. . .subject. Asking questions fills in the voids."

"Yes. This could be the basis for a good how-to story."

"Only when absolutely necessary for understanding."

7. Do you like to be taken on guided plant tours after press conferences? For which kinds of stories?

	Number	%
Yes	5	29.4
Qualified yes	7	41.2
No	5	29.4

(This question elicited the following comments:)

"Not necessary for the stories but of value for background info"

"Yes — for technical stories."

"Spend half a day in user plant, other half in yours."

"No! UGH. BLAH!"

"Yes — always interesting."

"Only if plant tour expands story meat."

"Possibly, if the plant is new or just remodeled, or if it is doing something new and different."

"Rarely."

"Yes — for case histories of company and its developments."

"Only if it shows something really new. Trip down into coal mine was great — no story, but quite an experience."

"I like tours to be optional, and prefer that they not run beyond the scheduled time."

8. Do you like to try a hand at operating new equipment yourself?

	Number	%
Yes	7	41.2
Qualified yes	5	29.4
No	5	29.4

(Comments included:)

"Usually, if I'm capable. Depends on the equipment. Using a gage or calculator is fine, but operating a locomotive — ?"

"Unless you are a technical writer, no. . .if the equipment looks like fun. . .then it might be a good idea."

"Not usually. Exceptions are cars, other vehicles that offer some thrill."

9. What are your pet gripes about press conferences? (Please let it all hang out.)

"One, speakers who read typewritten statements. Two, graphics that are too complicated or small to read, and no copies in press kit. Three, dark room. Four, overly warm room. Five, a lot of adjectives and pats on the back, but no technical facts. Six, speakers who dodge questions. Seven, editors who try to impress by asking asinine questions."

"Rehash of prereleased information. Reading press kit material. Company propaganda rather than substance. Not enough time or wrong people for questioning afterwards. Non-announcements." – John Kirkley, *Datamation.*

"Those featuring much ado about nothing." – Peter J. Sheridan, *Occupational Hazards.*

"Tendency toward too much puff about company."

"Too many speeches. Introduce the product, invite questions, and give out press package; then serve the refreshments without fanfare." – C.W. Beardsley, *Compressed Air.*

"Not new engineering design. Key engineers not available for questions." – Frank Yeaple, *Design Engineering.*

"Officials who make long and boring speeches. Conferences with more than 10 to 15 guests. Conferences where I really have no business being asked in the first place. Waste of my time."

"Poorly organized. People who talk have nothing to say. . . . Should not last over two hours with lunch, or one to one and one-half hours without lunch. Poor handouts. No pictures. No transportation to airport, or arrangements for transportation. Run-of-the-mill product that could be covered in a release." – Henry J. Holtz, *New Equipment Digest.*

"Those [press conferences] where you have to stay overnight; no real news; short notice; location hard to get to; longer than topic justifies; information too basic for trade press editors."

"If lunch is scheduled, a too-long lecture period can make me irritable – and hungry! If a morning press conference, the use of slides with the lights out tends to put me to sleep. Overselling one's products is poor practice – it turns editors off." – Milt Ellenbogen, *EE Magazine.*

"[PC] called for the expressed purpose of spending the budget. No news. Material not applicable to my readers."

"One, people who say 'no comment.' If you invite me to ask you about something, be prepared to answer questions; if not, you create more ill feelings than good PR. Two, say something worthwhile. Too many people try doubletalk; this gets you nothing and creates a negative impression. Three, don't try to make something 'off the record.' Chances are, one guy will still use it, the others will get in trouble, and there is more bad PR."
– Jack Trimble, *American Clean Car.*

"One, too many are simply ego trips for company execs. Two, too long because of trivial info. Three, I don't like general press conferences. Smart editors don't ask smart questions in front of competitors. Why help them with their stories?"

"There are not many [PC's] in my industry, so I don't have any particular gripes."

"Odd times for scheduling. Press conferences with nothing to say, nothing to show."

"I resent traveling to conference when it presents not really new info. Plant openings, for instance, are of little use – could be handled in news release – but they probably give PR agency an excuse to bill the client. Also resent long-winded speeches by company executives who like to spout off personal opinions on politics, economics, labor, religion, etc. – especially happens when townsfolk & local press are present."

". . .when companies apply pressure to get an editor to attend their press conference through the sales reps or the publisher. Of course I like to win 'brownie points' with a company when I attend their conference, but on the other hand I don't like to be punished when I can't attend."

10. What are the most important bits of advice you would offer to a beginner in PR planning his first press conference?

"Plan every item and have backup ready for everything – even if you test the PA system a dozen times on the evening before, it could be stolen during the night."

"Hold it in NY, Chicago or LA. Preferably NY. Make it short. Hold it *only for major announcements.* Call up a few editors from the primary books in the field, and see if they're interested — without leaking the announcement." — John Kirkley, *Datamation.*

"Provide publications ample advance notice." — Peter J. Sheridan, *Occupational Hazards.*

"Keep material brief — reasonably technical — with interesting facts, etc."

"First and foremost, provide something publishable. Make it easy to get there. Limit total time of trip to one evening, one overnight, one day. Show them [the editors] something they've never seen — and tell them ahead of time what it is." Frank Yeaple, *Design Engineering.*

"Call editors first to see if calendar looks clear — even if conference is up to three weeks away."

"Have a good reason for the PC. Fellowship before, but start on time. Keep talks short and to the point. Show visuals in a half-darkened room. Give ample opportunity for questions. Have persons with know-how present. Stop on time. Hand out good press packet, usually before PC starts.

"Location of PC is important. It should be in an easily reached place — city and location of city. Having it in Keokuk, Iowa, will limit attendance unless there is a good reason for having it there — plant dedication, for instance. Editors could go to a couple of PC's a week, but can't afford the time or expense. So we pick out the most important, and the ones we can get to with the least lost time from the office." — Henry J. Holtz, *New Equipment Digest.*

"Make it easy to reach, short, with top-flight technical speakers that know the subject. Forget the lunch — takes too much time."

"One, send personal and warm invitations. Two, follow-up phone calls. Three, a greeting by someone at the press conference. If the other attendees are strangers, there will be at least one person to relate to." — Milt Ellenbogen, *EE Magazine.*

(Milt brings up a good point about warmth and greetings by someone at the door. These editors are guests, human beings, potential friends! Don't treat them as though they were tax collectors.)

"Check audience info [on magazines] in SRDS [Standard Rate and Data Service reference books]. Does client's new product have a market in the magazine's field?"

"Start on time; have all your information there; don't debate with one or two reporters, as others have questions too. Don't call a press conference on 'nothing issues.' The guys who use this. . .will get just as much from a release, and they'll probably run it verbatim anyway." — Jack Trimble, *American Clean Car.*

"Don't. If required, keep it short."

"Avoid scheduling conferences that are advertising puffery."

"Keep it short; offer lots of information plus experts standing by. Make press kit complete with photos."

"Make it interesting. Hold it in a novel, unusual, entertaining place. Keep it short. Make sure you really have news. Impressive handouts or gifts often work; silly throwaways never do. Provide a thorough press kit with *good* photos, diagrams, etc. Either provide goof-proof, free transportation from airport, or do not try; I've seen many conferences fall apart because editors couldn't meet up with rides, buses, etc."

"Probably the worst mistake a beginner in PR planning can make in putting on a press conference is to try and do it on short notice. You've got to give editors adequate notice to allow them to fit the trip into their travel schedule and travel budget. If your elaborate invitation is running late, put in some phone calls advising some of [the editors on] your list that the invitation is on the way.

"Location is also important. Bring your conference as close to as many editors as possible. Chicago and New York are usually the top choices. Don't expect too many editors in the Cleveland area, for example, to hop on a plane for a press conference in Los Angeles or Tulsa."

Chapter 15

Merchandising the Results

Let's assume that you are keeping the company or client communications objectives in mind, producing materials skillfully, and scoring with high frequency in the print media of your choice. The clippings, tear sheets, and sales leads are piling up, and everyone involved seems satisfied. Isn't that enough?

No, there is more that you not only can do but ought to do. The additional efforts outlined in this chapter will pay off by furthering your own career and promoting the welfare of your company or clients.

PROMOTING YOUR PUBLICITY EFFORTS

How do you and your company's or client's management measure the effectiveness of your publicity efforts? One way is through the use of before-and-after awareness, attitude, and brand-preference surveys. A more limited means is the measurement of raw numbers of sales leads generated by publicity.

In addition, you have at your disposal a third means, one that is immediate, tangible, and impressive: the physical evidence, the clippings and tear sheets.

True, the production of X number of column inches of editorial exposure does not prove that you are helping the company to attain its primary marketing communications goals. What clippings and tear sheets can do, however, is to prove that you are skillful in achieving the intermediate goal of gaining editorial exposure.

Your superiors and other influentials will judge you in large part, rightly or wrongly, on the volume of exposure. This is particularly true in cases where company management has not seen fit to implement research that would measure changes in awareness, attitudes, and brand preference.

The physical evidence is important to you. If you want to secure your position and advance, exploit the evidence to the fullest; in other words, merchandise the results of your efforts. Here are some suggestions on how to do it:

Collect and Save All the Evidence

Some periodicals will religiously clip and mail to you the printed news stories and articles which have resulted from your publicity. Most periodicals cannot afford to go to such length, though, because it requires too large an expenditure of clerical time, postage, and materials.

In addition, you will not be able to spot and clip all the editorial pickups of your publicity. Even with assistance, you cannot possibly read every issue of every periodical on your publicity mailing lists.

Use a clipping service. It's the only means for keeping an accurate tally on your pickups and for thorough gathering of the physical evidence. Moreover, a careful perusal of all the pickups will show you who is using your stories, which kinds of photos reproduce best, and which kinds of illustrations the editors in your field prefer.

Reproduce and Distribute Clippings

Periodically — once every two weeks or month, depending on the number of clippings involved — sort through your collected clippings. Group them according to topic: product, catalog, personnel change, and so on.

Then, keeping them grouped, tack the clippings lightly with rubber cement or clear tape onto 8 1/2" x 11" sheets. Type up a standard cover memo. Run off facsimile sets and shotgun or route them to your superiors and to influentials such as the vice-president of marketing, the sales manager, product managers, the dealer or distributor sales manager, and the personnel director.

Fig. 15-1. Pages from a monthly clipping report. Page at far right reproduces a two-thirds page pickup of a case history.

Doing this will help to maintain visibility for yourself and your department, and will strengthen the perception that you're really doing your job.

Reproduce and Distribute Articles

Every time you score with a major printed news report or article — that is, one occupying three-quarters of a page or more — promptly run off facsimiles and distribute them as for your biweekly or monthly clipping reports.

In addition, send copies to any dealers, distributors, or customers involved. They will appreciate your thoughtfulness, and their good word will further your cause.

Maintain a Complete File

After you have made a mailing of a clipping report or article facsimiles, save the originals. Maintain at least a one-year file of all clippings and tear sheets, indexed so that you can readily retrieve what you want. You can put this material to many additional uses, as suggested later in this chapter.

Coordinate with Inquiry Handling

You say your news releases, case histories, and other publicity projects are generating large numbers of sales leads? How many, exactly? How can you and the influentials in the company tell with certainty which leads come from publicity and which from ads, direct mail, trade shows, and other sources?

Get together with the people who run the inquiry-handling system. Make sure it is set up so that you can determine the relative inquiry-producing power of your publicity.

Many industrial periodicals can help you in this task. They supply computer-produced mailing labels keyed to the ad or publicity circle numbers ("bingo card numbers") in the periodical. Someone in your own staff or the inquiry-handling crew can correlate each circle number with the printed item that generated the inquiry. Voila, you have your numerical evidence.

You don't want to stop after learning the numbers. Blow your horn! If you don't, who will?

PROMOTING THE PRODUCT AND THE COMPANY

In the preceding section we looked at ways to further your own career and boost the status of your department by merchandising the results. Now I'll offer ideas on how you can put that same material to good use in promoting the company and its products and services.

Some of the activities suggested here lap over into sales promotion, advertising, and personnel relations. To avoid tactical and political problems, coordinate your activities with the heads of the departments concerned.

News Clippings

Following are ways in which you can make good use of the news clippings in your file:

• Announcements of personnel changes. Take the largest or best-printed clipping and have it laminated between two sheets of clear plastic. Give this to the subject of the story. Since the average person doesn't receive much editorial exposure during his lifetime, your gesture will be appreciated and remembered. Lamination gives the clipping durability and long life.

• Announcements of new products and services. After most of the expected clippings have come in − and remember, sometimes pickups will appear 10 to 12 months after you mailed the release − reproduce the collection of clippings on a 17" x 22" broadside. Add explanatory, promotional copy, with a large main head saying something as, "Product X is BIG NEWS!" Then mail copies to your salespeople and dealers or distributors. Point out how your publicity efforts are assisting them in their sales efforts.

Also make copies of the broadside available in quantity to the salespeople. A broadside is unusual and impressive; it can be used as a poster, mailer, or conversation-starter.

Suppose you announced a new product at a press conference. Collect most of the clippings that resulted from the conference and reproduce them in a folder or booklet. Add explanatory copy plus the names and photos of the editors who attended the conference. The message: "Product X is real news! It drew 14 editors, got 22 mentions . . .," etc.

• Annual reports. Your company makes annual reports to stockholders, analysts, and employees on the company's financial condition, growth, changes, successes, and so forth. Similarly, you can make a report on your publicity activities during the year. Using the clips from your file, report on the number of stories reported, number of pickups, total inquiries generated, and total column inches. You can break out subtotals for individual story topics or products within each category.

Who gets the annual publicity report? Superiors and company influentials, certainly, but also salespeople, dealers, distributors, jobbers and so on. The report lets your field people know that the company is supporting them.

Reprints of Articles and Major News Reports

This category of physical evidence includes reprints made from tear sheets, plus reprints provided by the periodical's printer. Types of stories to be reprinted include major news stories, case-history feature articles, nonexclusive case histories, bylined technical articles, and other material you and company experts generated.

You'll also want to consider reprinting articles that were written by periodical editors and include prominent mention of your company or client. Look especially at installation profiles and roundup articles.

(For details on variations in reprints and how to reprint, see the next section of this chapter).

• Mailers. Reprints of articles and major news stories make excellent mailing pieces. Since they carry the editors' implied endorsements, the messages in reprints — as in the original articles — are more believable than are company-produced sales-promotion pieces. Furthermore, reprints contain information not normally included in promotional literature.

Fig. 15-2. Six variations in cover format for article reprints. Examples at top are, left to right: new photo and type not used in article, magazine cover with photo from article stripped in, and magazine cover as published. Examples at bottom are, left to right: type and line-art only, opening page of article as published, and new art and type on wrapper designed especially for reprint.

Your marketing communications people can use reprints effectively in rifle-shot mailings to many different types of prospects. In addition, you can provide reprints in quantity to dealers, distributors, and company salespeople, accompanied by instructions on why, where, and how to mail the reprints.

• Premiums. If you have made a reprint of a substantial "how-to" article or series, you can announce the reprint as new literature by means of a press release. This is one way to promote the company's expertise and to uncover new prospects.

• Salespeople's talk-pieces. Every now and then a salesperson needs a new, valid excuse for calling on a prospect or dormant customer. A reprint of a topical news story or article provides a good opener. Once the conversation is rolling, the salesperson can switch to other topics of his choice.

• Counter-top giveaways for dealers and distributors. Attractive, informative reprints afford a change of pace from the usual sales literature at the walk-in counters.

• Training manuals. The person who manages training of salespeople, distributors, and/or customers may be able to reduce the production costs of his manuals by using reprints for certain sections. Reprinting technical articles would likely cost less than writing, illustrating, and reprinting new material.

• Sales manuals. Even if a salesperson has gone through a product training seminar, can he remember all the technical data he needs? Used as supplements to brochures, spec sheets, and other informational pieces, reprints provide valuable pointers on topics such as product selection, application, installation, operation, and maintenance.

• Sales kits. Suppose a salesperson has a live prospect for a certain product line and wants to assemble a complete informative kit for him. Reprints provide useful information in a credible, impressive way.

• Application bulletins. Perhaps someone on your company's or client's communications staff wants to initiate a series of product and engineering application bulletins. If you want to avoid the costs of extensive typesetting and photo stripping, simply reprint case-history stories that have run in magazines. To code the bulletins according to product, customer, or industry, strip or paste indexing characters in the upper right corner of the first page.

• Envelope stuffers. Is someone in the company looking for fresh material to stuff into envelopes with other material going to employees, stockholders, distributors, or customers? Consider using reprints of timely, interesting case-history articles or news stories.

• A company-produced technical book. Plan your feature-article program with a book in mind, making certain to reserve book rights. After the last in the series has been published in a magazine, collect the articles and publish them as a bound book.

Let's say that the company makes laser scanners for industrial bar codes. You and the marketing director, chief engineer, and product manager could plan a three-year series of articles that would cover most or all major aspects of scanner technology. Article topics could include: introduction to the scanner, common variations, construction and operation, basics of bar codes, how to select codes and scanners, common peripherals, system software, basics of system planning, how to select a system supplier, and three or four representative case histories.

At the end of the three-year period, you would have the makings of a book that you could offer for sale, give away as a deluxe premium, and use as a training manual.

• The annual publicity report. Don't forget to promote yourself and your department. Reprints of all articles published during the year should be included in the annual report on your successes.

Reprints of House-Organ Material

Chances are that if you produce publicity you also play a role in producing one or more house organs for your company or client. Perhaps you edit these periodicals or write material for them.

Certain kinds of material are generated specifically for a house organ but are not offered to other periodicals. Examples include dealer success stories, executive profiles, and articles on new production equipment. Another example is the short case history or user report heavy in sales-talk and testimonials.

Regardless of any other uses to which it may be put, such house-organ material does not fall under the definition of "publicity," strictly speaking. I'm digressing here a bit from the general subject of publicity because we're on the topic of reprints, and there are many kinds of house-organ stories you can reprint and put to good use. You can employ the same procedures as for reprints of material that has appeared in industrial magazines.

Following is a list of some kinds of house-organ material you can reprint and merchandise. After each item are suggestions for uses of the reprints.

You will notice that not all the items and suggested uses pertain strictly to "marketing" — that is, if you restrict the term narrowly. I'm taking liberties in this instance because the term marketing can be quite broad; it can include certain aspects of public relations. Any experienced salesperson will affirm that his work becomes easier when the company he represents puts time, effort, and money into creating company visibility and good will toward the company.

The list:

• Profiles and success stories on dealers, distributors, wholesalers, and jobbers. Offer reprints to these organizations for use in their own promotion and public relations programs.

• Profiles of new company managers and executives. Mail reprints to civic leaders, lending institutions, and other individuals and organizations.

• Interviews with company executives on timely topics such as the state of the economy or the economy's impact on the company's industry. Local government and industrial leaders would be likely targets for reprints. Also consider the business editors of local newspapers and the announcers who conduct business-news programs on local radio and TV stations.

• Forecasts by company experts on the company's industry or the fields the company serves. Could the sales department use some fresh, different envelope-stuffers?

• Technical articles, case histories, and product news stories prepared exclusively for a house organ. Consider the possible uses of reprints in training manuals, sales manuals, and sales kits.

• Stories on new plants, plant expansions, new laboratories, new product equipment, improved office systems. Keep in mind that most of the companies that provided equipment, engineering, or materials for these in-company developments have publicity programs and house organs. Then, too, in some instances, reprints will make effective sales promotion pieces.

• Reports on improvements in test or quality-control procedures. Everyone in industry is concerned about quality. That particularly includes customer companies that have initiated or tightened their product-acceptance programs.

• News stories on company-sponsored donations, awards, grants, scholarships, and the like. Most people would rather do business with "good citizens" than with skinflints. Spread the word.

• The story behind the story: how a new material was discovered or a new product invented. Make a mailing of reprints to technical societies, technical periodicals, and the deans of engineering colleges. (Recruitment of topflight sales trainees comes under "marketing," doesn't it?)

• Stories on how the company's products are made, tested, packaged, etc. Stockholders know precious little about the company but would probably like to know more. Try using an attractive reprint as a stuffer to go along with the quarterly financial report.

You'll be able to come up with other ideas for the reprinting and effective use of house-organ material. Recycling this material stretches the return on investment in research, writing, photography, art, and typesetting. In addition, reprinting and merchandising house-organ material enables you to easily, inexpensively, and selectively enlarge your audiences beyond the confines of the house-organ mailing lists.

Counter Cards

Much of the point-of-purchase (P-O-P) material provided by industrial manufacturers is strictly sales-talk. Displays, posters, counter cards: these and other P-O-P materials typically tout product features and shout, "Buy me!"

Savvy dealers and distributors know, however, that at times subtlety and understatement provide useful, effective counterpoints to blatant sales-talk. Many salespeople also know the value of name-dropping.

The publicity counter card offers its message in a subtle, understated way and creates the perception that the message is endorsed by a major publication. Available from some magazine publishers and from specialty laminators, the counter card consists of tear sheets of a news story or article mounted on Masonite or heavy artboard. The board has an easel attachment on the back, permitting the unit to stand on top of a counter or cabinet. Plastic lamination protects the tear sheets and prolongs the unit's life.

The standard-sized counter cards accommodate one or two 8 1/2" x 11" pages. Larger cards that carry four pages or two spreads are also available.

If the use of counter cards fits into the company's marketing scheme, consider the potential benefits in mounting and displaying news stories, case histories, how-to articles, and photo features of one page or more.

As a rule, material used on counter cards should be heavy on graphics and easy to read. One of the page-size elements in the display can be the front cover of the magazine issue. If the cover illustration pertains to the news story or article being reprinted, so much the better.

In cases where you are displaying two or four pages of editorial material, you may want to add large type saying, "From the pages of Magazine A" and the issue date.

When you provide a counter card to a sales organization, also provide reprints of the material mounted on the card. The organization's manager of inside sales can place these on the counter next to the card. Some of the walk-in customers who find the mounted material interesting will pick up reprints and take them along.

TIPS ON REPRINTING

Obtaining reprints of articles and major news stories may seem simple at first glance, but the procedure includes some pitfalls and choices between many options. You can conduct a more efficient reprint program and avoid waste if you are at least aware of these pitfalls and options.

Determining Quantity

I've done it myself, and I've seen others do it: ordering too many reprints because the large quantity makes possible a low cost per copy. Once the initial interest and activity have died down, hundreds and perhaps thousands of reprints sit on the literature shelves, gathering dust. Eventually someone tosses them out. As a result, one of the more notable effects of the reprint project turns out to be waste.

How can you avoid this pitfall? I think the first and most important step is to plan the uses of the reprints carefully before you determine quantity. For example, you and the others involved in the project may decide that you want to:

1. Make a mailing of a reprint and cover letter to 650 customers and prospects. The list consists of buying influences in large companies – people to whom the company's own salespeople sell directly.

2. Bulk-ship 2000 copies to distributors. The quantity going to a given distributor is determined by the size of his mailing list.

3. Include one copy in each of 500 new training manuals being compiled.

4. Pass out 200 copies at an upcoming trade show.

5. Stock 500 copies for insertion in salespeople's kits and for miscellaneous uses.

There you stop, at a total quantity of 3850. You have covered the miscellaneous category with 500 copies, but you haven't gone overboard. The company won't be paying for thousands of reprints that merely take up space and gather dust.

Choosing the Process

Cheapest certainly is not always best, but you need to weigh total cost and cost per copy against budget limitations, the uses to which you'll put the reprints, and the effects they are supposed to achieve.

If the article ran in full color; if the topic of the reprinted article is of major importance in the company's marketing program; if the topic involves big-ticket equipment or systems; if the audiences for mailings have grown used to seeing full-color brochures and ads from the company – then colorful reproduction is likely the way to go. Here cheap, one-color printing may convey the message, "I'm not very important," and may actually work against the marketing communications goals.

On the other hand, suppose the chief uses for the reprints will be insertion in training manuals and salespeople's information kits. In this case, a good grade of one-color reproduction may suffice.

Of course, if the article initially appeared in only one or two colors, the choice has been partially made for you. Even here, though, the options include restripping the half-tones versus copy-dotting; restripping the art for the second color versus straight, one-color copying; adding type or art to dress up the reprint; and other possibilities.

Talk it over with the marketing director and the managers of sales and advertising before deciding on the printing process.

Choosing the Printer

If you plan to copy and print the job in one color only, and if the printing run will be small, you can probably save money by having an in-house printer or local commercial shop handle the job. But if you want a high-grade multicolor reprint that's faithful to the original as it appeared in the magazine, then you'll find it pays to at least ask for a quote from the magazine printer. This is particularly true in those instances where the reprint quantity is relatively small.

Like your local commercial printers, the magazine printer can add art for the front cover or back cover, make changes or additions in the type, run gatefolds, and so on. Once you have decided on the content, process, and quantity for the reprint, make up one or more dummies and ask for quotes from the magazine printer and from one or more local printers.

If the quoted prices are about the same, select the magazine printer. For one thing, he has already shot and stripped most or all of the negatives. For another, he has already run the job once (for the magazine), so he knows where he must make adjustments in ink coverage to achieve good results.

Obtaining Permission to Reprint

The publisher of the magazine that prints an article or news story owns the copyright to the material, or at least to the serial rights.

Generally speaking, once the material has been published in a magazine, only the publisher can grant or deny permission to reprint.

There are many subtleties in this area of copyright, however, including differences between North American and other serial rights, book rights, translation rights, and other rights.

Here's a rule of thumb:

If you plan to reprint an article or news story for consumption inside the company only — for example, in training manuals or salespeople's information kits — usually you don't need to bother asking permission to reprint. Should you feel nervous about it, call the publisher.

On the other hand, if you plan to mail the reprints to customers and prospects, make bulk shipments to dealers or distributors, or hand out copies at a trade show — in other words, if you plan to disseminate the reprint widely outside the company — then assume that written permission to reprint is required.

To obtain permission, write a letter to the magazine publisher. Indicate the planned quantity and uses for the reprint, and ask the publisher to specify the wording in the credit line.

A typical credit line goes like this: "Reprinted from the (month, year) issue of (name of magazine). Copyright (year) by (name of publishing company)." The credit line must appear on the first, second, or last page of the reprint. The type need not be large, but it must be clearly legible. Eight-point type is a size frequently specified.

Choosing the Format

Even though an article may appear staid in the magazine, you and your art director have plently of room for originality in designing the reprint. Many reprints have in fact been lifted from graphic dullness through the application of tasteful art direction.

The photos in this chapter show you a few of the myriad options open to you in designing reprints. We don't have room here to list all the generic types, but keep these in mind:

• Using magazine cover as reprint cover, with or without modifications.

- Using special, attractive photo or drawing as cover illustration. Combine with name of magazine.
- Using type alone on reprint cover. (Be careful with this one; keep it simple and tasteful.)
- Using photos, type, and company logotype on back of reprint.
- If material occupied an even number of pages in the magazine, running straight print. Add credit line, change page numbers.
- If article ran in one color, adding one or more colors.

And so on. Ask the magazines to send samples of reprints, huddle with the art director, and use your imaginations — within the bounds of the objectives and the budget.

Choosing Paper Stock

I have witnessed the murder of several articles. They were well printed in the magazine, but when ordering reprints the publicist turned the art director and/or printer loose. Like many art directors and printers, the people involved in these incidents had little regard for the legibility of the type and photos. Although the articles originally ran on a decent grade of white stock, the reprints were run on rough, antique-finish stock that virtually destroyed the legibility of the halftones, or on heavily tinted or screened stock that reduced the type to an unintelligible gray mass.

The saddest part of these woeful tales is that the publicists, sales managers, and ad managers involved didn't know any better. They let the art director or printer hold sway. Nobody knew the difference — except the recipients of the reprints. These people didn't get the whole message they should have received. I'm sure that in many cases the reprints were simply tossed unread into the round file.

Choice of paper is extremely important. Don't leave the choice to your art director or printer, regardless of how highly you regard their opinions. The murder they commit may be only third degree, but it's murder nonetheless.

Insist on review and approval of the paper stock. Make sure that it is smooth enough for faithful reproduction of photos and light enough in tint to allow easy reading. Beware of rough finishes and heavy tints in the paper itself. And don't allow the art director to injure or kill legibility by laying heavy ink screens or solids over the type areas.

Another factor to consider in stock selection is the end use or combination of uses for the reprint. If it is one 8 1/2" x 11" sheet printed on both sides, and is intended for use as a mailer, then printing on lightweight stock would allow two folds for insertion in a No. 10 business envelope.

If the reprint consists of six or more pages, however, or if you want it to endure as a reference piece, then consider a heavier stock. And if you want to strongly impress the people who will receive the reprints, look into some of the exotic, expensive stocks.

Whatever your choice, maintain legibility as the Number One criterion.

MANAGING THE PROGRAM

At this point you most likely realize that merchandising the results of your publicity efforts can become a sizable subprogram within the overall publicity program. Putting effort into merchandising multiplies the benefits of the initial successes. What's more, effective merchandising advances your cause and that of the publicity department, and helps you to establish strong, useful ties with influentials in marketing, sales, training, advertising, personnel relations, engineering, and general management.

To cap this chapter, here are a few quick, general pointers on managing the merchandising program:

Save the Evidence

Build and maintain complete files of clippings, tear sheets, and reprints. Cross-index the material in the files so that you can retrieve quickly.

Use Your Imagination

Look for ways to employ the evidence in various combinations. Categories may include events (e.g., press conferences and new-product introductions), products, technical topics, and time periods (e.g., month or year).

Budget for Reprints

When planning the publicity budget, include funding for reports and reprints. Remember the costs of artwork and typesetting as well as printing.

Promote the Use of Reprints

Educate the company influentials, and keep them educated, on the value of using reprints. Work closely with managers of marketing, sales, advertising, and sales promotion.

Blow Your Horn!

Don't be too modest about your successes. Watch the folks in advertising, and promote your triumphs as aggressively as they do.

Chapter 16

Fifteen Ways Publicity Can
Help Boost Sales

When you say the words "public relations" to managers in your company or client organizations, what meanings or images do those words trigger?

I think that to most people in industry, the words bring to mind a PR department manned by affable, literate staffers, plus the employee house organ, annual report, open house, bulletin boards, and perhaps a company movie or slide/tape presentation. Additionally, the term likely causes most people in industry to think of "publicity," meaning an occasional press release announcing a new product, catalog, or personnel change.

I've found that many folks, including a large number in ad agencies, say "public relations" when they mean publicity. You may have heard or used the expressions yourself: "Our agency has a PR capability," meaning the agency employs someone who can write a passable press release; or, "Let's do a little PR on this new product," meaning let's write a release, shoot a photo, and mail press packets to the key magazines in the field.

I could be wrong, of course, but I'm convinced that the foregoing describes the prevailing perception in industry of public relations and of publicity, PR's means of communication via mass media. Rare is the person who knows, even to a shallow extent, the power and diversity of publicity. Rarer still is the sales, marketing, or advertising manager who comprehends the many ways in which publicity can be used – in conjunction with advertising, direct mail, trade shows, and other means – to build and maintain sales.

That's why this book. If you get nothing else from these pages, at least get this: *Publicity should be used as a marketing communications tool because, properly employed, publicity can do much to help boost sales.*

Here are the 15 ways promised in the chapter title:

1. Prospect in new, known markets. Assume that one of these two conditions exists:

• The company offers a product that has become well established in certain industries and certain types of applications. The product may be anything: a machine, component, system, material, or method. Now the company wants to expand marketing of the product into other industries and other types of applications. Using some careful research, the company's marketing director has determined fairly accurately the nature and identity of prospects in the new, known markets.

• The company has developed a new product, that is targeted for one or more specific markets. Aside from a few field-test installations of prototypes, the product has not been applied. The ad manager ran some introductory ads, but the marketing director assumes that prospects in the target markets still know little about the new product, how it can be applied, its potential benefits, and so on.

Following are suggestions for actions that you, the publicist, could take. Naturally you would coordinate your planning and other work with the marketing director and the managers of sales, advertising, and sales promotion.

First, study the major periodicals serving the target markets. Do the periodicals give prominent play to new-product developments — for instance, in full-page, feature news reports, or in new-product or "design idea" departments? Do the periodicals use color illustrations, diagrams, graphs?

Plan your news copy and graphics accordingly. Tailor the material to the needs and practices of the periodicals. Prepare exclusive material for each periodical. In drafting the press release, tell how and why the product can be used in the target markets. Early in the release — perhaps in the second paragraph — give details on suggested applications. Use terminology native to the markets.

Then assemble a custom-built press packet for each of the key periodicals. Draft cover letters to go with the packets. In each letter, let the editor know that he is receiving a special, customized set of materials, and offer to provide additional information and graphics.

If the new product represents a major development for the company and lends itself well to demonstration, consider the possible benefits versus costs of a press conference.

So much for the news side of the effort. Now consider the feature side: the possible uses of case histories and other types of articles.

Look into the story value in the field-test installations and the first successful, normal application. Choose the best of these; then perform the following actions in the sequence indicated:

Call the editor of the Number One periodical serving the most important target market. Tell him about the terrific story out there, and offer him an exclusive if he or one of his staffers will cover the story and run it as a feature.

If he bites, you'll get feature-article exposure at little or no expense. The editor may request that your company or client provide photo coverage, but you would probably want that anyway.

Incidentally, you are more likely to get a "yes" answer to your proposal if you approach the editor of a magazine in which the company advertises regularly. Editors tend to favor advertisers.

If the first editor says "no," approach the editor of the Number Two periodical. If you initially get a "no" here also, then offer to prepare a feature-length case history article, complete with photos and other graphics, exclusively for the second periodical.

Keep calling, querying, and bargaining. Eventually you will land a feature case history. When the article appears in print, ring bells and blow whistles, but don't stop there. Urge the company ad manager to order reprints of the article and use them in a direct-mail campaign aimed at prospects in the target market.

I've employed this technique successfully myself, and have seen a number of companies do likewise. In one instance, a builder of industrial robots had engineered the company's first packaging application. A small electric robot was being used to pick plastic bottles of hand lotion from a conveyor and place them sequentially in the divided compartments of corrugated containers.

Seeing considerable sales potential in this type of application, the robot-builder wanted to reach other companies that might benefit from automation of packaging. So the PR director of the robot-manufacturing company offered a case-history feature article to a leading magazine. They ran the story as a two-pager. Then the robot company ordered reprints and used them in a direct-mail campaign.

In another case, a supplier of automatic storage and retrieval systems (AS/RS) sold a system to a large commercial printing company. It was the AS/RS supplier's first sale into the printing industry.

The supplier called a magazine editor and intrigued him with the story idea. Some months later, one of the magazine's staffers journeyed to the printing company and covered the story. The supplier's photographer, who had visited the printing plant on a previous occasion, provided an assortment of color photos.

After the story appeared as a five-page installation profile, the AS/RS supplier reprinted it as a six-pager with gatefold and used the reprints in a direct-mail campaign directed toward large printing plants throughout North America. Here again was the 1-2-3 combination: get the story published, reprint it, and use the reprints as ammunition in direct mail.

As you know from previous chapters, publication and reprinting of a case-history feature article does not exhaust the potential in the story. Following publication, you can condense the story into a case-history release, select one or two black-and-white illustrations, and shotgun the release with picture to a number of noncompeting vertical magazines.

Finally, let's consider one more option, the use of the "how-to" technical article. Suppose the company has for years marketed a system called the "ABC hot-melt gluing system," used in sealing corrugated containers. After some experimentation, the company's engineers have developed a modification that enables use of the system in assembling products made from paperboard, particleboard, and certain plastics. Now the marketing director wants to go after prospects in the broad, functional field of product assembly.

You may propose a series of case histories, but one problem remains: prospective users don't know how to use the modified system in assembly operations. A solution: write and place a how-to article, perhaps entitled, "How to assemble with the hot-melt gluing system." Note that you use the generic name, not the trade name.

After the article appears, reprint it and use it in direct-mail messages to large prospective users. In addition, ship reprints in bulk to the company's distributors and put reprints to work in training manuals, sales manuals, and sales kits.

2. Prospect in unknown markets. Assume that the company has developed a product — say, a component or material — that theoretically could be used in a broad range of industries and applications. Like so many products, this one was developed originally as a special for one customer and one application, but in recent years the product became sufficiently standardized that it was added to the line of cataloged products.

Now the marketing director wants to push outward with this product. Trouble is, nobody in the company knows where the prospects and applications may lie. How can publicity help?

Draft a press release announcing the availability of the product. Describe its construction and operation; then suggest industries and applications that could benefit from use of the product. In the copy, take care to use generic terms understandable in all industries.

You say you don't like the broad-brush approach? Well, if you can afford the time and expense, select 10 of the largest, most likely markets and tailor a release for each. Use application examples and terminology peculiar to each industry.

Either way, mailing of press releases gives an easy, quick, inexpensive way to "go fishing" for prospects in many unknown markets. You can mail releases not only to horizontal publications but also to dozens of verticals. After seeing the results, the company sales and ad managers can concentrate their dollars in the markets that seem to offer greatest promise.

3. Reach peripheral markets inexpensively. In this situation, the company's marketing people know where the prospects lie, but the advertising budget is limited. The ad manager must concentrate his dollars in a few horizontals. The challenge: to reach many additional vertical markets at low cost.

A solution: conduct a sustained, multifaceted publicity program. Mail new-product, new-literature, and case-history releases to the verticals serving all the markets. From time to time, throw in an exclusive technical article, followed by shotgun-mailing of a condensed version in the form of a how-to technical release.

4. Open doors for salespeople. Suppose the company is introducing a new product. The sales manager wants all company and distributor salespeople to step up their sales calls and push the new product intensively. Doors will open more readily if customers and prospects have read about the product in national periodicals.

Consider, too, that from time to time every salesperson needs a fresh excuse for calling on a customer or prospect. Publicity provides fresh excuses in the form of interesting news items, pertinent case histories, and useful "how-to" articles in the national and regional magazines. To make sure the salespeople have enough ammunition, the sales manager can order reprints.

5. Obtain sales leads. If ever you need a final, last-ditch justification for your publicity function, this is it. The mailing of press releases announcing new products and services can produce more sales leads, at a lower cost per lead, than can any other method. Published case-history releases and feature articles also generate sizable numbers of leads.

6. Establish credibility. Few units of published publicity have the impact of a well-conceived, well-executed ad, brochure, display, or audiovisual presentation. Design, layout, illustrations, type selection, copy: skillfully handled, these elements can give the sales message a force that no editorial material can match.

One key element that the sales message often lacks, though, is credibility. Upon encountering a message that overtly attempts to sell, the wary reader, viewer, or listener automatically raises the shield of skepticism. Overcoming that skepticism represents a major challenge to everyone involved in sales and marketing.

Publicity material — whether published as editorial material in periodicals or disseminated by other means — may not have the impact of sales messages, but it does possess the vital element of credibility. Even though generated to help achieve a marketing communications goal, the published news release, case history, or technical article appears in the same format as news stories and articles prepared by the editors.

In fact, except where an article carries a byline from someone outside the magazine staff, the reader usually does not distinguish between material from publicists and material that is staff written. Even in the case of bylined articles, the reader will usually accept the material readily because it appears in editorial format and thus carries the implied endorsement of the editors.

A sustained publicity program establishes, builds, and enhances the company's reputation for disseminating truthful, useful information. By virtue of its believability, publicity lends that quality to the company's sales messages. For these reasons, it behooves the marketing director to support a continuing publicity program centered on the company's products, services, and technologies.

7. Build and maintain a reputation for expertise. What is the perception of people in the marketplace concerning the expertise of your company or client? If you don't know, it would be to your advantage to find out.

I see in each industry two major categories of companies: one, the leaders or experts, and two, the companies that are also participants but are not noted for leadership. It seems to me that companies that are perceived as experts in their fields have at least three common characteristics:

• The company's research, development, application engineering, and field experience generate true expertise. This is something that no amount of sales-talk can successfully fabricate. Even the most skillful sales and advertising people cannot fake company expertise and get away with the fakery for long.

• The company executives, engineers, and managers — in other words, the company experts — give talks and present papers at important conferences and seminars. This activity creates a perception of expertise in the people who attend.

Equally important, the giving of talks and technical papers identifies the presenters as experts to the editors who cover the events. Perceived by the editors as experts, the presenters automatically become experts — sources of facts and opinions for news and feature stories.

• The company seems to receive mention regularly, and more often than other companies, in news stories, case histories, roundup articles, and other editorial material in the industrial press.

If you agree with my observation of these three conditions for perceived expertise, then it follows that the company wanting to establish and build a reputation for expertise should: (1) acquire genuine expertise through R&D, field experience, etc.; (2) see to it that company experts gain exposure for themselves and their company by giving talks and presenting technical papers; and (3) take additional actions that will yield large amounts of high-quality editorial exposure in the periodicals reaching the company's markets.

Our main concern in this book lies with the second and third categories, the giving of talks and papers by company experts and the gaining of editorial exposure.   As a publicist, you can't do much to influence the company's R&D or field activities.   On the other hand, you can do a great deal to influence the frequency and quality of oral presentations by company experts.   And of course, your charter as publicist can and should include the mandate to build the company's reputation for expertise through frequent, well-placed editorial exposure.

Which kinds of exposure?   News stories, certainly, but in particular case histories, installation profiles, and bylined feature articles, plus prominent, frequent mentions and quotes in roundup articles.

I've noticed that in many companies regarded as the leaders in their fields, the management as well as the publicity or public relations managers participate actively in press relations.   The company president, vice-president, chief engineers, marketing director, and others not only keep themselves accessible to editors but also communicate frequently and personally with editors of periodicals serving the company's markets.

In other words, the company experts themselves participate aggressively in press relations.   This may reflect a natural, intuitive bent in the experts toward maintaining good press relations. Whether that's true or not, openness toward and affinity with the press is a desirable attitude, that the publicist can cultivate in company experts.

Some publicists, especially those who are insecure, build walls between editors and the company experts.   "All press contacts are to be made through me and only through me," insist these publicists.

During the time that a newly hired publicist is defining his role and establishing his turf, the wall may be necessary.   Ideally, though, the publicist will set up and promulgate procedures for editorial contacts, commitments, and clearances, and then gradually dismantle the wall. Free interplay between editors and company experts — facilitated, not hindered, by the publicist — results in more and better editorial exposure. And that helps to build the company's reputation for expertise.

8. Build and maintain company visibility. Remember that classic ad from McGraw-Hill? The illustration shows a stern fellow, an executive type, sitting in a chair and saying, "I don't know who you are, I don't know your company," and a litany of other "I don't know's." Finally comes the punchline: "Now, what was it you wanted to sell me?"

The obvious but well-made point is that unless your company has irresistible salespeople, the prospect who never heard of the company, doesn't know its products, and so forth probably won't buy from the company.

The McGraw-Hill ad was directed mainly toward sales managers, marketing directors, and others involved in making major decisions concerning the use of advertising. Though intended to communicate the importance of advertising, the message actually applies to marketing communications in general.

How can your company build and maintain its visibility in the marketplace? Let me count the ways. Ads, yes, plus mailings, trade shows, conference talks, and many other kinds of exposure — including publicity.

Publicity can give the company more exposure, at lower cost per impression, than any other means of communication. Don't believe it? Well, build a concrete example based on reaching, say, two million theoretical prospects. Take out your calculator; pull the Standard Rate and Data Service (SRDS) directory from the bookcase; make a few calls to get quick estimates. Among the estimates, include one for the planning, preparation, and mailing of one press release.

You can argue convincingly about the nature and quality of an impression made by a news item versus that made by an ad, and I wouldn't contest. But if you limit the comparison to quantity and cost per impression, publicity wins.

Use publicity with, not instead of, ads and other communications formats. Keep up a steady stream of product, literature, and case-history releases, mailed not only to the major periodicals but also to the dozens of small vertical and peripheral periodicals where the company can't afford to fritter away precious advertising dollars. Doing so will give the company's visibility a scope and depth unattainable by any other means, and at relatively low cost.

9. Propagate sales literature. Your company or client may be producing the most attractive, informative, persuasive product literature in the industry, but literature sitting on a shelf does nobody any good. In fact, stored literature represents a waste because of shelf space occupied and dollars invested without a return.

Publicity offers an effective, low-cost way to propagate company literature, to put it into the hands of people who make or influence buying decisions. Use the new-literature release to announce new and revised bulletins, catalogs, and brochures. Other material you can propagate by means of press releases are manuals, facilities and capabilities brochures, slide calculators, films, and packaged slide/tape presentations.

Whenever it's practical and not too costly, send a sample of the new material along with the press releases. Many editors keep files of catalogs, calculators, brochures, etc., indexed by company and/or product category. The more an editor refers to your company literature, the better are your chances for mentions and for telephone calls requesting information or opinions from the company experts.

10. Help in recruiting dealers or distributors. Marketing people in industrial manufacturing companies will tell you that recruitment of qualified dealers or distributors is a critical, presistent factor in their marketing programs. Without exception, managers of dealer or distributor sales say they want to sign up "only the best sales organizations." By that they mean organizations that are well financed, carry respectable inventories, train their inside and outside salespeople thoroughly, use promotion and advertising effectively, etc.

The tale has two sides, though. In shopping for product lines to add to their arsenals, capable dealers and distributors look for "only the best manufacturers." And how do sales organizations choose their principals — that is, the manufacturers from whom they buy goods for resale?

Scope and quality of product line, discount policy, availability of stocks, delivery times, technical service, and factory training are major factors considered in the decision. Another is reputation in the marketplace, determined in part by the company's publicity efforts. Still another factor is visibility to the dealer or distributor: how often, how much, and how favorably the manufacturer is mentioned in industrial periodicals.

Like the company's customers and prospects, people who run sales organizations read magazines. They know which manufacturers back up sales efforts with advertising and publicity and which do not. They know that extensive, effective publicity by a manufacturer helps to build not only direct sales by company salespeople but also indirect sales by dealers and distributors.

Your publicity will be read first by the editors, then − hopefully − by the magazines' readers. These include customers and prospects, plus potential sales allies: dealers, distributors, wholesalers, jobbers, and reps. Successful recruitment of the best of these sales organizations depends in part on the scope and quality of the company's publicity program.

11. Support dealer and distributor sales. What are the methods by which dealers, distributors, and other independent sales organizations promote their sales? The primary methods are personal visits and telephone calls by outside and inside salespeople. Many dealers and distributors also put much time, effort, and money into direct-mail promotion. Usually the mailings make use of original material generated by the sales organization, combined with material provided by the organization's principals.

Other methods are regional trade shows, seminars, and Yellow Pages advertising. In some cases, sales organizations also advertise in state, local, or regional periodicals going to people in manufacturing, engineering, and purchasing.

Dealers and distributors look for support from their principals in many forms, including advertising and publicity in national periodicals. News stories, case histories, bylined technical articles − these and other forms of contributed editorials in national periodicals bolster the marketing efforts of the sales outlets. The higher the percentage of company sales made by dealers and distributors, the more important is support in the national media.

The initial appearance of news stories and articles in national periodicals is significant, but publicity can lend further support in the forms of:

- Reprints of case histories, bylined technical articles, and major news stories. Dealers and distributors can effectively put reprints to work as direct-mail pieces, trade-show handouts, training texts, handouts at walk-in counters, and in other ways.
- Modified, "canned" versions of product news releases for use by dealers and distributors in their marketing areas.

Assume, for instance, that you have announced a new model of photoelectric control in a general press release for your company or client. The release may begin with a sentence such as "A new type of waterproof, shockproof photoelectric control device for applications outdoors and in wet, dusty, hazardous installation indoors has been introduced by Brush Electric Co., Edison, N.J."

Your first step would be to mail the general release, accompanied by one or more illustrations, to national and perhaps major regional periodicals. You may also put the story and illustrations to work in the form of house-organ material and an initial new-product announcement bulletin.

Additionally, you could modify the general release for use by the company's dealers and distributors. The beginning of the release may then read as follows: "A new type of waterproof, shockproof photoelectric control device for applications outdoors and in wet, dusty, hazardous installations indoors is now available from (____, ____). Manufactured by Brush Electric Co., Edison, N.J., the device . . . " etc.

You reproduce this modified release, order a quantity of 4" x 5" illustration prints (quantity determined by total needed by participating distributors), and ship one release plus a quantity of prints to each dealer or distributor. Along with these materials you send a short, standardized letter of instruction.

Now let's zero in on one of the distributors — say, the fictional John Doran, marketing vice-president for Intermountain Electric Co., Boise, Idaho. Doran takes the release and retypes it on his company letterhead. In the blank spaces he types, "Intermountain Electric Co., 110 River Street, Boise, Idaho."

Following the instructions in your letter, Doran runs off facsimiles of his release. He assembles packets, each consisting of one release, one illustration print, and one piece of cardboard stuffed into a 6" x 9" manila envelope.

Next, Doran types or runs off labels from his own area publicity mailing list. These are addressed to the business editors of newspapers in his marketing area, plus the editors of local, state, and area periodicals directed toward buying influences in production, engineering, and purchasing. His press packets assembled, Doran makes his own publicity mailing.

I've used this technique myself, frankly with mixed results. On the negative side, the procedure adds to your costs, and some distributors who do not appreciate publicity will toss the materials into the wastebasket. On the positive side, however, those distributors who understand and appreciate publicity will use the materials and achieve good results.

I suggest you try this method with one or two product announcements, limiting your effort to a few sharp distributors. Walk through the procedure step by step with them; if necessary, help them to draft their publicity mailing lists.

After one or two distributors have used the method successfully, compile case-history success stories on their publicity projects and disseminate the stories to other distributors. As you proceed, keep notes for a pamphlet explaining why and how a dealer or distributor can conduct his own area publicity program.

You'll find this type of effort to be challenging and at times frustrating. You may end up dropping certain distributors from the program, but where you help a distributor to achieve success, you will see your company's publicity messages multiplied many times. It's worth a try.

12. Provide product-application ideas to salespeople. Some industrial salespeople — and this includes salespeople working for dealers or distributors as well as for the manufacturer — are highly imaginative. They have a knack for finding new applications for the company's products and services. Even these salespeople suffer blind spots, however; no individual can see all the possibilities.

Then, too, there are some salespeople who plod along in their familiar grooves. As long as the money is coming in and nobody topside is goading them, these reliable but unimaginative workhorses will not bother to seek out new applications.

Your company's or client's publicity program, if it is typical of industrial publicity programs, makes use of three formats that can provide new, useful application ideas for the salespeople. These formats are the case-history release, case-history feature article, and installation profile. The first two are written and disseminated by publicists; installation profiles, while promoted and facilitated by publicists, are written by magazine staffers.

You can help to bring about a free, voluminous flow of application ideas by taking these steps:

• Maintain contact with salespeople employed by the company and its sales outlets. Let the salespeople know that you are interested in obtaining leads to interesting applications.

• Provide incentives to the salespeople to forward story leads to you. Possible incentives include mentions of the salespeople in the stories they initiate, and some form of renumeration.

• Make use of as many of the submitted application ideas as possible. Some leads will develop into stories for national and regional periodicals, but many leads will not have that potential. Adapt the minor stories into house-organ material and application bulletins.

• Disseminate the application ideas in the most practical, economical formats. For major stories, the format may be reprints of the published articles. Minor stories can be published in house organs, application bulletins, and application-idea brochures: indexed, short case histories collected in brochure format.

Regardless of the format-mix you employ, keep a steady stream of application ideas flowing to the salespeople. This facet of your publicity program will do much to broaden the penetration of markets and increase sales volume.

13. Maintain enthusiasm in the sales force. What keeps salespeople enthused? Promotional efforts, sales contests, and tangible awards for meeting and exceeding sales goals are some of the devices often used by sales and marketing managers.

Many other factors affect enthusiasm in the field force, though. One of these additional factors is product innovation. How often does the manufacturer bring out new, imaginative, timely products that will meet an active demand, or can be talked about and readily sold?

Still other factors affecting enthusiasm in the field force are the company's technical leadership through R&D, search for new markets and applications, and participation in trade shows, seminars, and the like.

A vigorous, ongoing publicity program helps, too. The company's aggressiveness and leadership cannot be known intuitively; they must be perceived from tangible evidence. If the salespeople often see news stories and feature articles about company activities in important magazines, and if the home office keeps pumping out fresh, pertinent, useful reprints, then the salespeople will perceive the company's leadership and are more likely to remain "psyched up."

14. Enhance sales kits. Before making a pitch to a customer on a product or product line, the salesperson will often assemble a comprehensive sales kit. The kit typically includes product brochures or bulletins, specification sheets, and price lists.

All this material comes from the manufacturer, and is overtly aimed at selling. Both the manufacturer and the salesperson have an axe to grind; that is, they want to part the buyer from his money, and the buyer knows this.

It helps the sales effort if the salesperson can add to his kit reprints of major news stories, "how-to" articles, or case histories concerning the product. These materials ostensibly come from objective, disinterested third parties — the editors — and assist in building the credibility of the sales message.

15. Aid in recruiting topflight sales trainees. We can't act or form opinions on the basis of facts we don't know. If a bright, ambitious college student knows little or nothing about your company or client organization, he likely won't join it. Conversely, if your publicity has somehow reached him and formed the perception that the company is innovative, aggressive, and expert in its field, then the student may at least consider joining the company.

If the recruitment of high-caliber sales trainees has been a problem for your company, or if recruitment normally receives high priority, you can assist by doing the following:

• Provide reprints of impressive news stories, case histories, installation profiles, and contributed, bylined feature articles to the company recruiters. They will find your publicity materials to be useful supplements to brochures and other materials used in "selling" prospective employees.

- Compile a special mailing list of the editors of magazines published by leading engineering and business administration colleges, particularly those located near company headquarters. Whenever you disseminate releases about major new products or technical developments, use this list.
- Some students know little about the world outside college except what they learn from teachers. Encourage the use of press releases and reprints as informational direct mail to the deans and key instructors in targeted colleges.

Chapter 17

Managing for Economy

In the preceding chapters, we looked at the major formats for product publicity — and suggested ways to get more with each dollar spent for publicity in those formats. In this chapter, I am suggesting some methods by which the publicity manager — whether in a manufacturing company, service company, or agency — can realize greater economy through administrative and management techniques.

1. Build and maintain photo files. Appoint someone a librarian, and have him assist you in building and maintaining complete, up-to-date files of black-and-white photo negatives and reference prints. Using file cards or another convenient method, cross-index the envelopes or file folders by file number, product, and — for application photos — name of customer.

In addition, build similar files of drawings, graphs, charts, retouchings, renderings, and other art that may find additional uses. With large and odd-sized pieces, shoot copy negatives and make prints for the reference file.

A handy addition to the picture library is a set of print books containing reference prints from all the negatives on file. Be sure, though, to stamp "FILE PRINT" or "DO NOT REMOVE" in large letters across the face of each print. This will minimize the borrowing and loss of file prints.

Initially, planning and setting up a picture library is a long, involved, and tedious chore. Once you have the files and procedures established, however, daily maintenance is easy and routine.

Why bother? Because for every one request from an editor for an original article, you'll get many requests for stock photos or artwork to be used in roundup articles, directories, buyers' guides, or other editorial productions. Having a complete, up-to-date, well-indexed picture library will enable you to fill these requests promptly and efficiently. Editors will appreciate your assistance, and as a result of giving it, you'll get more and better editorial exposure. For a small expenditure of time and money, you'll realize a big return.

2. File transparencies, too. Just as you did for black-and-white pictures, build and maintain a file of color transparencies in 35-mm and larger formats. I recommend a separate filing and indexing system for color transparencies for two reasons: 2" x 2" slides must be handled differently from prints and negatives, and the uses of transparencies are somewhat different from those of black and white prints.

With a good collection of transparencies, you'll be able to provide editors with illustrations for their color editorial pages. Once in a while, you'll be invited to submit transparencies for consideration as cover shots. As you probably know, landing a front cover – and then merchandising it fully – can be worth a lot to you and your organization. Then, too, having a library of color slides will enable you to help people in training, sales, employee relations, and other company functions.

Take care, however, to retain the original, master slides. If a slide is to be used for projection only, order duplicates; don't lend the master. If an editor wants an original transparency for reproduction, send the largest-size original in stock, and ask that it be returned after the picture has been published.

As with black and white, the key to effective use of your color transparencies is a well-maintained, well-indexed filing system. It will pay for itself many times over in good will and editorial exposure.

3. Communicate, communicator! The following point was mentioned in preceding chapters, but it is important enough to merit expansion:

Do your best to overcome personal differences and territorial jealousies with regard to the people in training, sales, sales promotion, advertising, and other communications departments. Communicate openly and often with them, watching always for opportunities for cooperative ventures. Any time you can split the costs of field trips, writing, art, etc., with another communicator, you both come out ahead.

Then, too, watch for and actively seek opportunities for co-op ventures with your company's customers, suppliers, dealers, and distributors. You and your company profit, not only in getting more publicity for less, but also in a growth of good will and cementing of relationships between the people involved.

4. Specials outside, routine inside. "Should we buy it outside, or do it ourselves inside? Do we now have the people to do it, or should we hire? And if we hire, what kind of person and talents are we looking for?" If you haven't heard these questions yet, you will eventually. Every company and agency, large or small, faces the problem of "inside vs. outside" at one time or another.

The answers are never simple, because you're dealing not only with dollars-and-cents mathematics but also with personalities, talents and — inevitably — politics.

No set of answers will apply equally to every company or situation. You have to work out the particulars to suit the situation. Nonetheless, at the risk of some oversimplification, I offer these general guidelines for manufacturing and service companies:

Go outside for these publicity services:

• Specialized knowledge, writing, and photography, such as that needed for technical articles, case-history coverage and articles, and complex news releases.

• Editorial contact and placement of articles.

• Selling of article ideas to editors, and also to company officials. Experienced outsiders can often sell where the insider has rough going.

• Compilation of mailing lists for nonstandard press releases.

• Mailing of special releases to nonstandard lists; also, any mailing that requires special handling, such as those involving exclusive color transparencies.

• Mailings of standard releases, if your company doesn't have in-house mailing capabilities.

Staff up to perform these publicity functions inside:

• Simple, standard press releases, including the tasks of research, interviewing, writing, and supervising of reproduction and mailings.

- Compilation and maintenance of standard mailing lists and plates for press releases.
- Establishment, indexing, and maintenance of photo and artwork files.
- Editing, production, and distribution of house organs, application bulletins, and other printed literature closely related to or dependent on the publicity function.
- In-house photography, where volume warrants.

To sum up: Go outside for advanced, specialized knowledge and talent; staff up to handle the simple, routine chores. You'll get better results and save money, too.

5. Work on major cost factors first. Look for ways to economize without sacrificing quality. Begin by determining the major cost factors in each type of activity; then work on those costs.

Examine your case-history activities, for example. What are the major cost factors? Probably the travel and writing; reproduction and mailing are not significant factors here. Can you cut the writing costs, without loss of quality? Not likely, to any extent. What about travel? Yes, you can make sure the people covering your case histories take in more than one story per trip, so you can spread the travel costs.

What about technical and feature articles? Here the major cost factors are research and writing. Where can you save? Well, are you motivating company engineers, technicians, and managers to write articles themselves? Are you looking for co-op ventures with your training people? Do you watch for ways to revamp and get more mileage from existing materials, such as technical papers, manuals, old articles, etc.? These are all valid ways to save.

Finally, your press releases. In this case, the largest costs are usually incurred in the writing, reproduction, and mailing. Are you handling the simple releases internally, or do you automatically job them out? Have you shopped for the best price/quality combination for release printing and quantity photo prints?

What about the mailings? If your company has an in-house mailing capability, do you take full advantage of it, or do you automatically job out mailings to an agency or lettershop?

How much mail-room overhead will you have to pay for out of your publicity budget? Would you come out ahead by using a mailing service for even your standard release mailings? Only a sharp pencil will tell you for sure.

Don't spend a lot of time on minor cost factors in an attempt to save nickels and dimes. Rather, look first at the major cost factors. That's where you can save real money.

6. Plan ahead and brief thoroughly. Before buying outside services for a project, pause. Define your objective, write out a plan of action, and note important details, including:

Complete names, titles, addresses, and phone numbers of people to be contacted and/or interviewed
Who's supposed to do what: make appointments, get clearances, assign photographers, etc.
Key elements of the story
Deadlines

Then, when you talk to your suppliers, brief them thoroughly. Tell them exactly what you want to accomplish and how you want the job handled. Make sure all the details have been transmitted and understood.

Take a little time for planning and briefing before the job gets under way. Doing so will help prevent mixups, call-backs, ruffled tempers, red faces, and muffed assignments. The job will go more quickly and easily, and so cost less.

7. Do you really need a press conference? Before you decide to conduct a press conference, make sure that the development really warrants a conference.

Editors work on tight schedules. Their time is limited and valuable. Calling them to a conference and then feeding them a ho-hum story — or worse yet, a lot of puff — will irritate and alienate them. You'll lose their good will and end up getting less exposure in their periodicals. (See Chapter 14.)

Unless you have a truly big story, do the job by mailing out a press kit and making follow-up calls. If you're sure you have a really big one, though, go ahead and call your conference. You'll get much exposure, good will, and prestige for the money you invest.

It's a matter of economics.

8. Watch for special opportunities. Keep on the alert for special publicity opportunities. Ask your advertising people to pass along publisher's promotional literature, particularly calendars and other pieces that announce upcoming special issues, roundup articles, selection guides, and other major productions.

When you run across an upcoming feature that may involve your company's products, services, or technologies, get in touch with the editor. Volunteer to provide information, photos, drawings, tables, or whatever else he may want.

For a small expenditure of time and money, you'll get valuable exposure in material that may be saved for reference by your customers and prospects.

9. Put one person in charge. Does your company − or if you're in an agency, your client company − have *one* person who's in charge of contact with the press? Or do the editors have to guess whom they should contact, because they've been hearing from so many company individuals at various times?

The problem can grow especially acute in large, diversified companies with many product lines and groups, divisions and manufacturing facilities. Well-meaning product managers may take a fancy to becoming publicists; they call the editors about their own pet projects, and soon the editors lose track of who's doing what in the company.

Do a big favor for yourself, your company, and the editors: Appoint one person as the press-relations manager. Announce that appointment to all the editors on your mailing lists and, equally important, to all managers and staffers within the company. Make it clear that all contacts with editors will be made, or at least initiated, by the press-relations manager.

Centralizing this responsibility will make the job much easier for editors serving your field. They'll need just one name and one phone number to get what they want from your company. As a result, you'll get more calls from editors and more exposure on their pages.

This doesn't mean that only the press-relations manager talks to editors. On the contrary, you should encourage direct communication between editors and company officers, managers, engineers, etc.

Just make certain that all involved understand that the press-relations manager is the appointed go-between, with authority to say yes or no to commitments for articles and expenditures. Doing so will help you to avoid embarrassing conflicts in commitments and excessive strain on your budget.

10. Allow for "targets of opportunity." How do you budget for publicity?   One often-used method is to forecast total expenditures for X number of articles, Y number of case histories, Z number of press releases, plus something for overhead and mechanical expenses.   Or perhaps you budget by product group or division, with special allotments for planned programs and campaigns.

Whatever your method, don't forget to set aside a generous amount for "targets of opportunity."   These are the chances for articles, cover spots, participation in roundups, and other specials that invariably pop up during the course of the year.

There's no way you can foresee or budget specifically for these opportunities, but they're every bit as valuable to you as planned publicity.   Why? Because frequently these unpredictable opportunities give you a chance not only to land some space, but also to help an editor who's in a bind.

It happens at every periodical from time to time: An article must be killed, someone who promised an article didn't deliver, a hole must be plugged, the cover was forgotten till the last minute and so on.

With his clock ticking, the editor calls a reliable source and asks for help.   If that source is you, you'll not only score in terms of space, but you'll also strengthen your ties with the editor.   Imagine your chagrin, though, if you must tell him, "Sorry, we can't help; we didn't budget for that project."

Be sure to earmark some funds for targets of opportunity. True, this practice may look vague and speculative to your accountants, but it's sound economics over the long term.

Chapter 18

Attitudes for Profit

Most of the pointers given in the preceding chapters pertain to techniques as applied to publicity formats and management. To get the most and best editorial exposure from your publicity investment, you need to learn and apply those techniques. Equally important, though, you should learn and cultivate certain attitudes.

In fact, you won't receive all the potential benefits from your learned techniques — nor will you be able to develop new or modified techniques for changing circumstances — unless you have developed the proper attitudes toward publicity.

Your fortunes as a publicist may rise, hopefully, but they could fall, too. PR budgets get cut; advertising budgets are slashed, and companies lose influence with publishers; editors retire; and talented writers turn to raising sheep.

When these things happen, many of the techniques you've learned or developed may prove inapplicable. Then you must develop new techniques to suit the new circumstances. Only with well-ingrained, proper attitudes can you adapt successfully.

Here are some pointers that, in my opinion, show the way to developing profitable attitudes in a publicist:

1. Play it straight. Always be open and honest with editors. Never try to pawn off old material as new, or offer an exclusive on a story to more than one periodical, or try to use advertising money as a lever to place weak, puffy material.

Play it straight, and you'll do well with editors. Try to pull a fast one, though, and you'll be branded, perhaps for life. Editors remember.

2. Strive for excellence. The words sound like a class slogan from grade school, but they're critical to your success in publicity. The task is perhaps more difficult for you than for people in some other fields, because, first, there aren't too many people around who know good publicity from bad, and second, most editors are too polite or busy to tell you when your material is substandard. They simply discard or reject bad material.

Rather than cursing the editors or merely guessing at why you're not getting as much editorial space as you'd like, make an effort to find out what makes good publicity. Read books, take courses, practice, and seek criticism from qualified people on your methods and output. The competition for certain kinds of editorial space is keen. Good material has the best chance of getting printed, so spend time on finding out how to plan, produce, and place good material.

Search out news that is truly news, and feature material that is interesting and useful — to the readers, not to people within your own or your client's company. Always strive for the highest quality in writing, photography, artwork, typing, printing, and so on.

Material that is weak or poorly prepared may get published, for one reason or another, but the odds aren't favorable. Sound, professional editorial material will get published. Make it a habit to send only good material, and your batting average will grow along with your reputation.

3. Treat editors as people. Basically, there are two ways to deal with editors. One is with a cool, impersonal, businesslike manner. One functionary, a publicist, deals with another, an editor. The other way is to develop warm, personal, first-name relationships with the key editors in your field, and to treat them as people rather than as functionaries.

The former method does work, but poorly. Often it is founded in a self-seeking attitude. The publicist wants to take from the editor. "What can you do for me?" is the underlying question. In contrast, the latter method springs from an attitude of service, of giving. "What can we do for you?" the publicist asks the editor. "What do you need or want, and how can we help you?"

Pressure, manipulation, raw technique: these are tools of the self-centered publicist. As I said, they do work, but only to a point, and only for a while. Better to build your publicity efforts on a sincere attitude of service. Give and offer assistance — information, pictures, or whatever — even when no immediate reward is in sight. Hustle when an editor is facing a tight deadline. Pass along tips on possible stories, even though your company or client may not be involved. Keep the editor informed on developments, not only in your company but also in your industry as a whole.

Every once in a while, visit the editors of key magazines at their own offices. Take along outlines for articles, or at least ideas for articles, that you can produce for them as exclusives. The fact that you bothered to travel in order to see them in person will be appreciated and remembered.

In short, extend yourself to help the editor. Cultivating this attitude of service, of helpfulness, will enable you to build warm, close friendships with editors. You'll find your life as a publicist much more rewarding, not only in your personal relationships but also in the quality and quantity of space you receive.

One more point: Don't forget to thank an editor after he has done something good for you, such as publishing one of your articles or using one of your photos on a cover.

4. Think profit, not savings. Much of this book is devoted to methods by which you can gain more editorial exposure for each unit of time, effort, and money you invest in publicity. In part, these methods must be founded on an attitude of thrift.

Like losing weight, though, thrift can be carried too far, to the point at which it works against you. Hasty and careless typing, poor printing, cut-rate writing — these and other so-called budget measures may save pennies short-term, but in the long run they waste your publicity dollars. Here's why:

The primary goal of your publicity activity is to gain as much favorable editorial exposure as you can for you company or client. Achieving a high rate of return — a profit — on your investment depends to a large extent on the quality of your product.

What is "quality" in this context? News that is news, and useful, interesting feature material, to begin with; but beyond that: professional research, interviewing, and writing; clean, crisp typing and printing; eye-stopping photography; high-grade prints; and so on.

Quality costs money. True, smart buying enters the picture, but by and large, in publicity services as elsewhere, you get what you pay for.

The way is clear. Insist on professional services to put into your product. A high-quality product will yield a good return in number of pickups and amount of editorial space. Cut corners, though, and you'll find yourself saving pennies but losing potential dollars' worth of exposure.

Beyond that, learn when to spend a little in order to gain a lot. Pay for periodic critiques of your work by professionals, such as editors or PR pros. If the volume of your publicity warrants it, invest in a clipping service. It's most helpful, not only for measuring your editorial exposure but also for refining your techniques and lists.

To sum up: Save but don't skimp. Think of long-term return on investment rather than of how much money you're not spending.

5. Work with the interest. Each time you expend or authorize time and money for new, original research, interviewing, writing, and illustration for a feature article, you are spending the principal of your budget. You will realize much more value from your budget, however, ir you develop a knack for working with the interest as well. Here's how:

Save article manuscripts, artwork, photos, and research notes. Build files of published articles and a library of pertinent technical papers and reference books. Become familiar with what your company or client has written for training and sales promotion: bulletins, manuals, brochures, and scripts for movies and slide presentations.

Save and scavenge, cross-indexing the material so you can easily retrieve what you want. Then develop the habit of looking for ways to reuse and find new uses for existing material. Update old topics, give them a new slant, refresh them with the latest facts and opinions. Seek ways to combine parts of two or more old articles into a new one. Pick up a topic, turn it sideways or upside down and treat it from a new angle.

Is it redundancy to dust off old topics and reuse them? No, it's simply recognition of the fact that the market for ideas is always new, always changing. Writers and editors may grow blasé as their tenures lengthen, but new readers — and also important, new editors

— are constantly arriving on the scene. What was "old hat" to some five years ago is brand-new to the novices of today.

So start making use of the interest you're earning from the principal — the work already done — and you'll double the return from your article budget.

6. Prune, don't mutilate. Periodically, every publicity director, whether in an agency or client company, receives an order from on high to "cut the publicity budget." When this happens — and it will — it's important that you interpret "cut" to mean prune, not mutilate.

If you've ever cared for trees or shrubs, you know that pruning may be harmful to a plant if the pruner is a hacker. The life of the plant is jeopardized; nobody, including the pruner, likes the results; and the plant takes a long time to recover.

So it is with a publicity budget. Indiscriminate chopping may reduce expenditures, but it also may seriously reduce the program's effectiveness. In extreme cases, this kind of budget cutting may even cause the program's total demise.

It's important, therefore, both to the program and to the jobs of the people involved, that you apply a deft touch when reducing allotments. Here are some tips you may find useful:

- Reduce the quantity of projects but never the quality of the remaining projects. Maintain your high standards of writing, photography, printing, and so on.
- Don't reduce the number of news releases. Every company needs continuing exposure of its name, products, and personnel, and this exposure is best provided by releases.
- Trim the mailing lists, eliminating the names of periodicals with only marginal value to the marketing effort. Check the clipping files; drop listings of periodicals that apparently ought to be valuable but have consistently ignored your releases.
- Reduce the number of case-history articles generated. Produce only those having specific, well-targeted marketing goals. Convert the articles into product application releases that can be shotgunned at low cost.
- Initiate fewer new, original technical articles. Look for ways to reuse existing technical papers, research, and other data at low cost.

Concentrate on short how-to technical pieces you can shotgun to a number of vertical periodicals.

No doubt you'll find other techniques to suit your own set of circumstances. What's important here, though, is not specific technique but the professional pruner's attitude. Prune with an eye toward the program's vitality and effectiveness. The results will benefit not only the publicity effort but also the people involved. In the process, you'll all learn to work smarter, not just harder.

7. Welcome "zero-base." Publicists, sales managers, product managers: all of us become infatuated with our work, our routines, our ways of doing things. Programs grow with wild abandon, the reasons for their existence are forgotten, and we run on for the fun of running.

The proliferation of projects and zestful activities can be fun. Enthusiasm runs high. We glow in the excitement of "doing it" and of seeing all that editorial space we've generated.

Such times are dangerous. All too easily, we lose sight of the why: why we're publicizing, why the program, why our very jobs. Along comes a recession, or a carnivorous accountant, or — good grief! — an advocate of zero-base (ZB) planning, and our whole little world seems in jeopardy. Anxiety haunts us, and in the hallways run rivulets of perspiration.

There's no need for anxiety, though, once you accept the ZB concept. In fact, adopting the attitude behind ZB — that of periodically justifying activities and expenditures — will help you to do a better job.

Perhaps the healthiest concept to hit publicity — and, in fact, the other branches of promotion as well — in many years, zero-base planning will prevent you and your marketing associates from flying ahead blindly and stupidly, inviting cutbacks. ZB will force you to get back to basic analytical and creative procedures, so vital but easily forgotten.

For each program, campaign, and project, including perennial pets such as house organs, you'll have to start with the marketing communications problem (or challenge, or opportunity, depending on how you see things). You'll find yourself and your marketing people sitting down to define the problem, explore the general situation, look at the tools available, etc. — just as the book tells us to do.

After all, isn't that the smart way to operate? ZB gives purpose to everything you do. Before long, you'll find that ZB actually makes your job easier. Everyone involved – marketing executives, product managers, you, and your colleagues – all will function on a sound base of knowledge and justification. All will be fully aware not only of what you're doing but, more important, of why you're doing it.

Annual ZB planning and budgeting refresh that awareness. ZB exercises also provide valuable education in marketing communications for new sales managers and product managers. These people usually arrive full of enthusiasm and knowledge of field-sales techniques, but sadly undertrained in marketing communications. Further, a yearly ZB session gives you a chance to show off your expertise and to impress the people you'll be serving.

So when ZB comes along, don't panic. It's a friend; embrace it, adopt the ZB attitude and make the most of it. You'll become a better publicist.

8. Cooperate. Set out deliberately to establish an attitude of co-operation with your peers in advertising, sales promotion, training, and sales. Open, frequent exchange with these people will broaden your horizons, giving you many times more ideas and opportunities than you could ever realize working alone.

It isn't always easy. In many companies and agencies responsibilities are ill defined, fear is the prime motivator, and politics runs rampant. A climate of anxiety drives people to build walls and become reticent in order to protect their own little enclaves.

Nonetheless it pays you to make an effort to break down the fears and petty jealousies. Try to develop an attitude of bold openness, exchanging ideas freely. You'll receive more than you give, and everyone, including you and your company, will benefit.

9. Sell yourself! Observe the colorful folks in advertising; see how they promote not only their successes but virtually all their activities. Reprints, mailers, award plaques, dinners, presentations, kickoffs, campaign reports – sometimes it seems that as much time and effort (and money?) go into the merchandising as into the advertising itself.

What about you and your publicity programs, campaigns, and projects? Do you tell loud and clear what you're going to do, then do it, and then tell what you've done? Or do you, as do so many publicists, settle for a modest scrapbook of clippings and tear sheets, and perhaps an article reprint now and then, printed on the cheapest paper available?

That's not the way to get ahead. In fact, that's not the way to survive. When budget cuts come, your publicity budget may get the worst of it simply because management doesn't know what you're doing and what publicity has accomplished for the company.

You must become aggressive and develop the attitude of the promoter. Learn to promote habitually not only the company, its products, and its services, but yourself and your programs as well.

Some discretion is needed, of course. Promote obliquely, so as not to appear too self-serving. Resentment by your superiors and jealousy in your peers won't further the cause. See to it that each piece of promotion has an obvious usefulness, a purpose other than your own aggrandizement. Couch the language in cool, objective terms, and shun the personal pronoun "I."

There are many tools you can use to promote your publicity efforts and achievements. Just a few of them are:

• Clearly define the goals, tools, procedures, and timetable for your publicity campaigns. Make sure publicity has an identity separate from, and on the same plane as, advertising, direct mail, and other big-ticket activities.

• Report periodically on news releases, giving numbers of pick-ups, column inches, and inquiries produced. This kind of data always makes a hit with sales and product managers.

• Circulate reprints of case-history and technical articles soon after they appear in print. If you work for a client company, give credit to the agents or freelancers who do the work, of course, but don't forget to make known who initiated and guided the project.

• When you land a front cover, have it mounted as a counter-top display and put it out for all to see. Often the publisher will do the mounting for you.

• About once a year, compile your published case histories into a booklet and make it available widely. Salespeople, dealers, and distributors appreciate receiving tips on where they may apply and sell the company's products and services.

- Reprint technical articles, too. The major ones can stand on their own, perhaps with newly designed covers. Shorter how-to pieces can be collected annually and republished in booklet form.
- At budget time, don't spend all your hours telling people what you're going to do and how much money you want for the coming year. Summarize your achievements from the preceding year, and publicize the summary. This will help you to get what you want and perhaps more.
- Watch for valid opportunities to hold press conferences. They not only yield more space per dollar than do mailed releases and articles but they also enable you to put managers, engineers, and other influentials in starring roles as speakers or panel members. Besides, they'll appreciate the opportunity to converse tête-a-tête with editors. Make sure, though, that you yourself are visible during the preceedings.
- Conduct an annual publicity training seminar for sales managers, product managers, and — depending on the number of people involved — district and field salespeople. Direct the seminar particularly toward the new people. Show and tell what publicity is, what it can and cannot do, what you've done for others, and what you can do for them.

Prepare a take-along kit or booklet that explains what a news release is, for example — how it's produced, where it goes, what it does, how much it costs, and so on.

- Develop close personal ties with many dealers, distributors, and field salespeople. Their comments have a lot of influence on the attitudes and actions of sales, product, and marketing managers.

In your case-history articles, be sure to mention the salespeople and companies involved in solving the case and closing the sale. Mail reprints of case histories and technical articles to dealers and distributors as well as to company people.

When you land a front cover on a magazine, make reproductions available — preferably mounted on counter cards — to all appropriate sales organizations.

Cultivate the folks in the field. Being on the front lines, where the dollars change hands, dealers and distributors appreciate whatever you do for them. Usually they're quite vocal with their appreciation. Their support will aid your cause.

• Conduct periodic PR seminars for your company's dealers and distributors. In these seminars, tell what PR is, how to stage events that merit publicity, how to deal with the press, etc.

Dealers and distributors have many marvelous opportunities for local PR. Help them to plan and build their own PR programs, and they'll reciprocate.

• Capitalize on opportunities to have editors visit your offices. Be seen with them, and introduce them around. Report on your trips to visit and consult with editors. Your closeness to them is an impressive asset. Moreover, their requests for articles carry more weight than do your own unaided requests.

• Just in case the big boys from advertising should start beating up on you, be ready. Have facts and figures available to show how many pages of valuable editorial space you've obtained, how many dollars were spent to get them, and the average cost per page.

That last one is the ace. Ask, "Now, what's the average cost per page for advertising, including preparation and production? . . . OK, for space alone? Have some dollar figures ready just in case your adversary counters with "Yeah, but's" or chokes up.

Then administer the coup de grace. Ask, "How much is a page of editorial space worth, in terms of credibility and information content, compared with a page of advertising? Twice as much? Three, four times as much?"

• Touch base often with the marketing, sales, and product managers who approve your budgets and projects. Keep them posted on your progress and achievements. Remain visible, always projecting yourself in a positive manner.

• Show how you're getting extra value from your publicity budget by applying the tips given earlier in this book. Tell what a "profiteer" you are: how you're gaining extra exposure from articles, saving money on quantity prints, and so on.

Blow your horn! Nobody else will do it for you. Besides, being the expert publicist you are, who could do it better?

Index